A NEW MIMESIS

A NEW

A.D. Nuttall

MIMESIS

SHAKESPEARE AND THE
REPRESENTATION
OF REALITY

Methuen London and New York

First published in 1983 by
Methuen & Co. Ltd
11 New Fetter Lane
London EC4P 4EE

Published in the USA by
Methuen & Co.
in association with Methuen, Inc.
733 Third Avenue
New York, NY 10017

Printed in Great Britain at the
University Press, Cambridge

British Library
Cataloguing in Publication Data
Nuttall, A.D.
A new mimesis.
1. Realism in literature
I. Title
809'.912   PN56.R3

ISBN 0-416-31780-4
ISBN 0-416-35870-5 Pbk

Library of Congress
Cataloging in Publication Data
Nuttall, A.D. (Anthony David)
A New Mimesis.
Includes bibliographical
references and index.
1. Shakespeare, William,
1564-1616 – criticism and
interpretation. 2. Mimesis in
literature. 3. Realism. I. Title.
PR 2976.N83   1983   809'.912
83-5415

ISBN 0-416-31780-4
ISBN 0-416-35870-5 (pbk.)

Contents

Preface

This book is an attempt to show that literature can engage with reality. Despite its thrasonical title, it offers no direct challenge to Erich Auerbach's *Mimesis*. *A New Mimesis* is more theoretical, much more argumentative, much narrower in its range of literary reference than Auerbach's great work (in all this some readers may see the marks not only of a lesser author but of a degenerating culture). Where Auerbach pursued his thought through centuries of fiction, I have chosen to concentrate on a single, loved author: Shakespeare. But in the first part of the book and again at the end I range freely among theorists and critics ancient and modern, though even here I do not discuss every writer who is relevant to my case. I say nothing, for example, about Whorf. My argument is directed against formalism, that is, against the resolution of matter into form, reality into fiction, substance into convention. Where structuralism is formalist, I am antistructuralist; otherwise not. I am conscious that my target is in a way unreal; no one can really live with the kind of fundamental, epistemological formalism which this book attacks. But current critical discourse has adopted a certain style. This style admits or even welcomes metaphysical absolutes, and these absolutes themselves directly imply a wholly disabling conclusion. Meanwhile one of the immemorial ways of praising a writer, that is by saying that he or she is true to life, has become obscurely tabu, as if it involved some fundamental misconception of the nature of literature and the world. In such circumstances it seemed fair to take the fundamental postulates a little more seriously than they are often taken by their proponents. My own position, which is that the word *reality* can legitimately be used without apologetic inverted commas and that literature may represent that same reality, is in itself scandalously simple; but to argue for this view in the 1980s is to be involved in complex 'in-fighting'. The result stylistically is an alternation of donnish knowingness with aggressively simple assertion which is slightly repellent even to me, the author.

This book has been growing in my mind, with a sort of slow violence, for the past twenty years and there are inevitably points of overlap with work I have published during that time. I have included material from a paper I wrote for an Oxford conference of the Higher Education Group (subsequently circulated in the form of a newsletter); from a paper delivered at Cumberland Lodge (published in 1982 by the King George VI and Queen Elizabeth Foundation of St Catharine's, Cumberland Lodge, Windsor); from my article, 'Realistic convention and conventional realism in Shakespeare', which appeared first in *History of European Ideas* (1, 1981, pp. 237–48) and then in a revised form in *Shakespeare Survey* (34, pp. 33–7): from my review in *Review of English Studies* (32, 1981, pp. 113–14) of *Psychoanalysis and the Question of the Text*, edited by G.H. Hartman; from my review of E.B. Gilman's *The Curious Perspective* in *The British Journal of Aesthetics* (19, 1979, pp. 375–7); and also from an essay on Virgil and Shakespeare (not yet published at the time of writing this preface). There are also some points of contact with my books, *A Common Sky* (1974) and *Overheard by God* (1980). My debt to my friends both for opposition and reinforcement is incalculable, especially to Jonathan Dollimore, Bernard and Dorothy Harrison, Frank Kermode, John Lyons, Stephen Medcalf, Alan Sinfield, George Watson, Cedric Watts and Sir Denys Wilkinson. I have a similar debt to various audiences, to whom I read papers. Not one of these people, of course, agrees with everything I say. I also owe a great debt to Denise Smith, for typing a manuscript horribly pestered with afterthoughts.

A.D. Nuttall
November 1982

1
Shaking the concepts

Contexts

Ideas ebb and flow. In seventeenth-century England the harder heads were all in favour of putting notions on one side and attending firmly to *things* in themselves. They granted that the structures of ordinary language suggested a somewhat more complex state of affairs, but that was because ordinary language was variously corrupt. A reformed language and a reformed natural philosophy would, it was supposed, simply correspond to reality, that is, to the *things*, in a one-to-one fashion.

Thus stated, the idea is almost self-evidently absurd. A language thus reformed would consist of an indefinite series of proper names and the consequent natural philosophy would be forced to content itself with mere litanies of pious reference. As soon as the simplest classification enters (note that this takes us to the level of ordinary common nouns, like 'dog', as opposed to 'Rover', but says nothing about such things as verbs), the simple postulate of one-to-one correspondence is broken. 'Dog' superimposes a higher web of relations, linking Rover to Fido and by direct implication separating him from Jumbo, Dobbin and Kitty (I name further individuals whose classification may be guessed). The various draft schemes of linguistic reform, from Leibniz's *a priori* clarification to Bacon's empirical, ideogrammatic compromise, from

Descartes's mathematical dream to Bishop Wilkins's concept-notation, all discovered, within moments of their inception, that they must allow not only for things but also for the relations between them. Yet the initial thrust of the movement remained strong: the universe consists of things, and to this great truth, after years of metaphysical spinning of cobwebs, we must return; we must learn to display a wise passiveness; we must, so to speak, allow ourselves to be imprinted once more, as we were in our first infancy, by reality. To advance this thesis was to carry an automatic conviction with the most intelligent people of the time. It had the kind of immediate potency which should always be mistrusted, but *ex hypothesi* hardly ever is.

It is therefore unsurprising that the philosophic gladiators of the seventeenth century should have joined in a grand denunciation of metaphor, since it is metaphor which most relentlessly, most reck-lessly presupposes the relational character of reality:

> Bare ruin'd choirs where late the sweet birds sang.
>
> (Shakespeare, Sonnet 73[1])

This line licentiously perceives not only a relation between tree and tree, but between all trees in late autumn and the architecture of churches, and then, beyond that, a relation with, of all things, the sad condition of the poet himself. Hobbes called metaphor the *ignis fatuus* of scientific reasoning.[2] Thomas Sprat in his *History of the Royal Society* (1667) described how the new élite, the leaders of the scientific revolution, deliberately disdained the use of figurative language.[3] Locke thought children should be protected from poetry (and, for some reason, made to wear wet shoes).[4]

It is impossible to date with any precision the reversal of this move-ment. The Cambridge Platonist Ralph Cudworth in his *True Intellec-tual System of the Universe* (1678) questioned the whole myth of the mind's passivity in cognition. In 1725 Vico published his *New Science* in which he called out to the unborn soul of Lévi-Strauss to invent the modern discipline of anthropology: the myths of primitive peoples are not, he suggests, ludicrously erroneous history; they are rather a sophis-ticated coding or metaphorical ordering of reality. Vico adds, more radi-cally, that what we call 'true' is always in fact a shape first imposed by the mind. Vico disliked Descartes's insistence on absolute, timeless certainties, and felt that one could understand nothing if one did not understand how it came about in time. In his *The Most Ancient Wis-dom of the Italians* he presents his celebrated equation (playing on two senses of *factum*, 'fact' and 'thing made'), *verum factum*, 'truth is something made'.[5] Meanwhile in England Swift wrote *Gulliver's Travels* in which the hero finds his way to a land so philosophically enlightened that its greatest sages have dispensed not only with notions but also with words; they converse entirely with *things*, the said things being carried on the back in vast, unwieldy burdens.[6]

Swift's 'Laputa' is perhaps the most powerfully philosophical satire ever written, but it did nothing to deflect the orthodoxy of the age. Indeed the 'atomist-objectivist' orthodoxy I have described survived comfortably, easily weathering formidable attacks from German idealists and English Romantics right through to the twentieth century.

And then it suddenly seemed as if the critical voices had become too clamorous to ignore. Things happened in physics of which few could speak directly but which nevertheless led many non-physicists to suppose, vaguely and yet seriously, that the physical basis of the universe was not the solid, stable thing it had seemed to be. Wittgenstein, by common consent the greatest philosopher of the century, asked, 'Have you considered what language-game you are playing?' The question is both baffling and obscurely congenial, even now. It suggests that apparently substantial problems may melt away when it is once seen that they arise from a confusion of conventions. There is, so to speak, one 'game' in which we talk about physical causes and another in which we talk about, say, moral freedom; each game has its rules and all is well as long as the two sets of rules are not confused.

To the model of the game (with its strangely austere insinuation of triviality) Wittgenstein added the model of language. Where earlier philosophers had spoken of logic, Wittgenstein tended to speak of 'grammar', as if conflicts between premises or conclusions were somehow to be tamed by a new species of philology: a new linguistics seemed all but ready to usurp the throne of logic. This movement in philosophy may seem at first sight to resemble the humanist revolution of the Renaissance, when Scholastic philosophy was rejected and all nerves were strained to produce a stylistically pure Latin (with the result that Aquinas was condemned on the curious ground that his Latin was unlike Cicero's). But most Renaissance humanists felt no compulsion to rationalize the new emphasis on style; they simply abandoned metaphysics for Latinity. Wittgenstein, on the other hand, did what philosophers have often done; he produced an antiphilosophical *philosophy*, that is, he offered a way of dealing with philosophical problems which elegantly undercut the usual, dogged enterprises of rational corroboration or opposition, but nevertheless powerfully addressed fundamental philosophical difficulties. Nor would he rest before his problems were truly solved (in this proposing higher standards for his own attempts than have been applied by some of his followers). Which is as much as to say he never rested.

Wittgenstein left a certain taste behind. After Wittgenstein, again vaguely but also seriously, more seemed to belong to language than had before. Within the formal discipline of linguistics Saussure had stressed the fact that the elements of language are intelligible and significant only in so far as they form part of a system. 'B' alone says little or nothing, but when it occurs in the word 'bar' it means more. But 'bar' is unmanageably ambiguous and in any case does not *assert* anything; but with a fuller systematic context, e.g. 'The bar is now open', these ills are remedied; we have meaning; we understand. Of course there are different kinds of meaning. Literary people, who are trained to love polysemy, find it easy to express the transition from 'bar' to 'The bar is open' as a reduction or restriction of 'bar' to the poverty of a univocal sense. But, whether one prefers the rich potentiality of the *noun* as yet unconstrained by syntax or the sharper, operational significance of the *sentence*, each is utterly dependent on conventional relations for its force. No one mounts a case for the phonic elements; no one elaborates on the rich meaningfulness of 'b–'. It is not that, for Saussure, the linguistic whole is more than the sum of its parts; the atoms do not of themselves *begin* to compose language or meaning. Everything inheres in the systematic character of the relationships; the atoms are nothing, could be varied freely without injury to the major organism.

In anthropology Lévi-Strauss answered the implicit invitation issued so long before by Vico. He examined the myths and totemic systems of primitive peoples as a kind of relational logic, almost a secondary language. Metaphor assumed a very considerable cultural efficacy. By metaphor, for example, everything within a given culture can be seen as either raw or cooked, and thus a running binary opposition is created. To divide the world up in this wanton, arbitrary manner may seem futile. But it is the merely serial enumeration of things implied by atomism which is truly futile. To institute a variable running comparison, of whatever kind, is to create genuine meaning.

At this point certain critics writing in English begin to enter the picture. Ernst Gombrich in his brilliant *Art and Illusion*[7] showed the startling extent to which the character of the most 'realistic' painting was determined, not by the brute 'facts' of nature or visual experience but by artistic response, whether docile or disruptive, to the formal stratagems of previous painting. In literary studies Northrop Frye sought to arrest the current practice of piecemeal, 'one-poem-at-a-time' criticism, and led a return to ancient exegesis, involving allegory, genre, tradition, *context*.

All these voices may be loosely associated by virtue of a shared hostility to atomist objectivism. There are other, consequent movements which are more powerfully unified and work to the same end. Of these the most notable is structuralism, a movement of the early twentieth century, now enjoying a second lease of life. Summary characterizations of structuralism abound, but nevertheless one must be attempted here.

Structuralism, as its name suggests, recommends a shift of emphasis from origins or causes to structures. Its own origins (if we may nevertheless unregenerately notice them) are roughly threefold: first Saussurean linguistics, second that species of anthropology which stresses the organizing metaphors and metonymies of different cultures, and third formalist literary criticism, as practised by the Russian formalists and the Prague circle. Since the world attains significance and intelligibility through relationship rather than by a merely serial imprinting of the passively receiving mind, our task must be to learn the language, so to speak, of whatever activity we are seeking to understand; that is, to identify the codes, the structures of similarity and contrast which alone confer significance upon its discourse.

The enterprise is marked by a certain *esprit de système.* Here Saussure's distinction between *langue,* the general linguistic system operated by a given culture, and *parole,* the speech of an individual person, was a crucial influence. Evidently, if one wished to find the sources of meaning, it was necessary to get behind the comparatively trivial modifications introduced by the individual to the underlying system, which is at one and the same time the common possession of us all and the most potent determinant of discourse. Here, it seemed, was an insight which was susceptible of a wider application. 'For every process,' wrote Louis Hjelmslev, 'there is a corresponding *system.*'[8] At the same time it is not entirely clear how this insight is to be applied in, say, the study of literature. A.J. Greimas strove to demonstrate that literature might be deduced from language, as a further prepersonal generation of systematic structures, consequent upon the first system which is language itself. Roland Barthes, more prudently perhaps, suggested in 'Science versus literature'[9] that literature had emerged, had disengaged itself from its linguistic origins (though its medium remains linguistic) and therefore the system of literature will be analogous to that of language, rather than deducible from it. Barthes thereupon adds that the student of literature should not attempt a pseudo-scientific 'objective' study but should rather practise 'writing' himself; thus, by entering the fluid world of literature he may gradually subvert the false ideal of objectivity pursued by scientists:

> Writing alone can smash the theological idol set up by a paternalistic science, refuse to be terror-stricken by what it wrongly thought of as the 'truth' of the content and of reasoning, and open up all three

dimensions of language to research, with its subversion of logic, its mixing of codes, its shifts of meaning, dialogues and parodies.

There is more than a hint here of the freely 'poetic' criticism which has become common at Yale. Yet, despite Barthes's suggestion that the critics should cease to analyse and simply 'practise literature', structuralists continued doggedly to seek the governing codes of literature, to look for the second language which is literature, rather than looking for literature within language.

Yet this instruction also is ambiguous. Does each individual work have its own 'language', its underlying system of generative relationships, or is it, somehow, the entire corpus of literature which alone provides the web of significance without which no single line of verse could have any kind of force? The second approach (which Barthes called *science de la littérature*[10]) seems closer to the spirit of structuralism, but it remains curiously difficult to do (raising in some the chill thought that language and literature are not only separate, they are different sorts of things, serving radically different purposes – not even 'analogous').

The impetus of the movement however is not lost. Its vigour is evident in certain joyous tabus, tabus which to our forefathers would have reeked of reactionary obscurantism, would have been the last thing to be expected from the young or forward-looking; empiricism is rejected, and so is truth–to–life and the free creative sovereignty of the author over his own work. Instead we have certain Gallic epigrams: literature writes itself, people are read by the books they suppose themselves to be reading, thought (not people) thinks, speech speaks and writing writes.[11]

Thus the fundamental thrust of structuralism is conservative: what is done is done and our trivial individual interventions are mere expressions of a system which is other and greater than we. Yet at the same time it holds an extraordinarily exciting promise of possible revolution. For those who have identified the mechanism of culture may be the first free people in the world, may prove to be the harbingers of a revolution so profound as to be more than merely social, a revolution in our very categories of thought. The promise is not always firm or clear – indeed, on occasion it is austerely withdrawn – but its flickering presence to some extent explains why a movement which the old find suffocating should mysteriously liberate the young.

Meanwhile there is a perfectly ordinary, sheerly intellectual attractiveness in structuralism which is both powerful and well-founded. To those educated in a doctrinaire and perhaps corrupt version of New Criticism in which attention was artificially confined to one poem at a time, the new freedom to expatiate over varying contexts was exhilarating. Even one as far removed from continental theory as C.S. Lewis showed his responsiveness to this great source of explanatory power when he insisted, in his *Preface to Paradise Lost*, that anyone who wished to understand Milton's poem must first inform himself on the nature of epic.[12] Lewis did not clearly adopt the metaphysical thesis that Epic is prior to any particular epic poem, but chose rather to suggest that a historical sequence of individual works may gradually compose an identifiable genre, having heritable conventions, and that these conventions in their turn condition the works which follow. But the thesis that context confers meaning is clearly acknowledged.

T.S. Eliot wrote in 1919 that works of literature form 'an ideal order' such that the addition of a new work always implies a modification (which may, indeed, be almost imperceptible) of the entire system.[13] His earlier assertion in his thesis on Bradley that 'the real is the organized'[14] is full, metaphysical structuralism. We might compare with this his insistence that we must know all Shakespeare's work in order to understand any of it.[15] If we wish to go still further back, Matthew Arnold's contention in *Culture and Anarchy*[16] that those who know only the Bible do not really know even *that* recognizes the same intellectual imperative.

Those students of Greek literature who were excited in the middle years of this century by Bruno Snell, Ė.R. Dodds and John Jones remember the extraordinary sense of a new instrument in the hands, a new power to lift immense masses of material. When Snell noted the almost complete restriction of mental terms in very early Greek poetry to ideas of *multiplicity* and the fact that the idea of mental *depth* came later, he seemed at a single stride to have travelled leagues beyond those scholars who had always asked, 'What did Sophocles mean, here?' The presuppositions of the text told one so much more than the presumed suppositions of the author. Here, again, was a method which undercut previous methods.

But all the while there is the danger of prophetic absolutism. Perhaps the most typical vice of twentieth-century 'prophets' has been the abuse of such 'undercutting' explanations. One accounts for the discourse of an opponent, not in terms of that opponent's knowledge or ignorance of reality, but as determined 'from below' by factors of which he is unconscious – say by his pot-training or his economic origin – and then, by ascribing to such explanations an absolute, exhaustive efficacy, one simply neutralizes his opposition: 'You think you are saying that because you have noticed something; in fact it is because of the way you were reared.' In structuralism the reference to an extrinsic causative substratum is often dropped, but an equal potency is ascribed to the very forms of discourse, and these, in a similar manner, are placed outside the control of the individual speaker or writer. It is not especially characteristic of structuralists, as yet, to apply this weapon to hostile critics. But the tendency to absolutism is noticeable, together with associated prohibitions.

It is to these prohibitions rather than to structuralism itself that this book is addressed. Structuralism and poststructuralism still present an intuitive unity, but are at the same time richly dialectical and various. I am concerned not with the positive content of structuralism, except where it assumes a peculiarly absolute metaphysical form, but with its negative aspect. I shall have little good to say of the second, so let me say now that the first has been a kind of second birth for literary studies. I could almost say that literary conferences are live or dead as they are touched or untouched by 'the new movement'. But I propose to fret at the new tabus. It is after all common sense to welcome a gift and to resent a theft.

The strand in structuralism and poststructuralism which I shall oppose can be represented by a series of brief theorems.

1 The world consists not of things but of relationships.[17]
2 *Verum factum*: truth is something made.[18]
3 The ultimate goal of the human sciences is not to constitute man but to dissolve him.[19]
4 Language is prior to meaning.[20]
5 Verisimilitude is the mask in which the laws of the text are dressed up.[21]

Relationships, not things: verum factum

In the eighteenth century the word 'nature' carried an automatic credit; to use it was to be absolved from any necessity to argue or demonstrate and the approval one received seems to have come equally, so far as one can now tell, from the learned and the unlearned. The five propositions I have given have a similar quality but with an important difference. They carry a charge of automatic credit; they are immediately congenial to the intelligentsia. But they are not congenial to anyone else. To the man in the street each is either unintelligible or else obviously false.

Atomist objectivism has been thoroughly overthrown. It does not follow, however, that one must instantly fly to the polar opposite and affirm that only relationships are real. Something is obviously badly wrong with the first theorem, 'The world consists not of things but of relationships.' The notion of a relationship presupposes the notion of things which are related. A world consisting of pure relationship, that is, a world in which there are no things, is *ex hypothesi* a world in which no thing is related to any other and in which there could therefore be no relationship. The proposition is thus fundamentally incoherent and one can watch it dismantle itself, like a self-destructive work of contemporary art.

We may choose, then, to withdraw for a moment from the full metaphysical denial of 'things' and instead assert a more modest claim: that it is the relationships between things which make for meaning and intelligibility. After all, whenever we say anything about an individual person or thing we find that we cannot avoid saying something about other persons and things at the same time. If I say that Margaret is generous I say (at the same time) that she gives more than other people do and so directly imply that they give less than she. If I say that a book is red I have said that its colour is like that of a pillar box and unlike that of a clear sky. The impulse to drop the endless comparisons and talk instead about the individual itself turns out to be one which can never be satisfied. Only by trusting relationship can we establish our understanding of things.

This truce enables us to proceed to the second theorem, which is that all these patterns of relationship (than which human knowledge has no better material) are themselves the work of the human mind. This immediately generates an extreme consequence. So called knowledge is really fiction: *verum factum, verum fictum,* 'truth made is truth feigned.'

Vico himself would have welcomed the jingle. Tacitus's cynical observation (*Annals* v, 10) *fingunt simul creduntque,* 'They feign and at the same time they believe', struck him, somewhat oddly, as 'noble'.[22] Vico, we must grant, did not consider that all knowledge was a human construct. He distinguished between *scienza* (which comprehended mathematics and 'the human sciences') from *conscienza,* which was of physical objects.[23] Only the first is constructed by human beings. But the concession is less than it seems. For only God has knowledge of physical objects.[24] What we know is the civil world, and this is ourselves. Thus 'in a sense men have made themselves'.[25] It remains difficult to judge how absolute Vico's thesis really was. He seems as time passed to have hesitated over the example of mathematics but at the same time to have felt more and more strongly that history was the fundamental, typical form of human knowledge, and history, he is clear, is construct. Max H. Fisch says that in *La nuova scienza* history essentially replaces mathematics as the exemplary science of what is 'humanly true'.[26]

The implicit conclusion that knowledge is fiction is to some extent obscured by the structuralist emphasis on impersonality and convention. Something which is not made by you or me but is rather the work of *Homo sapiens* or *Homo occidentalis* may seem a little firmer or stronger than a mere fiction. In fact, however, though it may thereby have a greater claim to stability, it has no greater claim to truth. If one says 'But that is what truth *is*', one merely concedes the reduction of truth to the status of a cultural fiction. A story which three people agree to tell is not *ipso facto* truer than a story told by one person.

To be sure, there is in philosophy no position so untenable but that some intrepid spirit will be found occupying it. B.F. Skinner in his *Verbal Behaviour* seriously declared that proposition to be most true which is enunciated most loudly and most often by most people.[27] Chomsky in an annihilating review[28] mildly suggested that Skinner might try to make his theories true by training machine guns on large crowds of people and forcing them to chant the basic propositions of Skinnerian psychology. More commonly the question of truth is simply dropped. Jonathan Culler proposes without a tremor that we cease to pretend that the ordinary world is real: 'First, there is the socially given text, that which is taken as "the real world".'[29] Notice that Culler places inverted commas round *the real world* but none round *text*. The traditional relation of object and representative is silently reversed.

Thus, the fact that a given 'truth' is a construct of a whole society rather than an individual, though that may seem to confer a saving 'otherness' or independence on the supposed truth, cannot begin to confer veracity. Structuralism is clamorously opposed to Cartesian subjectivism of the individual; but that which is subjective to an individual culture it eagerly accepts and indeed accords an uncontested authority.

Another sort of screen is provided by the fact that anthropology commonly treats the practices and discourse of remote peoples. The idea that the 'truths' honoured by these peoples are a fiction is subliminally reinforced by the reader's sense of the grasp on fact afforded by his own culture. It is easy to diagnose cultural fiction in the story that the world rests on the Great Tortoise when one 'knows' privately that the earth is located in space. It is thus fairly easy to postpone the moment when the principle of *verum factum* is retorted against oneself. But its ultimate application to oneself is unavoidable, as long as the principle is maintained as a metaphysical absolute. Tell your structural anthropologist that his structural anthropology is a subjectively generated myth (subjective, that is, to his culture) and he, or she, will often commit the highly venial sin of resistance, will show signs of wishing to claim objective truth, of the old-fashioned kind, for structural anthropology if for nothing else. And at once the trap closes. Either the absoluteness of *verum factum* must go, or else must its claim to be believed.

For if the anthropologist did not claim objective truth, did not avail himself of the usual twentieth-century stratagem whereby the expert exempts himself from the non-cognitive determination which enslaves all the rest, we should once more be confronted by the spectacle of a self-dismantling philosophy. If the truth of a given system inheres solely in certain arbitrary, collectively agreed conventions and patterns, once we perceive this, our innocence is lost and we realize that there is no reason to believe statements made within that system to be true; they may be consistent with the rest of the system, but not true. But what tells us that all reference has this purely conventional and contextual character? Structural anthropology, say. And what is structural anthropology? A cultural system of patternings like any other. So the contention that 'truth' and 'falsity' are functions of an imposed system of patterning may be consistent with other elements in the patterning system known as structural anthropology, but there is no reason to regard it as true. But in that case we need not have set out on this journey at all.

The picture is familiar. It is, as I have suggested, characteristic of modern thought in its more philosophically daring moments to see all human culture as merely epiphenomenal to a set of factors available only to the investigator. But the 'self-exemption of the expert' can produce some oddly contorted sentences. For example here is Terence Hawkes:

> A wholly objective perception of individual entities is therefore not possible: any observer is bound to *create* something of what he observes. Accordingly the *relationship* between observer and observed achieves a kind of primacy. It becomes the only thing that *can* be observed. It becomes the stuff of reality itself.[30]

Notice first the relative modesty of 'a *wholly* objective perception . . . is not possible', which might imply some sort of meagre Indian reservation for objectivity, for a *verum* which is not *factum* but merely *est*. But then, note, this modesty is abruptly replaced by stark assertion: the relation between observer and observed is the *only* thing that can be observed. Which is flat contradiction. If the relation is the only thing that can be observed, what does 'observer' mean in the first sentence? Obviously not the enlightened watcher of relationships. Logically we are back in the desolate landscape of 'pure relation' where no thing is related to any other. The 'accordingly' of the second sentence is especially piquant. The cynic observed that the English phrase 'as a matter of fact' is normally used to introduce a lie. 'Accordingly' here denotes inconsequence.

What is implied is nothing less than a collective cultural solipsism. This is at first sight horrifying but at second glance absurd since it can advance no claim upon our assent. The monster has no teeth.

Where, then, do we go from here? The philosophy of brute facts or still more brutal *things* has been dislodged and its replacement, apparently, can never establish itself as a replacement. But we have not exhausted the possibilities. It is necessary to distinguish two meanings of the phrase 'objective truth'. If 'objective truth' means 'truth which, so to speak, states itself, without regard to the nature and interests of the perceiver', we must grant at once that objective truth has been superseded. If, on the other hand, 'objective truth' means 'truth which is founded on some characteristic of the material and is not invented by the perceiver', there is no reason whatever to say that the notion of objective truth has been superseded. Indeed its supersession would mean the end of all human discourse, not just Newtonian physics but even *Tel Quel*. Objective atomism is dead but objectivity is unrefuted.

The distinction, however, is not often observed. It is as if people had noticed that all vision is perspective and then (because of some rhetorical colour in the word 'perspective') had forthwith slid into the very different contention that the visual world is subjective to the individual.

In fact, as anyone who reflects on the history of European painting will realize, the iron rules of perspective combine the admission of an individual viewpoint (for no two people in a room does the furthest corner make the same angle) with a fully comprehensible objectivity (if one of them changed places with the other, the angle for the second would be the same as the angle for the first, so long as they were the same height and neither was astigmatic).

Indeed, it is not so much that Renaissance perspective somehow ingeniously combined these things. A firmly predictable objective reference is actually derived from the preliminary specification of viewpoint. Thus in the work of a Renaissance artist like Domenico Veneziano we can infer securely what a person on our right would see, but no such foundation for inference is available in an iconographically parallel work by a much greater artist – the last great artist of the Gothic middle ages – Jan Van Eyck. It is not that Van Eyck is incapable of visual realism. His command of varying texture, fur, gold, linen, velvet, skin, is breath-taking and perhaps still unmatched. But his command of perspective is uncertain, and in consequence the world presented in his pictures is spatially infirm and not fully intelligible. Thus, although individuality of viewpoint is more carefully pointed in Domenico's work, it is to his painting rather than to Van Eyck's that we tend to attach the cool adjective, 'impersonal'. Instead of 'although' we should really say 'because'.

It may be objected that my parenthetical concession that astigmatics may see differently betrays my entire case. In fact, it is not that astigmatics *may* see differently; they *do* see differently. We should not know this if the facts of visual perspective had not first been ascertained. Pathological divagation from a norm cannot be demonstrated if there is no demonstrable norm. Radical or 'Cartesian' subjectivism, whereby it is suggested that each individual may inhabit an utterly private universe, is an entirely separate issue, and can never be corroborated by particular demonstrations of idiosyncrasy any more than it can be refuted by apparent cases of agreement. The astigmatic does not embarrass the visual objectivist.

Again, it may be objected that the classical perspective employed by Renaissance artists is at bottom a convention. Not all societies have represented the world in this manner. Meanwhile 'what we actually see' is itself quite separate. The objection is plausible.

In *Art and Illusion* E.H. Gombrich quotes a story told by the Japanese artist Yoshio Markino of his father.[31] To follow this story it is necessary to understand that in the art practised by Markino's father a rectangular object would be shown by parallel, not converging lines, that is, by axonometric perspective rather than by the classical perspective laid down for the Renaissance by Leon Battista Alberti in his *Della pittura*. Apparently, when the father was first shown a picture which employed the converging lines of classical perspective, he thought the box in the picture must be irregularly shaped. Readers seize on the story as illustrative of the conventional or arbitrary character of classical perspective. But in fact the latter part of this story suggests a somewhat different state of affairs. I quote Markino's father: 'I used to think this square box looked crooked, but now I see this is perfectly right.'

Of course he may have meant only that he had adjusted to a different visual game with different rules. But the phrase 'Now I see' strongly suggests that he noticed how classical perspective approximates better to the facts (I deliberately omit the now almost compulsory inverted commas) of visual perception. The image obtained by a primitive camera exhibits all the characters (with certain very minor differences) of Albertian perspective. The history of *trompe l'oeil* painting tells the same tale. A perspective view of a room painted on a wall would not deceive the eye were it not that we do indeed see perspectivally.

It may be said that it deceives *our* eyes merely because we are so habituated to the graphic convention that we project it back upon the ordinary world, and that a Japanese would be similarly deceived by an axonometric representation, since he sees axonometrically.

But what can it mean to say that someone sees axonometrically? If you draw a picture with Albertian perspective and then try to draw the same picture with axonometric perspective, one clear difference emerges at once; in the second picture more of the background is occluded by the foreground. In the first picture nine little trees show in their entirety; in the second only six show.

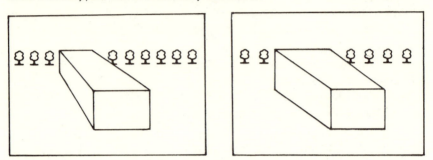

Do the Japanese see six trees, in real life, where we see nine? I think not.

Indeed, if we are to be really strict, the trees should not be small in the second picture since the law of diminution by distance is precisely what is denied in axonometric perspective. The full application of this austere denial has extraordinary consequences. We would not see trees against a background of distant hills, since if the hills were represented on the same scale as the trees we should not see the hills at all, but only a portion of one of them. It is perhaps very revealing that Japanese or medieval pictures which approximate to axonometric perspective often do so in a piecemeal fashion, treating particular objects axonometrically, but subjecting the recessive planes of the picture to a brisk series of summary reductions in scale. Once again one suspects that they are compelled to do so because perception does so systematically and continuously.

It might be thought, however, that my distinction between visual facts and conventions is much too cut and dried. It is well known that if another person stretches out a hand towards one's face, that hand does not look as large as it ought to according to the laws of classical perspective. However much of the background it occludes, it obstinately retains the known size of a hand and does not look three times as big as the face which is two and a half feet behind it. The great painters of the Renaissance tactfully accommodated this factor when they refused to represent foreshortened recumbent bodies in full perspective.

That such involuntary modification of the datum does happen was shown clearly by R.H. Thouless in an admirable series of experiments carried out fifty years ago.[32] Thouless asked subjects to look at a disc set at an angle to the field of vision so that its retinal image was (as in classical perspective) a narrow ellipse.[33] He then asked the same subjects to choose from a series of ellipses varying from the very narrow to the almost circular that which most nearly resembled the shape the object had presented to the eye. Pretty consistently the subjects chose an ellipse which was thicker than the retinal image; that is, they chose a compromise shape, somewhere between the retinal shape and the known circular shape the disc presented when viewed directly.

Thouless, commenting on this, remarked that when a child is taught to draw in strict perspective, it is wrong to say that he is being taught to draw the way he really sees: 'his drawing response is on the contrary being reconditioned to the stimulus object instead of to the phenomenal object.'[34] But in fact Thouless makes it clear that what he somewhat misleadingly calls the stimulus object is in fact phenomenally available – that is, available *as an appearance* – to the subject. One does not have to cut open a subject's head to view the retinal image. 'The way the subject sees' is in fact an ambiguous phrase and can with equal propriety be applied to the datum (which with an effort of concentration can be accurately reported on) or to the *modified* datum. We therefore do not have a simple contrast between a retinal stimulus and a phenomenon available to the subject. Rather the contrast is between a 'hard' given phenomenon and a phenomenon which has been involuntarily modified.

The modification occurs only when subjects know that the object is really circular. Unconscious modification to the real shape was less in art students who had been trained in perspective. Thouless notes that in practice a draughtsman can preserve the 'retinal stimulus character' (or, as I would say, the hard phenomenal datum) by holding a pencil at arm's length and measuring the size of objects against it (this test is exactly parallel to my 'occlusion' test). Thus the final implication of Thouless's work (contrary to that whole panic-stricken movement of the twentieth century which sought to deny the very existence of *sensa*, but in line with the more recent work of philosophers like Frank Jackson[35]) is that the classical perspectival shape is available to the subject *and* that it is unconsciously modified. That modification occurs he shows very clearly; but by the same token he shows that there is a datum which is modified (otherwise modification, or, to use Thouless's term, 'regression', simply would not apply to the case). The entire demonstration which an unreflective person might take to corroborate conventionalism in fact does no such thing. The perspectival facts of perception are alive and well.

Gombrich himself (my source for the anecdote about Markino's father) recorded his warm appreciation of Thouless's work but subjoined a curious criticism. It is the word 'real' which worries him:

> A penny is not more real when seen from above than when looked upon sideways. But the frontal view happens to be the one which gives us most information. It is this aspect which we call 'the characteristic shape' of the object, the one (or sometimes two) which exhibits most of those distinctive features by which we classify and name the things of our world. It is on these distinctive features. . .that primitive art will concentrate, not because it draws on knowledge rather than sight, but because it insists on clear classification.
>
> Now this same insistence on distinctive features also influences our reaction in real life whenever we are confronted with an uncertainty. It is therefore inexact to speak of our knowledge which influences our perception of the oblique penny. Rather, it is our search for knowledge, our effort after meaning. . . .[36]

Of course it is true that a penny viewed directly is no more real than a penny viewed indirectly. But it by no means follows that Thouless was wrong to call the shape presented in direct viewing the real shape. He meant by this that it was round, as a penny is round. A penny may be described as 'really round' if every point on its circumference really is equidistant from the centre. This (with microscopic variations) actually is the case with pennies.

Gombrich implicitly admits as much when he says that the direct view gives us more information and exhibits those features on which our classification is based. 'Information' and 'features' are here implicitly objectivist terms. Yet he nevertheless smarts under a mysterious pressure to withdraw terms like 'real' and 'knowledge'. The prerational influence of the *Zeitgeist* was never more evident. Moreover, its next move can be confidently predicted. Gombrich is visually sophisticated enough, or nervous enough, to shy away from any confident ascription of reality to the shape. But he can still write the words 'in real life' without inverted commas. It is on this phrase that the modish reader can now be expected to pause and ask, 'Does he not know that "real life" is a problematic concept?'

Gombrich has shifted the level of our discussion from the reality of the phenomenon *qua* phenomenon to the reality of the physical object. It is easy to be tripped by a confusion of these levels. Dreams are both real and unreal. They are real *qua* dreams but their contents are not real outside the dream. My dream that a lion was driving the bus was real in that I actually had such a dream, but unreal in that the lion did not really drive the bus. Phenomena are not the same as the physical objects of which they are phenomena. A percept of a penny is not a real penny, though it is a real percept.

Plato made use of the necessary gap between object and percept to decry the validity of the senses. In the *Republic* (598A) Socrates extorts from Glaucon the wholly undamaging concession that a bed viewed from different angles presents different shapes. He concludes, correctly, that the appearance is different from the physical object and, incorrectly, that the artist who adheres to such an appearance is a liar. In fact, because the range of variations in apparent shape is systematically related to the real object and this relation is intuitively intelligible to the observer of the picture, truth may be preserved in a picture organized according to appearance.

In an admirable study, *The Curious Perspective: Literary and Pictorial Wit in the Seventeenth Century*,[37] Ernest B. Gilman tells how perspective, proudly presented by Alberti in his *Della pittura* as a source of truth, gradually became as the years passed an instrument of deception. Gilman tells his story well, with a running implicit suggestion that the initial claim upon truth was somehow 'found out' or exposed by those who came later. Here as elsewhere it is necessary to distinguish between the formal modifications which are essential to perspective as such and those which are exploited to produce a disturbing effect. In Albertian perspective no less than in Dubreuil a round wheel may be represented by an oval. The Renaissance artist must have been clear about this or he could not have drawn his perspective picture. So far from being untruthful such forms are a means of accurate representation. No one who has assimilated the language of perspectival art (and, for certain reasons to do with the way our eyes actually work, it is easy to assimilate) is deceived by an oval representation of a wheel. On the contrary, as we have seen, he is able to infer roundness with a certainty never before available. Just as in ordinary perception we are rarely given a precise, frontal presentation of a wheel but can nevertheless see, in terms of the visual organization of the context, when a thing is round and when it is not, so Albertian art can confer relative certainty, where older 'conceptual' art, with its literalist method of conveying shape (a square-in-fact must appear as a square-on-paper) frequently leaves the viewer bewildered. Gilman writes as if the claims of Albertian perspective are somehow overthrown when the fact of 'distortion' ('systematic modification' might be a better phrase) is honestly acknowledged. The fact that the defence against such attacks was occasionally mismanaged (as by Filarete) does not mean that the attacks were truly formidable.

The use of perspective to deceive is another matter. Borromini's diminishing colonnade in the Palazzo Spada deceives because in it representation is doubled with reality. Borromini, in order to make the colonnade look longer than it really is, used actual columns of decreasing height, knowing that they would be taken for columns of equal height. It is only because like columns in a single structure are normally the same height and in ordinary perception a line of equal columns diminishes as it recedes that Borromini's deception works. The fidelity of perspective art to the facts of visual perception is nowhere more evident than in such *jeux d'esprit*. Clearly, it is fidelity to the laws of spatial perception rather than to a particular concrete place which is claimed in the (usually ideal) scenes of Albertian perspective. Again and again, the so-called deceptions of perspective turn out to be deceptions as to what is concretely real and what representation. The room which seems to continue is really a painted wall. Only a language capable of veracity can be used for deception.

The Platonic condemnation in the *Republic* is thus doubly absurd. Not only are the modifications by which percepts or representations differ from their objects reconcilable with veracity, the distinction between vehicle and tenor is actually essential to every act of representation. Here as elsewhere it is Augustine who streaks ahead of his peers: *unde vera pictura esset, si falsus equus non esset*? 'How could it be a true picture, unless it was a false horse?'[38]

Meanwhile the cardinal truth stands: specific demonstrations of subjective or ideological modification always presuppose an objective referent against which they are plotted. One may show subjectivity in musical taste by the fact that Jane likes Tchaikovsky though Jill does not. But this demonstration presumes that in the 'hard phenomenal' sense they are hearing the same thing. For, if we were to allow that, if Jane were to hear Tchaikovsky the way it sounds to Jill, she would say 'But this is awful!' their *tastes* could be identical; Jane's smiles and Jill's frowns would then be appropriate, by identical canons of taste, to the differing private displays confronting them. If you want to say that their tastes diverge, you have to be able to say that their perceptions do not.

Here I can imagine a structuralist objection which might run as follows:

> Your musical example is trapped in the old metaphysical assumptions of subjective privacy and objective publicity which have now been swept away. You presume that there is a distinctive, individual 'sound' called Tchaikovsky for each individual perceiver, and devoutly *hope* that it is always the same. The characteristic sound which language calls 'Tchaikovsky' is really a node, a point of intersection of thousands of relationships; its 'identity' is constituted e.g.

by the fact that Tchaikovsky lies somewhere between the Russophile music of Glinka, Balakirev and Mussorgsky on the one hand and what he himself spoke of as southern or Italian influences on the other. When a person 'hears' Tchaikovsky this intersection of relationships *is* what he hears. It is therefore not just practically impossible but inconceivable that a person, admitted to another's experiential field, should say 'That's not Tchaikovsky, that's William Boyce!' The most that could occur would be a momentary disorientation followed by a 'twigging' of the usual system. Take the analogy of colour perception. Suppose that A, admitted to B's visual field, sees a pillar box and says, 'Well, well, that's what *I* call "blue".' This reaction is perhaps conceivable but it cannot survive for long; he will rapidly lose any sense of cerulean distance in the colour (I am striving to catch what might seem to be the intrinsic phenomenal 'affect' of blue) but, as he learns that it is now the colour of hot coals and blood, will associate it with heat and urgent danger. At the same time language will lead him to call the pillar box 'red'. So with a musical transference of consciousness: even if we were to allow that the entire relational field of music were somehow represented for each subject by different primal sounds, the auditory character, the auditory *identity* of any musical experience, before we get on to such secondary questions as its aesthetic impact, would be determined by the rest of the system. An initial puzzlement followed by a recovery of the usual system is perhaps conceivable. A wholesale *inversion* of auditory characters which are themselves dependent on the pre-personal system is utterly inconceivable.

Such is the objection. My answer is that I do not intend the idea of a radical transfer of one mind into another's experience as a serious possibility. I say only that, if *per impossibile, per contradictionem*, it were to occur, it would at once prevent any inference of subjectivity in taste. Meanwhile, as long as we do infer that tastes are subjective, we implicitly commit ourselves to the existence of common objects of perception (which may indeed be richly structured). The disquiet expressed above is merely an elaboration and a particular sort of comment on a difficulty already acknowledged in my phrase *per impossibile*. In fact the general tendency of such an argument, the tendency to rule out the idea of *radical* subjectivism, is welcome to me, but its credentials would require separate scrutiny. Perhaps the most obvious difficulty in the counter-picture here proposed by structuralism is the psychological one; if identity invariably depends on context, so that the nature of a context will depend on the context of that context, and so on, where is the point of entry? How does one begin to learn if one must know everything before one knows anything?

The problem is especially acute in aesthetic perception as opposed to practical perception, because the urgent hints and pushes supplied by practical reality are largely absent when, say, we are listening to music. Yet, in my own personal recollection, Elgar's music had its distinctive 'taste' or quality most vividly of all when I first heard it as a small child in a state of pretty complete musical ignorance, so that for years afterwards it always rose unbidden in my mind as an obvious example of a translinguistic individual.

Meanwhile, what might be called 'the objectivist correlative' remains inescapable. If you want to say that a society imposes its cultural forms on reality, you must have a conception of the reality with respect to which the imposition is detected. The alternative is a Derridian flux of *écriture*.

Much of what I have been discussing can be traced to one or other of two philosophical sources; first, relationalism, according to which identity can always be resolved without remainder into relationship. This theory became prominent in English philosophy with criticisms of Locke's doctrine of substance. People observed knowingly that seemingly solid objects were really mere bundles of qualities (as if solidity were not itself a quality, and as if an object so qualified were not solid!). This was the first of my 'brief theorems' and evidently stands squarely behind structuralism, though most structuralist enquiry can function just as effectively with a less absolute metaphysical underpinning.

The second doctrine, which underlies my second 'brief theorem', *verum factum*, is the romantic doctrine that the imagination may actually be *constitutive* of the objects of knowledge. This doctrine, if taken in its full rigour, implies that knowledge is not really knowledge but a mode of fiction: *verum factum, verum fictum*. The doctrine of the constitutive imagination is certainly not proved by the demonstrable element of interpretation or 'configuration' present in all perception, since, as I have tried to show, all the excellent demonstrations of configuration presuppose independent access to visual facts, otherwise we should not know that configuration had occurred. We understand the common example of the lines which can be interpreted either as an overhanging cornice or a set of steps because we can *see* that the lines remain the same while our interpretation varies.

Certainly Bacon was wrong in suggesting that we could put our notions to one side and attend to 'things' in themselves; 'thing' is a normative concept; we decide what counts as a thing or it is decided for us by our inherited perceptual apparatus. The question, 'How many things are there in this room?' is a nonsense question. Do we include the neutrinos? Do we include twinges of nostalgia? But the fact that we are 'set' to register other human beings very swiftly and miss utterly the blictris which so engross the eyeless Alpha Centaurians does not mean that we *make* the other people we see.

The shapes we bring to bear on the world are interrogative rather than constitutive. We trawl with the human net and therefore catch only what can be caught in its mesh, but it does not follow that we are the sole inventors of the catch. I and the history of my species may decide what counts as a chair, but if I then 'trawl' for chairs in this room I shall find so many, and no more. Human astronomy is perspectival in the sense that it is from a given point of view, but this does not imply that the knowledge so gained cannot be objective. A whale would, I imagine, be unlikely to notice my ears, but may conversely be aware of gradations in the character of seawater of which we are unconscious, but this does not mean that my ears are an anthropocentric fiction or conversely that the gradations of the sea are a myth of the whale race, a phallaenocentric fiction. In this book the word *object* will occur frequently, without apologetic inverted commas. This, inevitably, will 'smell of' Locke and the benighted epistemology of the seventeenth century. But in fact I shall be using the word in a 'baptized' sense, that is, with full acceptance of the fact that human needs condition the schemata by which we elicit certain characters from the world. As I use the term, there is no implication that the universe will admit no other organization than that implied by human language, or that other intelligent beings with different needs and therefore different perceptual equipment would nevertheless obtain the same set of 'things'. But there is an implication that reality is such that our terms can be used referentially in a fruitful manner, which is the kind of cumbersome metaphysical periphrasis which can be dispensed with in practice. If reality is such that *horse* can be used referentially, there are horses. This we ought to have learned from the hiccough in seventeenth- and eighteenth-century philosophy over Primary and Secondary Qualities. The matter is most easily explained by a short dialogue:

A   There is no Red without eyes.
B   Then colour is a subjective phenomenon.
A   But some objects are so constituted that they appear red to our eyes, and others are so constituted that they do not.
B   But in that case 'Being so constituted as to appear red *is* ''Being red''; those are the red objects, and they *are* red.'

The reader is invited to construct a similar dialogue, beginning with, 'There are no horses without human beings to conceptualize (or say) ''horse''.'

Orthodox Darwinians agree that biological adaptation is the product of natural selection, not design, yet they freely use teleological language among friends, where it will not be misconstrued; e.g. 'That tooth is for rubbing, not cutting.' My use of *object* is in certain respects like their use of *for*. There remains the difficult question, 'What does it mean to say that reality is *such* that it can be referred to in our language?' Can that 'such' be unpacked further? Some writers have tried to describe phenomenally the reality which lies beyond our concepts, calling it a 'darkness' or a (positive) 'Nothingness' or '*Néant*'. But how could we know that what lies outside our conception is 'dark'? The alternative is to construe 'dark' as merely a picturesque way of repeating the fact that we do not know its nature, but in that case the purported description collapses into tautology. But the open word *reality* makes no pretence of description, yet at the same time its proleptic openness greatly assists the whole business of *extending* our conceptions, the work of *learning*. The presumption that talk of the darkness which lies beyond our concepts is fundamentally honest while talk of specific objects carries a taint of falsehood can and should be reversed. Meanwhile, however, the idea that transconceptual reality corresponds structurally to our concepts seems to involve an immediate metaphysical absurdity; the terms of the supposed correspondence are *ex hypothesi* unavailable. Facts are not hypostatized propositions (hypostatized for us by an accommodating deity). But facts are not mere propositions either. When language successfully describes reality, it is not that the relation between the two is something *less* than structural correspondence. It would be truer to say that it is *closer* than mere correspondence. We do not say 'That corresponds to "duck" '; we say, 'That is a duck.' We can only describe the world, phenomenally, in terms of our current colonization of it. Thus far, it has proved to be richly structured, relational and full of marvels. Obviously, we do not know what we do not know; who, then, is to say whether the unknown is a mess of shadows or a fabric of inconceivable richness? Meanwhile that which we know *is* as we know it, or else the knowledge is not knowledge.

Dissolving man: the priority of language to meaning

I turn now to the third and fourth of my 'brief theorems'.

The third theorem was taken from Claude Lévi-Strauss's *The Savage Mind*: 'I believe the ultimate goal of the human sciences to be not to constitute but to dissolve man.'[39] The context of this observation is a difference of opinion between Lévi-Strauss and Sartre, a Sartre who by this time had moved from 'pure' existentialism in order to grapple with the implications, for one who had been a radical individualist, of Marxism. Despite the modifications Sartre was making in his philosophy, it is to Sartre's individualism that Lévi-Strauss finds himself opposed.

Existentialism, in so far as it had affirmed that authentic humanity consisted in a radical freedom, prior to any predictive law or regularity, had from the start ruled out the possibility of a 'scientific' psychology, that is a psychology which laid down scientific *laws* of human nature. At the same time, by its very emphasis on this dark, ineffable freedom, existentialism throws up a residuum of formalized conceptions of human nature, the variously defined and labelled 'selves' we operate in social existence. These selves, which are external to our authentic instability, require a separate explanation. The answer is that we are the authors, or feigners, of these essentially fictitious selves and can modify them at will; nevertheless most ordinary discourse about man in society is quite properly concerned with this highly formal system of 'proposed identities'. When structuralism takes over from existentialism, its easiest course is simply to drop all reference to the dark, authentic self (which was always in any case ineffable), to accept the essentially fictive character of the proposed social 'selves' and to investigate these as a fluid system. Here certain laws of fiction, of generation, of metonymy and distinction may after all be discovered. There is a slight but irremovable clash with existentialism in the renewed hope of system, even at this secondary, 'grammatical' level, since for the radical existentialist the freedom to modify the 'proposed self' is ultimately without any constraint; nevertheless, in so far as the structuralist is willing to acknowledge that the general structure of society is a vast web of fictions rather than a series of brute facts he may appear as the direct heir of the existentialists.

With Lévi-Strauss, when he was writing *The Savage Mind*, the transition from existentialism to structuralism had not assumed this form. Rather, he was preoccupied with the elementary (and as we have seen ultimately irremovable) difference between those who would study human beings 'as if they were ants',[40] that is the scientists who gaze down in an impersonal manner and reduce human behaviour to predictable patterns, and those who acknowledge the real humanity of man and therefore his real elusiveness when pursued by 'scientific law'. Lévi-Strauss, faced with this, sides with the scientist. His remark about 'dissolving' man is, as he says himself, 'intentionally brutal'.[41] He accepts that the role of the anthropologist must be to discern patterns and is so far a loyal descendant of the existentialists as to agree that to do so is to substitute for free, individual humanity something which is prepersonal and inhuman. The effect of anthropology is not, so to speak, to compose before our eyes anything which we would recognize as a person; anthropology will

never give us Margaret or David. Rather, it gives us the nature of humanity, and resolves individuals into the patternings from which they are
generated as cultural beings.

The thesis, though expressed with all the seeming absoluteness of
Gallic 'metaphysical epigram', is in fact quite modest. Lévi-Strauss is
not denying the existence of individual human beings. In fact his book is
pungently 'thingy', full of substances and richly distinctive examples. At
one point only do we scent radical relationalism, namely at the point
where he observes, as an empirical fact, that herbivores are not interested
in grass but in the difference between species of grass.[42] It would be more
accurate, given the nature of his evidence, to say that herbivores are
interested in varying grasses. The abstract form of words Lévi-Strauss
chose is inapposite to his example but congenial to one of the metaphysical impulses of structuralism. In its form it is a remote echo of
Saussure's 'In languages there are only differences without positive
terms.'[43]

A second powerful agent in the dissolution of the human subject is
Freudian psychoanalysis. The main element in Freudian psychology
which concerns us is of course, as might have been predicted, its anti-
existentialist emphasis on prepersonal laws of human nature. The tension between existentialist radical freedom and the Utilitarian conception of man as governed by the principle of maximizing happiness begins
with Dostoevsky's *Notes from Underground*. Freud, having sophisticated the Utilitarian happiness principle as a partly unconscious pleasure principle, essentially reaffirmed the law-governed character of
human nature (sometimes even reviving the extreme determinist model
with expressions like 'psychic *mechanism*').

There can be no suggestion that Freud, any more than Lévi-Strauss,
denied the existence of individual human subjects. For a long time the
principal difference between Jung's psychology and Freud's appeared to
lie precisely in the fact that Jung addressed vast cultural movements
while Freud discussed individuals. Yet the mechanisms Freud isolated as
psychologically crucial are prior to the individual; the differences between people are relatively superficial accidents. One man's Oedipus
complex is the same as another's. Indeed there seems to be no clear reason for not calling the Oedipus complex a repressed *archetype*. Thus,
while Freud does not deny the existence of individual human natures, he
removes the efficacy and lowers the status of those elements in people
which are specific to the individual. In that he repeatedly reduces apparent reasoning to the mere rationalization of views held because of
prepersonal forces of which the subject is unaware, he may be said to have
dethroned the rational subject. In the exciting language of structuralism,

psychoanalysis shows us how the prepersonal psyche does its work behind and through individuals, who no longer preside as sovereigns of its process. One really needs a verb to echo the noun 'psyche': 'The psyche psyches', if somewhat odder than 'Thought thinks' or 'Literature writes itself', is linguistically only a little more barbarous than Heidegger's notorious 'Das Nichts selbst nichtet' ('The Nothing itself nothings').[44]

Moreover, in Freud the metaphysically loaded word 'real' is pressed hard: 'You think you love your father but *really* you want to kill him' and so on. Here the presumption must be that the modifications of desire introduced by the super-ego, instead of being part of the fabric of reality having equal status with the original unconscious drives, are themselves unreal. 'Delusive' might have been arguable, 'unreal' in its full sense is absurd – but is nevertheless used.

At this point we are faced with a curious historical slippage. The cultural 'story' of psychoanalysis in England and its 'story' in France are badly out of phase and have at last come together in a very odd fashion. In England the literary impact of psychoanalysis was powerful in the 1930s. Lawrence, though he found Freud unpleasingly scientific, responded to the general idea of dark forces and carefully noted the disappearance of 'the old stable *ego*' of character which had dominated the traditional novel.[45] His own works show, with far more subtlety and tenderness than we find in Freud, the nuances of individual personality intermittently threatened and engulfed by the prepersonal. People as they talk or feel are momentarily seen as columns of blood or fire, archetypal, unexorcized.

But then in England psychoanalysis was itself undermined by a wave of positivist criticism. Freud (it was claimed) so framed his theories that no conceivable instance would ever falsify them; or, where they were susceptible of an empirical check, they turned out to be false. Controlled tests of the efficacy of psychoanalytic therapy were, with the exception of certain tests run with hysterics, largely negative. Indeed it was hard to see, in terms of the theory itself, why psychoanalysis should be expected in any case to work: if repressive oblivion is a 'natural' way of staunching an intolerable psychic wound, why should the mere 'removal of the dressings' in the presence of an analyst constitute a cure rather than a repetition – fainter perhaps but still a repetition – of the original trauma? The patient is asked to relive his or her original disabling experience on no better rationale, it would seem, than the common notion of facing up to things, since they may not seem so bad after all. Where was the evidence of the Oedipus complex or, more radically, could there ever in fact be clear evidence of the Oedipus complex, as Freud described it? What on earth happened in Freud's self-analysis? How does one justify the wanton manipulation of evidence in the case of 'little Hans'?

Prepubertal sexuality is real enough but is strongest in what Freud lucklessly termed 'the latency period'.

It became the fashion in enlightened circles to chuckle over especially extravagant passages, like the notorious footnote on female guardianship of the hearth in *Civilisation and its Discontents*. For the curious, the argument there is that human beings, confronted with fire, experience a primordial desire to urinate on it; two primitive men, left alone with a fire, would instantly extinguish it 'in homosexual competition'. Women were not exempt from this impulse, but because of their anatomy, were more likely to be burned. Accordingly, restrained by the Reality Principle, they became the trusted guardians of the fire and the original locus of stable civilization.[46]

There can be little doubt that by the mid-1960s the intellectual reputation of psychoanalysis in English academic circles was low. In France the rejection on essentially empirical grounds of Freudian theory seems to have been much less pronounced. As a result the Freudian 'dethroning of the ego' was assimilated as if it had been rigorously demonstrated and exerted a largely unimpeded influence on literary theory. The influence of Freud is powerful in Lacan and Derrida. Meanwhile in England literary theory either did not exist at all or existed in a curiously ossified condition. Young teachers of English were hungry for theory and suddenly it seemed that France could supply that hunger. By the time the movement took firm root in England, its radical metaphysic was potent enough to disarm in advance the old empirical criticisms of psychoanalysis. In England and still more in America the game was rather to reorganize the 'text' of 'reality' and the text of literature with reference to the 'text' of psychoanalysis.

As a specimen of the revived influence of psychoanalysis we may take the 1978 selection of papers from the English Institute entitled *Psychoanalysis and the Question of the Text*.[47] The volume contains essays by Murray Schwarz, Cary Nelson, Neil Hertz, Geoffrey Hartman, Jacques Derrida and Barbara Johnson. Parts of the book are traditional enough. For example, Cary Nelson discusses the defensive postures adopted by critics and the difference between the text as ideal, autonomous object and the text as a 'matrix of our desires'.[48] This is the ancient problem of the subjectivity of literary understanding. Norman Holland suggests that we shift attention from the text and start looking at the needs of readers. He then suggests that Dr Johnson's disapproval of the death of Cordelia in *King Lear* springs from the psyche's running need to see virtue rewarded. This succeeds in being both old-fashioned and inept at the same time. The thesis that it is agreeable to see virtue rewarded hardly requires an elaborate psychoanalytic dress, and the quasi-scientific generalization of the notion merely exposes it to disproof; for if there is some sort of prepersonal psychic law which moves people to disapprove of cases where virtue is not rewarded, why is it that so many people actually approve aesthetically of the death of Cordelia?

The other essays in the book exhibit the marks of the new movement rather more clearly. Murray Schwarz notes a structural similarity between the patient–analyst relationship and the text–critic relationship, and suggests that in either case there is a hypothetical 'third person' with reference to whom discourse is 'triangulated'.[49] The thesis is far from clear when it moves beyond the mere noting of an analogy. He explains that he does not regard the findings of psychoanalysis as affording a stable set of truths:

> The psychoanalytic side of my subject is as changing as the literary. We are no longer in a position to appeal to the formulae of metapsychology without recognizing that they, too, are provisional and inseparable from the needs and fears of their formulators and users.[50]

To reason thus is in a manner to psychoanalyse the psychoanalyst. The more traditional form of this move is to say, 'If reasoning is really rationalization and psychoanalysis is a body of reasoning, psychoanalysis is itself a mere rationalization of views held, not because of objective insight into reality but because of the pathology of the theorist.' The usual inference from such an analysis was that either some portions of psychoanalysis must be exempt from the reduction to mere rationalization or else psychoanalysis itself has no claim to be believed. But it is characteristic of what might be called the Derridian phase of poststructuralism that this conclusion is not drawn. Instead the critic launches himself into the maelstrom. The fluid is interpreted by the fluid. As we watch, however, certain propositions recur, as that the author is a fiction created by the reader and that the critic constructs his definition of himself with reference to this fiction.[51]

Neil Hertz in his essay contrives a reasonably neat matching of structures, by likening Kant's notion of the mathematical sublime (in which the mind is first checked and then released) with various kinds of (enjoyed) psychological and critical blockage. This might have ripened into a psychological *explanation* of certain aesthetic pleasures, but one senses an ideological unwillingness to permit such a ripening. The author is happier with a more neutral world of analogous structures. Geoffrey Hartman, in a brilliantly written piece, takes from Lacan the notion that the child, having seen himself in a glass, thereupon assumes

the proffered, externally constituted identity, and suggests that literature is produced when language, so to speak, catches sight of itself. Here
a psychological analogy is used to illustrate a formalist theory about
literature. The psychoanalytic material is ornamental (Hartman's stylistic taste inclines to the Baroque) rather than corroborative.

The formalist theory is clearly derived from various post-Romantic
views of literature: 'Poetry is not the thing said but a way of saying
it. . .meaning is of the intellect, poetry is not.'[52] 'A poem should not
mean/But be.'[53] Yet Hartman's illustration may go some way to explain how life and interest may be sustained in a medium thus divorced
from the object; his implicit answer is that reference *is* sustained, but it
is reference to language itself. One is left (still toying with the imagery
of mirrors) wondering how, if language is to bear no colour from the
world of meanings, it can ever receive from a mirror a visible image of
itself. Will it not be confronted by a mere absence, as ghosts are when
they pause in front of a glass? Or, if language is itself a medium normally
reflective of non-linguistic realities, are we then left with the picture of
one mirror facing another?

Jacques Derrida, in the same volume, meditates on the structural
similarity between a baby's throwing away and then recovering a toy
and Freud's own manner of proceeding when he tries to analyse this
infantile behaviour. There is a feeling of audacious 'undercutting', of
psychoanalysing the very process of psychoanalysis, but once again
there is little sense that we may consider anything at all to have been
either explained or demonstrated. Derrida himself is emphatic that we
cannot even raise the question of the objectivity of Freud's method
since Freud was himself then and there engaged in investigating the
origins of subjectivity. This sounds very fine but is wholly without
cogency. One might with equal force maintain that it is impossible to
train a telescope on a lens factory. Barbara Johnson suggests, in her
essay, that Derrida's readings do not so much analyse the impossibility
of a final interpretation as enact that impossibility. This is very close to
what I would say myself, with the difference that for Barbara Johnson
the situation thus disclosed is considered highly satisfactory. There is a
curiously similar passage of complaisant nihilism in Geoffrey
Hartman's *Criticism in the Wilderness*[54] where he calmly observes that
Derrida's demonstration (in *Glas*) of Genet's non-significance itself
attains to full non-significance.

The relaxing of the ordinary empirical referents, of the usual recourse
to possible fact, ground and consequence, cause and effect, premise and
conclusion, is finally strangely enervating. Cary Nelson in his essay
wonders whether it would be 'useful'[55] to say that the reconstituted

body of literature as it appears in the work of Northrop Frye is 'the Mother' as presented by psychoanalysis. 'Useful' is here a word of deliberate and dreadful vagueness. The word 'true' might have elicited from both writer and reader a greater precision of mind (incidentally, the answer to Cary Nelson's query would then be, 'Probably not'). Again Barbara Johnson reminds us that Derrida has surmised in Lacan's reading of 'The purloined letter' that for him (Lacan) the letter is a symbol of the *mother's* (missing) phallus. In all this welter of intelligent supposition the sheer improbability of the central notion is not noticed. This is rather a refusal to notice than an inability to do so. An ideological hostility to the very idea of probability is gradually being displaced by a more neutral mode of mental juxtaposition.

To read *Psychoanalysis and the Question of the Text* is to realize that the reintroduction of Freudian notions in a poststructuralist critical environment can afford little more than a set of mental toys. Without the ordinary restraints of objectivism there is little for the first intelligences of Paris and Yale to do but *play* – with a sort of sub-Nietzschean hilarity, parsing and reparsing the texts, laying map on map and listening to the sound of their own voices (or typewriters).

Occasionally, indeed, such play closes any gap which might once have existed between European philosophy and parodies of it (I think of the difference between *L'Être et le Néant* and Paul Jennings's brilliantly funny send-up, 'Report on resistentialism'[56]). For example, Lacan says darkly that the child is an 'hommelette', that is both a 'little man' and a sort of broken egg, lacking identity.[57] Light-years of intellectual distance lie between this and the sort of linguistic anomaly relished by Wittgenstein. Lacan's remark is strangely lugubrious. He is not joking. Nor is he thinking. The difference between the two is perhaps no longer apparent to him.

It is in Derrida that the dissolution of the subject is most complete. He joins the Freudian critique of the responsible, initiating subject to Heidegger's more radical critique in *Being and Time*. Hume observed two centuries before that, whatever is given in introspection, it is never a single being which we can recognize as a self.[58] One finds memories, mental images, passions, thoughts, but never this mystical Self. Yet, if the Self is not forthcoming, there is still experience. Husserl's great attempt, however, to 'bracket off' all presuppositions and to attend to pure experience as it passes, Derrida considers to have failed[59] (in this he stands plainly in the tradition of Sartre). The flux of 'pure experience' turns out to be a tissue of relations; remove the 'merely conceptual' presuppositions and you have nothing left. One feels the continuing power (even by negation) in French thought of Descartes's famous

cogito, 'I think therefore I am.' For the French the experience of subjective thought is the strongest guarantor of individual identity. If that
goes, individuals go.

The dissolution of consciousness into relations ought to remind us of
the dissolution of the objective world into relations. If we doubt the
necessity of the second dissolution we may perhaps permit ourselves to
doubt the first. A consciousness which is endlessly and intelligently
related to reality is still a consciousness. Such relation indeed involves
presuppositions and essentially interrogative schemata. This
anticipatory apparatus is manifestly operated from a single centre (this
is the old argument that, if the unitary self is not available to
introspection, it may nevertheless be identified as 'That which
introspects'). It is true that such a conception of the Ego or subject will
be hard to distinguish from the ordinary idea of a person, but that I count
as pure gain. On the other hand a consciousness without any such
relation to the world would not be a consciousness at all.

I have tended to assume that the thought of Derrida moves inexorably
towards absolute scepticism. This interpretation maybe wrong. Certainly, if one reads Derrida with Merleau-Ponty in mind, certain passages suggest not so much free-floating formalism as a peculiarly tense
engagement with reality. In *Writing and Difference*[60] Derrida cites a
passage of Merleau-Ponty in which the writer is seen as himself 'a new
idiom', constructing fresh means of expression. The words of Merleau-
Ponty are themselves a summary of work set out at greater length in the
same author's *La Prose du monde*. There Merleau-Ponty makes it clear
that the reader is able to understand the new meanings inaugurated by
the writer only *by way of* the great stock of ordinary given meanings.[61] It
is hard to be sure how much of this is to be read back into Derrida
himself. While Sartre, following Heidegger, had argued that meaning
was a simple feat of fiction, proceeding from a Kantian pure will,
Merleau-Ponty argued in *The Phenomenology of Perception* that structures of meaning are unintelligible without physical conditions, and
vice versa; meaning presupposes our own embodiment in the real
world; *être pour soi* (*Sein*) and *être en soi* (*Dasein*) are essentially
incomplete categories, each requiring sustenance by the other. Without doubt, Derrida is aware of this counter-movement in French
philosophy. Yet in his writing as in the earlier work of Sartre there
is a bias towards idealism. We must remember that there are many
idealisms – of image, concept, language, text – united by their
common opposition to material substance. For Derrida the sign is the
structure of consciousness and, since he rapidly concludes that there
is no substantial boundary between reality and signs, at the far end,

and no similar boundary between the mind and its signs, at *this* end, there is really little point in speaking of consciousness at all. At this point Derrida might have dropped back into the language of material substance. Instead, he went the other way: there is nothing, he writes, except text.[62]

It is evident that we have reached our fourth theorem: the priority of language to meaning. Here once more we may approach the radical theorem by a series of unwilling steps.

Jonathan Culler in his *Saussure*[63] points out that languages are differently organized. In English a *stream* is distinguished from a *river* by size; in French a *rivière* flows into another *rivière* or a *fleuve*, while a *fleuve* flows into the sea. From this it may be inferred that things do not exist 'before language'; that is, we cannot, if we fairly acknowledge the variations of linguistic usage, continue to believe that the world consists of a set of things which language merely names; if that were so, although languages might vary in the sense that they might have different words for the same thing, they would not vary in *meanings*; the lexical senses would coincide exactly; *fleuve* would do for the French what *river* does for the English, that is, it would name That Object. But in fact we find, not only simply differences of vocabulary but also endless differences in the *things* proposed by languages. It is therefore concluded that 'things' are, precisely, a proposal of language and have no prior existence. This is commonly taken to be the fundamental theory of the *Cours de linguistique générale* ascribed to Saussure.

The picture is of course familiar. The reader should recognize it as a late version of the critique of objective atomism. It will also be apparent that each of my first four theorems may at any moment assist any or all of the others. Nothing in the example of semantic variation could surprise a humanist of the sixteenth century or a classicist of the eighteenth. Those of us who were educated in the fag end of this tradition spent most of our waking hours learning how Greek, so far from being a mere nomenclature in easy and exact correspondence with English nomenclature, had in fact a different conceptual structure. The whole game of prose and verse composition turned on the need to discover ingenious conceptual equivalents which were never exact. Yet members of this tradition felt no compulsion to infer that either ὄρεα or 'mountains' (our nearest equivalent) did not actually exist, independently of the words. On the contrary, Jonathan Culler could not have described – could not even have identified – the difference between the *fleuve-rivière* contrast and the *river–stream* contrast, had he not had access to substantial clarifying existents.

It is exciting to isolate variations in linguistic mapping of things apparently fundamental like physical bodies – rivers or mountains –

and it is very easy to generalize one's results. But the truth is both duller and, to some of us, more intellectually comforting. Language includes nomenclature and, while it is variable, it often coincides. The lexical sense of ἵππος, *equus* and *horse* is identical. The fact that horses may have grown or shrunk through selective breeding is immaterial. In any case individual horses had always varied. An ancient Greek, looking at the winner of the Derby, would have no difficulty fixing on the word. Nor would an ancient Roman.

Furthermore, there are obvious areas of *overlap* between the terms of different languages. It might be possible to demonstrate that the French for 'flow into' which Culler relies on in his explanation of the distinctiveness of *rivière* differs in various respects from the English; yet, as long as there is an overlap, we may explain ourselves to the French. Indeed, *fleuve* and *river* themselves overlap substantially and therefore in most situations one word translates the other successfully. Translation, seldom automatic, an art rather than a science, is thus not wholly impossible. The AA road map of England employs not only different colours but also different conceptions from those used in the *Times Atlas* physical map of England. But no sane person concludes from that that England does not exist. In any case I agreed long ago that 'thing' is a normative concept, but insisted that the objects elicited by our varying classifications may nevertheless still be said either to exist (in most cases) or not to exist (in some).

In ascribing this theory to Saussure I am forced, like all commentators since his death, to trust in the general authenticity of the *Cours de linguistique générale*. The book which we know by this title is in fact a posthumous construct, put together by Charles Bally and Albert Sechehaye from students' notes of lectures delivered by Saussure in Geneva in 1907, 1908–9 and 1910–11. Whatever its genesis, the *Cours* has come to be considered as a major work. Thus I write 'Saussure holds' and so on, but in this case at least it really is the book itself which is the (strangely isolated) authority. Here at all events is a 'dissolved author', but the dissolution is a local accident of history.

It is also claimed in the *Cours*, rather more mysteriously, that in language 'there are only differences, *without positive terms*' ('il n'y a que des différences, *sans termes positifs*'[64]). By 'positive terms' Saussure seems to mean 'terms which have substance independently of the system', or even 'terms whose meaning is guaranteed by independent reality'. He says, 'Whether we take the signified or the signifier, language has neither ideas nor sounds that existed before the linguistic system' ('Qu'on prenne le signifié ou le signifiant, la langue ne comporte ni des idées ni des sons qui préexisteraient au système linguistique, mais seulement des différences phoniques issues de ce système').[65] Saussure's formulation is innocent so long as he allows that ideas issuing from the linguistic system may be tested for usefulness on the world (though this involves that in the long run a process of natural selection will stamp a certain character on any actual language). Without this saving concession the linguistician is left with no other material than the plotting of variations in lexical and syntactic usage. Nothing remains but a strangely empty series of differences. In practice of course the plotting of significant variation and difference will always presuppose common referents, as in Culler's analysis of the variants of *river*; if there was nothing but language in a void we should not detect a variation between a French speaker and an English speaker upon their both being confronted by an x, but would be faced with a world even more desolate than the field of differences envisaged by Saussure; we should be faced merely by an endless list of words; we could not detect interesting variations in equivalent terms because there would be no way of showing the initial general equivalence. The reader may by this time be growing a little weary of this running objection.

Saussure's theory is sometimes represented as an assertion of the arbitrary character of language. The concept of arbitrariness does indeed play an important part in his thought, but in a peculiar way. It has long been pointed out that (apart from onomatopoeia) any sound will do to represent any thing. A rose might have been called a blug. The initial relation between the word and the object is arbitrary, but the linguistic structure which grows from this mere fiat is systematic and rule-governed. Saussure, however, pushes the concept further. He suggests in effect that not only the sound but also the sense is arbitrary. What we *mean* by 'rose' is a fictive proposal only, having no foundation in reality. This is not so much an extension of the usual doctrine of linguistic arbitrariness as a reversal of it, for whereas by the traditional view the initial relation between a word and its meaning is arbitrary, by Saussure's doctrine the relation between word and meaning becomes very tight indeed (*fleuve* means 'fleuve' and does not really translate *river*) and it is the connection with real objects which becomes elusive.

It is likely that Saussure never clearly foresaw any such black metaphysical implication. If he had been pressed on the point he might have argued that just as phonic differences presuppose the existence of sound itself as the substantial medium of difference, so semantic differences presuppose an initial universal reference to a reality which is substantial though as yet undifferentiated. The clipped, tantalizing phrases which have come down to us will certainly permit such a reading. But they also permit – and have received – a reading which is

much nearer to metaphysical scepticism. And indeed he seems sometimes to go out of his way to invite such an interpretation. For example,
he suggests irrationally that where 'positive terms' have been rejected
'negative terms' may somehow survive. He declares that the only in-
herent characteristics of linguistic features are to be found in their being
'what the others are not' ('Leur plus exacte caractéristique est d'être ce
que les autres ne sont pas').[66] Such a conception will yield a linguistic
classification as opposed to a merely serial enumeration of items only if
there is some *point* in saying that *fleuve* differs from *river*, and such
'point' is normally supplied by an overlap in usual reference. Otherwise
the 'not' shrinks to a mere observation that this word is not that. No one
needs a course in general linguistics to learn *that*. Moreover, if *nothing*
can be predicated of an element beyond the fact that it is not another
element, and this principle is extended to each element as it is successively encountered, we are confronted with a vacuous infinite regress.
In fact even an English dictionary, say, which might seem to be necessarily regressive in that English words are endlessly referred to other
English words for their explanation, is useful to human beings. It is
useful to them because they and the dictionary inhabit the same real
world.

The seventeenth-century scheme is indeed overturned. Bacon said,
'Matter rather than forms should be the object of our attention.'[67] Lacan
says conversely, 'It is the world of words which creates the world of
things'[68] and Saussure says that language is a form, not a substance.[69]
Putting these two together we may arrive at a metaphysical simpli-
fication: 'There is only form.' This is fundamentally incoherent, since
form could not be understood as form without an answering, well-
founded conception of matter or content. A structuralist after all should
be the first to realize the necessity of appropriate context as conferring
meaning. The last context is and must be the world itself.

I remarked a few pages back that none of these fluid features of language would surprise a classically educated eighteenth-century man.
The same argument may at this point be turned round. None of my
critical inferences would surprise Jacques Derrida. Seeing clearly that
meaning depends on the existence of stable termini of reference Derrida
simply gives up meaning. Just as Saussure found that even bare 'difference' was too ambitious, too rich a concept, so Derrida finds that even
the reduction to signs might be subject to a further reduction, since
'sign' implies too much: 'Cela revient, en toute rigueur, à détruire le
concept de ''signe'' et toute sa logique', 'This, strictly speaking,
amounts to destroying the concept of ''sign'' and its entire logic.'[70]
Anticipating my criticism in terms of the presuppositions of 'form' and

the like, he confines himself to the ostensibly neutral term *écriture*, 'writing', a word which no longer suggests the old duplicity of representative and object. He welcomes all the subversive elements in Saussure, the denial of 'positive terms', the theory of arbitrariness (Derrida prefers to say 'unmotivation') but castigates his master's occasional weakenings, his continued hopes for a linguistic system. Saussure's negative system of *différences* assumes in Derrida a double sense. First there is the play of differences which produces the illusion of meaning (how, it is not clear), second there is *différence* in the sense 'deferral': since meaning is never given in a single linguistic element, meaning is deferred until the required context is supplied. But no such specific context will ever provide a substantial terminus of significance; its meaning in turn must wait on some further context, and so on *ad infinitum*.

Here Derrida lays his finger on what was described earlier as the difficulty of entering an essentially contextual system (in which in order to know anything we must first know everything). In Derrida this difficulty is erected into a sceptical principle. But instead of accepting that his premises must have been wrong, he accepts a conclusion so disabling that he cannot even enunciate it without violating it (since to enunciate is to *mean*). This manifests itself early in *De la grammatologie* in a queer, convulsive trick of style which rapidly becomes very recognizable and characteristic: 'La "rationalité" – mais il faudrait peut-être abandonner ce mot pour la raison qui apparaîtra à la fin de cette phrase – qui commande l'écriture ainsi élargie et radicalisée, n'est plus issue d'un logos . . .', "Rationality" – but perhaps that word should be abandoned for reasons that will appear at the end of this sentence – which governs a writing thus enlarged and radicalized, no longer issues from a logos. . . .'[71] The doubling-back is violent, and yet it fails. For as long as one is rejecting rationality for *reasons* (whatever they are) one has not rejected rationality. Once more, in saying this one is not telling Derrida anything which he does not know; he is aware that the solvent he has applied to the works of others is applicable to his own work. At one point he writes, with clear reference to his own critical practice,

> I set down here as an axiom and as that which is to be proved, that the reconstitution cannot be finished. This is my starting point: no meaning can be determined out of context, but no context permits saturation.[72]

The usual 'tic' of style is present here in the deliberate clash of 'axiom' and 'that which is to be proved'. Similar is his habit, at first very exciting but in time merely tiresome, of writing *sous rature*, that is, of crossing out a word but instructing his printer to retain the crossing out (the correction of Derrida's proofs, one surmises, must require at least three colours of ink).

One might suppose that, given the dissolution of the self, of experience, of Platonic forms and of meaning, at least the notion of the text might survive. 'Text' perhaps may, but not 'the text'. Derrida writes of 'a text that is henceforth no longer a finished corpus of writing, some constant enclosed in a book or its margins, but a differential network, a fabric of traces referring endlessly to something other than itself, to other differential traces'.[73]

Perhaps the oddest thing about the thought of Derrida is its manifest allure. This must consist chiefly in the promise of undercutting, the suggestion that the initiate will somehow have 'got behind' the thought of everyone else, and in the sheer novelty. But there is little here which is genuinely new. Derrida is curiously like the Pyrrhonians described by Diogenes Laertius in his *Lives of Eminent Philosophers*, written at some point between the end of the second century AD and the time of Constantine. In all these ancient writers 'convention' (a better neutral term, surely, than *écriture*) accounts for everything. Pyrrho himself, according to Diogenes, 'denied that anything was honourable or dishonourable, just or unjust. And so, universally, he held that there is nothing really existent, but custom and convention govern human action; for no single thing is in itself any more this than that.'[74] Our 'running question' must here be, 'And is this statement itself merely conventional?' The third of Agrippa's 'five modes of perplexity', the 'mode of relativity', neatly encapsulates the history of structuralism and its resolution into scepticism: 'The mode derived from relativity declares that a thing can never be apprehended in and by itself, but only in connexion with something else. Hence all things are unknowable.'[75] Agrippa's second mode of perplexity mirrors Derrida's principle of indefinite deferral: 'The mode which involves extension *ad infinitum* refuses to admit that what is sought to be proved is firmly established because one thing furnishes the ground for belief in another, and so on *ad infinitum*.'[76] Agrippa applies the principle to rational demonstration, Derrida to semantic confirmation. The end result in either case is virtually the same.

Such Pyrrhonian eristic victories end by being merely Pyrrhic. The philosopher who thus undermines others ends by undermining himself. Diogenes, commenting on the Sceptics, is anxious to reassure his reader that they led happy, well-adjusted lives, Hume himself emerged from his blackest bouts of scepticism to play backgammon with his friends until he felt normal again.[77] Derrida, despite the dissolution of the author, continues to appear on title pages and to sign letters. Perhaps he does so with a Jesuitical mental reservation, a saving private consciousness of fiction. The method of *Glas*, however, suggests a less sophisticated state of affairs. Here he seems deliberately to have withdrawn the normal, reassuring authorial presence, to have allowed the words to play their own games. The stratagem is ill-conceived in at least three ways. First, it makes the book extraordinarily difficult to follow or even to read (the concept of 'following' is perhaps inapposite). Second, a general metaphysical theory cannot be corroborated by special, outstanding examples; if you have *really* dissolved the author, the dissolution applies equally to *Middlemarch* and *Glas*. If on the other hand *Glas* provides a brilliant example of the 'dissolved author', then other books provide less good examples, and so the author as such has not after all been dissolved. Thus Derrida has perhaps repeated the naive error of the Russian formalists who affirmed that all literature was about itself and offered *Tristram Shandy* as a *typical* novel,[78] or Sartre's error of supposing that he could demonstrate the universally histrionic nature of man by pointing to an obviously and unusually histrionic waiter.[79] Third, it is difficult to think of any way in which Derrida could have stamped his personality more firmly on a book than by such an idiosyncratic and wholly artificial withdrawal of authorial presence. Every page is clamorously eloquent of its author's identity.

There are other, more modest ways of 'dissolving the author' but these tend to collapse into wholly familiar propositions. For example, it was a commonplace of New Criticism to observe that, when we say 'Jane Austen is an ironic rationalist' we are referring to the identity constituted by the novels plus their title pages; we mean only that the books are thus. If biographical research revealed that the living, breathing Jane Austen was in fact a humourless, drug-crazed mystic, this would have no power to dislodge the earlier pronouncement. In this sense, the 'authors' we discuss are constituted by books and not vice versa. This doctrine is reasonable so long as it implies only that criticism should concern itself with the work rather than with the genesis of the work. But if it is held to imply the overthrow of the ordinary account of the genesis of the work, we must answer that it does no such thing. Real people write books and an authorial personality is then inferred by readers. The inferred personality, naturally, frequently resembles the personality of the living author. It does so because most people are reasonably consistent personalities. Even when the inferred literary personality seems totally distinct from the personality exhibited socially, it remains a real component, an aspect of the living personality to be weighed against the others (for the kind of fiction we produce is just as much a part of our character as the way we treat our friends). But such wild discrepancies are comparatively rare. That is why the discovery that Jane Austen was a drug-crazed mystic would in fact surprise people very much. Lewis Carroll wrote *Alice in Wonderland*; C.L. Dodgson wrote *Symbolic Logic*. Here, it might be said, are two utterly distinct authorial identities, and the biographical fact that Carroll and Dodgson were one and the same person is simply irrelevant. But the examples given in *Symbolic Logic* betray the same imagination, daemonic yet deeply Victorian, that we find in *Alice in Wonderland* and *Alice in Wonderland* is full of free-floating logic. The old-fashioned way of describing this situation would be to say that the inferred personality behind *Alice* resembled the inferred personality behind *Symbolic Logic* because both works sprang from the same living mind; that is, according to the old-fashioned way of looking at these things, one is willing to suppose that the inferred personality might actually *be* that of the author, or be part of that of the author, and this supposition is wholly reasonable.

The writer who would criticize sceptical theory today finds himself in a rhetorically odd position. He is conservative and that word alone carries an automatic charge of disapproval. The fact that what he wants to conserve is meaning and reason, without which socialism, for example, could not exist, is not noticed. The highly 'acceptable' popularizers of poststructuralist scepticism sometimes flinch or hesitate when they run up against the radical meaning of the texts they expound. D.C. Wood, after a dogged and very able exposition of Derrida's philosophy (condemned in advance by the master, who has said that summary is impossible) ends by affirming, with conscious cheerfulness, that Derrida is useful because he implicitly destroys existing institutions. Wood only very faintly perceives, in a hesitant reservation concerning the text-centred character of Derrida's work, that he is equally fatal to everything else.[80] Yet Derrida himself says,

> ce que nous appelons la production est nécessairement un texte, le système d'une écriture et d'une lecture dont nous savons *a priori*, mais seulement maintenant, et d'un savoir qui n'en est pas un, qu'elles s'ordonnent autour de leur propre tâche aveugle.
>
> What we call production is necessarily a text, the system of a writing and of a reading which we know is ordered around its own blind spot. We know this *a priori*, but only now and with a knowledge that is not knowledge at all.[81]

Christopher Norris, perhaps the best of Derrida's defenders, attempts to meet the objection that, despite the deconstructionists' 'professed scepticism towards logic, truth and the very possibility of communication',[82] they continue to demand that their texts be read with intelligent attention. His answer is in four parts: the objection is inapplicable to Paul de Man, at least, because he interprets texts scrupulously; second, it is similarly inapplicable to Derrida, for Derrida is capable of accusing his critics of unscholarly inattention to detail; third, Derrida arrived at his sceptical conclusions only after strenuous intellectual labour, and, fourth, 'Deconstruction neither denies nor really affects the common-sense view that language exists to communicate meaning. It *suspends* that view for its own specific purpose of seeing what happens when the writs of convention no longer run.'[83] And that is all. The entire absence of cogency, in a writer of Norris's ability, is almost embarrassing. The first three parts of his answer merely recapitulate the gist of the objection: that deconstructionists implicitly rely on canons of truth or reason which their theory rejects. The fourth part of his answer is the only part which *confronts* the objection and it is both false and absurd. The person who suspends a rule concedes by implication that it is normally in force. Deconstruction is a bizarre philosophy but at least it never descends to the tautological vacuousness of pointing out that, if we remove the component of rational communication, language will turn out to lack rational communication. It does not ask, 'What if there *were* nothing outside the text?' Derrida himself would never have provided this sort of limply concessive answer. His own reply to the philosophical criticisms of Searle,[84] for example, is wildly 'ludic', and so remains true to its own Nietzschean irrationalism. When, some three years before, Norris reviewed *Grammatology*, his response to the fundamental logical challenge was less bland, more anxious and perhaps more candid. He wrote,

> Towards the end of his book Derrida seems increasingly aware of the difficult – perhaps impossible – character of his task. To attempt *in language* such a radical critique of language itself is surely to lay oneself open to charges of inherent duplicity and failure.[85]

It is indeed. Derrida is inconsistent. He has failed.

Of course no one can really 'think with' the ideas proposed by Derrida. They are rather a way of ending thought. But there is manifestly a Derridian influence, perhaps most obviously associated with his term 'deconstruction'.

In Derrida himself the term is evidently metaphysical. To 'deconstruct' a work is to detect in it the myriad metaphysical assumptions generated by the erroneous assumption that meanings exist outside writing. It is Derrida's special gift to apply this technique not only to standard 'logocentric' authors like Macaulay or W.P. Ker but to seeming allies, like Rousseau, Lévi-Strauss and Saussure. He loves to dismantle their work in order to show that their scepticism is less than pure, or less pure than his.

In the American friends and followers of Derrida, most clearly of all in Geoffrey Hartman, 'deconstruction' assumes a more modest, less lethal force, owing more than a little to the Romantic tradition. Hartman roots deconstructive criticism in the doctrine of the priority of language:

> The priority of language. . .plays a crucial role in these essays. It expresses what we all feel about figurative language, its excess over any assigned meaning, or, put more generally, the strength of the signifier vis-à-vis a signified (the 'meaning') that tries to enclose it. Deconstruction, as it has come to be called, refuses to identify the force of literature with any concept of embodied meaning and shows how deeply such logocentric or incarnationist perspectives have influenced the way we think about art. We assume that, by the miracle of art, the 'presence of a word' is equivalent to the presence of meaning. But the opposite can also be urged, that the word carries with it a certain absence or indeterminacy of meaning. Literary language foregrounds language itself as something not reducible to meaning: it opens as well as closes the disparity between symbol and idea, between written sign and assigned meaning. . . . To suggest that meaning and language do not coincide, and to draw from that noncoincidence a peculiar strength, is merely to restate what literature has always revealed. There is the difference, for instance, between sound and sense, which both stimulates and defeats the writer. Or the difference which remains when we try to reduce metaphorical expressions to the proper terms which they displace. Or the difference between a text and the commentaries that elucidate it, and which accumulate as a variorum of readings that cannot all be reconciled.[86]

Here it might be claimed that it is the notion of deconstruction itself, rather than that of meaning, which is really the vanishing quantity. The removal of metaphysical supports is played down. The notion of the priority of language collapses into the old Romantic thesis that poetry is essentially mysterious, so that it will always elude translation or paraphrase. The urbane elegance of Hartman's prose seems deliberately to disdain any attempt at scientific precision; the *esprit de système* of structuralism is now thoroughly out of fashion.

When Hartman speaks of an excess over any assigned meaning, can we be sure that he does not really mean that poetry bears a different kind of meaning? His contrast immediately evokes entirely traditional contrasts between rudimentary, factual communication and poetic expressions which uniquely convey a complex of meanings, emotional, factual, hypothetical, evocative but, for all that, meanings. Indeed, what else can he intend? He appeals vaguely to mere sound. Onomatopoeia is the one area in which sound is really potent in poetry and onomatopoeia is an occasional and eccentric thing. Moreover it has long been observed that even the heaviest onomatopoeic affects are noticed only when a clue is provided by the ordinary meaning of the line. 'The murmuring of innumerable bees' is onomatopoeic to English ears because those English ears are told that the reference is to bees. Outside onomatopoeic effects *mere* sound is merely unimportant. Housman, a plain member of the same critical tradition, commented that the Miltonic line, 'Nymphs and Shepherds dance no more' (*Arcades*, 96) can draw tears from the eyes when 'the actual sense of the passage is blithe and gay'. No reason can be given beyond the fact that such lines 'are poetry, and find their way to something in man which is obscure and latent, something older than the present organization of his nature, like the patches of fen which still linger here and there in the drained lands of Cambridgeshire'.[87] But when Housman decides that the *sense* of the passage is happy, has he really exhausted the range of *meaning*? Housman relies on the fact that the *context* of this line is an invitation to the nymphs and shepherds to come and live on 'a better soil' (101) and is therefore optimistic. But meanwhile it is entirely possible – indeed it is a fact – that the line carries its own insulated meaning, a meaning which is both more immediate and more evocative than the general invitation in which it occurs. Would Housman have wept if he had thought that the word 'nymphs' meant 'fire-extinguishers', that 'shepherds' meant 'meat-pies', that 'no more' meant 'shrilly'? The plangency of the line arises from the ordinary lexical meanings of the words and acquires further meaning from the manner of their arrangement.

Again, the idea of 'foregrounding' language to its meaning is almost unintelligible unless we allow that what is really intended is the foregrounding of immediate, evocative meanings to factual, paraphrasable meanings. Hartman's phrase is not entirely clear; he says that in literature language is foregrounded 'as something not reducible to meaning'. Perhaps he is not confident that meaning can be wholly banished from the language side of the antithesis. If so, the great project of deconstruction has almost disappeared. The hesitation between 'absence' and 'indeterminacy' in the next sentence tells the same tale. Philosophically the hesitation is intolerable. Two entirely different theories are simultaneously implied. The reader who is sensitive to warning signals should not be surprised when he comes to the extraordinarily limp statement of the critical programme: a relentless focus on 'certain questions' (what questions?) and good old rigorous 'close-reading'. Perhaps Hartman was aware that, if he located literature too firmly in the ineffable residuum which is left after all efforts at interpretation have been exhausted, he could not by definition have anything to say himself. The post-Romantic doctrine in its strong form is a kind of minor scepticism; it confines its attack to interpretation and paraphrase but, if taken seriously, really does outlaw expository criticism, while perhaps permitting continuous theoretical explanations of the prohibition. But Hartman seems to be in doubt about even this, which makes him both much less original and much less destructive than Derrida.

Hartman's mode of deconstructive criticism involves a return to a loose form of Romantic existentialism and therefore gives us, with its emphasis on ineffable mystery, the melancholy obverse of system-governed structuralism. I said earlier that existentialism denied that authentic humanity had any *definable* nature at all. Its nature is to precede such definitions, to be their creator but never their servant. Lying behind this is the fundamental postulate of existentialism, 'Existence precedes essence', that is, we merely *are*, before we are ever defined, and the definition always lags behind the reality. The principle is normally applied to human beings but is occasionally extended to objects. In Sartre's *La Nausée* the chestnut-tree root gazed at by Roquentin likewise exists before its definition; words fall short and can only falsify the ineffable reality.[88] But for things as for people we produce fictive, schematic, clearly defined identities and these are the matter of ordinary discourse. I suggested that structuralism is the child of existentialism in its implicit acknowledgement of the fictive character of the structures it investigates, but, as it proceeds with its work, it is necessarily the un-Romantic, formalist side of the mind which is engaged. With Hartman the ineffable Real once more assumes the centre of the stage, but it is the ineffable reality not of man, nor of trees, but of *poetry*, which commands his allegiance. Like others who face such an extinction of their best skills, Hartman grows strangely verbose, elaborately eloquent, as he approaches the point at which he must confess that nothing can be said.

Here there is a link, after all, with Derrida. The central impossibility of *La Nausée* is its attempt to convey in words that which is *ex hypothesi* transverbal. Sartre seeks to partition the universe ontologically into two fundamental categories, existence and essence. It is to essence alone that words are applicable. Yet 'existence' is a word and is certainly not applied by Sartre to essences (though there is in *La Nausée* a very revealing slip, when he writes, 'The *essential* thing is contingency'[89] (my italics); contingency belongs of course on the 'non-verbal' side of the division. A very similar absurdity can be found in Derrida when he attempts to tell us, having divined that he cannot consistently attack concepts with concepts, that *différance* (he has his own reasons for spelling it with an *a*) is 'neither a word nor a concept'.[90] Quite obviously it is both.

But with Hartman it is only literature which is 'dissolved'. One does not seriously fear a metaphysical extension to people and things. In general, he is simply a late-born Romantic. Of other members of the 'school' Paul de Man is fiercer but then Hillis Miller is gentler than Hartman. Miller is willing to affirm that all interpretations have equal authority (does *he* think 'nymph' in Milton can be accurately glossed as 'fire-extinguisher'?) and can therefore find himself in dispute with M.H. Abrams,[91] but most of the time one finds in Miller nothing but the best kind of sensitive intelligence, working as sensitive intelligence always did. Harold Bloom, meanwhile, is frankly antideconstructionist. They do not look like a conquering army.

I have drawn but one strand from a rich fabric of critical discourse. It should not be mistaken for the whole. The progress of structuralism and poststructuralism has not been univocal. On the contrary, internal arguments raged from the beginning. Some of these were themselves directly antisceptical in tendency. Roland Barthes argued that a fully modernist, objectless text would be sterile: 'Le texte a besoin de son ombre, c'est *un peu* d'idéologie, *un peu* de représentation, *un peu* de sujet: fantômes nécessaires'; 'The text needs its shadow; this shadow consists in *a little* ideology, *a little* representation, *a little* subject-matter – necessary ghosts'.[92] These things are necessary, if only as the material of subversion. 'Representation' and 'subject-matter' momentarily renew old relations with the world, even if 'ideology' does not. Althusser allows that science affords a form of knowledge which exists outside ideology and is therefore able to define and comprehend ideology.[93] The argument is parallel to arguments advanced in this study. Indeed what we may call the materialist wing, with its emphasis on history, must be – and at its best is – clearly opposed to absolute formalism. Yet even among the materialists, formalist cultural subjectivism is for ever breaking in. Althusser's guarded objectivity was soon attacked (with particular reference to his concept of 'scientific history').[94] Moreover one finds that useful and highly influential 'guides' to the movement, like Terence Hawkes's *Structuralism and Semiotics*, tend in their summaries of complex material to simplify in the direction of scepticism. Hawkes cites a passage of Edward Sapir[95] in which it is suggested that 'human beings do not live in the objective world alone. . . but. . .are very much at the mercy of language', and that the ' "real world" is to a large extent built on the language habits of the group.' I, as a critic of sceptical structuralism, feel obliged to notice the direct implication of 'alone' and 'to a great extent', which is obviously that the objective world does exist, though in a threatened condition. Hawkes, on the other hand, sums up the passage as affirming that 'there is no such thing as an objective, unchanging "real" world.'[96] If we may withdraw from the sentence 'unchanging' (for surely no one but a Platonist believes in an unchanging world) the proposition is merely Pyrrhonian. The stock apologetic inverted commas appear round *real* even where reality is being explicitly denied, so that they are either redundant or else imply that there is after all a *real* 'real world' (surely the opposite of the author's intention). Similarly, Catherine Belsey is clearly mildly distressed by the persistence in Wolfgang Iser's *The Act of Reading*[97] of common-sense, specific interpretations, as if he were not yet liberated from reference to the object.[98]

The part played in this entire story by the concept of experience is a curious one. In continental and continentally influenced critical writing 'empiricist' is now a common term of mild abuse. But on this side of the Channel many clung to the notion, and empiricism itself became, more and more clearly, a technique for losing reality. The seemingly candid word 'experience' is profoundly ambiguous, meaning either 'that in the world which is experienced' or 'a mental presentation' (which may or may not be linked to reality). It became apparent in the eighteenth century that idealism was latent in British empiricism. Bishop Berkeley, in his grand effort to turn 'ideas into things'[99] was the purest of empiricists and the purest of idealists at one and the same time. Matter, he perceived, was a metaphysical conception. It is important to remember that Berkeley saw his philosophy as a bulwark against scepticism. The distrust of metaphysics, of entities beyond our conceptual reach, is fundamental with him. His response was to locate reality firmly – by definition – within our concepts, to build reality from our ideas. The outcome of his enterprise is notorious. Reality so constructed is mere fiction.

Yet philosophy since Berkeley has conspicuously failed to learn from his brilliant failure. The horror of the metaphysical (even of the concrete metaphysical so essential to the physicist) continued to dominate thought. Thus Hume, finding himself unable to check our ideas against reality, no longer explained the difference between perceptions and fantasies as resting on the fact that perceptions are of the real, but instead proposed a wholly internal distinction: perceptions are vivid, mental images less so. Ordinary usage allows us to say, summarizing Hume, 'There are only vivid and less vivid images', which betrays the fact that the plain difference between percept and image has not been explained but merely surrendered. Thus the Hume of the first book of the *Treatise* confesses that, however strenuously we 'fix our attention out of ourselves. . .we never really advance a step beyond ourselves, nor can conceive any kind of existence but those perceptions, which have appeared in that narrow compass'.[100] The pattern of Hume's thought has been endlessly repeated in the centuries which have followed, in various idealisms variously masquerading as bluff common sense. The medium of idealism is at first the flux of ideas, later the flux of language.[101] In fact ideas and that of which they are ideas must be logically distinct, or the term 'idea' would never have evolved. It is open to anyone to redefine 'idea' lexically so that it simply means 'thing', but to do so is to collapse the grand thesis 'Things are made of ideas' into something very close to tautology. Meanwhile any culture which accepted such a semantic revision would soon have to work out a word for specifically mental presentations. Similarly language and the reality it describes must be logically distinct. Yet I. Dilman writes, 'The source of the objectivity of our judgements is language itself (and that brings in the way we live, act and react) and not anything independent of this.'[102] The parenthesis is a transparent attempt to smuggle non-linguistic realities back into the scheme. The tone and the hesitation are thoroughly English but the inner impetus of the argument is Derridian.

C.S. Peirce strove to locate reality in the ultimate agreement of human beings.[103] W.V. Quine was firm that Greek gods were unreal and physical objects real, but confessed that this very firmness was dependent on a mere 'posit', a theoretical base which is itself prior to and therefore unsupported by any set of credentials. Thus, epistemologically, the science which teaches the reality of physical objects need be no more correct than the religion which teaches the reality of gods.[104] Quine's firm belief is reminiscent of Hume's firm (but confessedly irrational) faith that the sun would rise on the following day. Objectivity is replaced by a more or less coherent, more or less extensive intersubjectivity. The philosophers who opt for language rather than consciousness as ontologically fundamental eagerly inhale the new atmosphere of suprapersonal rules and conventions as if its very impersonality somehow conferred substance but a rule which obliges no one and relates to no material circumstance external to itself is quite as vacuous as the most fugitive and private mental image. Neither Peirce nor Quine, meanwhile, is able to draw the elementary distinction between what is true and what is generally held to be true.

If we ask what drives philosophers to embrace views so nakedly counter-intuitive we shall find that, for them as for Berkeley, it is fear of scepticism – and with the same profoundly ironic outcome. If we suppose a reality independent of our concepts or our language, we suppose that which *ex hypothesi* we can neither conceive nor describe. Hence the real becomes the metaphysical *Ding an sich* of Kant, the mumbo-jumbo of the Platonists, a place of utter night (the obvious middle position, that we know *some* of reality and *much* of it remains, indeed, obscure is commonly left out of account). Recoiling from this melodramatic dark-ness philosophers simply closed their shutters and declared one little room an everywhere. Nicholas Rescher puts the matter succinctly:

> We cannot profitably argue 'Our concept of reality is legitimate because it (actually) corresponds to "authentic reality".' This line of argument runs into the road-block posed by the question: just what manner of 'reality' is at issue in this correspondence? (1) Is it reality *an sich* construed in altogther mind-independent terms? That reply won't do, because how could one possibly support it? (2) Is it reality-as-we-think-it? Of course a correspondence obtains here, but that is just trivial (circular).[105]

The mode of reasoning here employed is incompatible with Tarski's Correspondence Theory of Truth, which turns on the (luminously cor-rect) possibility of removing inverted commas in one half of one's demonstration: 'The cow is in the meadow' is true if the cow *is* in the meadow. But for Rescher (and Quine, and Peirce, and Hume, and Berkeley) everything is in inverted commas. Equally, Rescher's theory is incompatible with learning or any sort of progression in knowledge.

Yet to say that Rescher's argument will not square with truth-as-correspondence or with the palpable fact of learning is only to say that it generates unpleasant consequences; the internal cogency of the argu-ment is unrefuted. But in truth the argument is, internally, extremely coarse. Obviously one knows only what one knows. We do not know how far our knowledge corresponds with reality. But the possibility that it does or does not so correspond is easily conceivable. Rescher runs together definite knowledge and open conception. The mesh of concept can be left deliberately wide. The far side of the moon was a perfectly clear though pretty empty conception before spacecraft brought back observations. Neither language nor conception is a system of minute, atom-by-atom correspondence. We hazard before we win, cast nets before we catch, but if we had been doing all this in a vacuum it would have felt very different. For a start, there would have been no ascertainable failures. An objector might answer, 'But you cannot check – *independently* – the correspondence of even the most "certain" knowledge with reality.' Indeed there are no absolute guar-antees of factual truth and one 'terminal possibility' implied by realism is the possibility that *all* our 'knowledge' is erroneous. Neither of these propositions shocks (or dismays) common sense. But epistemological atomism either paralyses knowledge or begets, as its ill-nourished but rebellious child, conceptual idealism. Once again, the Greeks were there first:

Meno	How will you look for something, Socrates, when you have no idea what it is? What sort of thing, out of all the things you don't know, will you postulate as the object of your search? Or, if you have the luck to find it, how will you know that this is the thing you did not know?
Socrates	I see very well what you are up to, Meno. You see this as an opportunity to draw out a deliberately contentious argument. A man can neither discover what he knows nor what he does not know. He can't look for what he knows, because he already knows it, and therefore has no need to search; and he can't look for what he does not know, for then he wouldn't know what he was looking for.
Meno	Don't you thing that's a good argument, Socrates?
Socrates	I do not.

(Plato, *Meno*, 80D-E, my translation)

In the course of this prolonged 'shaking of the concepts' I have moved from a rejection of atomist objectivism to a still more vehement rejection of cultural or structural subjectivism. If meaning is not imprinted by things nor yet evolved in advance through merely mental or linguistic pressures, how is meaning constituted? Meaning is of two kinds, operative and semantic. Operative meaning occurs when an individual intentionally says something in a material context (truth is usually either claimed or presupposed in some form on these occasions). Semantic meaning exists before specific occasions in the form of lexical senses (and larger units) but these are themselves formed with regard to their potential use in real situations. Operative meaning is a function of systematic convention operating with reference to the real (thus reference may be direct or hypothetical, of which more anon). Lexical meanings and syntactic patterns are culturally variable but the various forms are all designed for use upon the real world and indeed some are more useful than others; English pronouns, for example, are notoriously weak and ambiguous, so that locutions like 'He, that is, Lacan' are forced upon us.

Meanwhile, truth is other than meaning. We may consider the matter in three phases. First, relations are proposed and in so far as they are merely proposed are subjective to the person and/or system which proposes them; but then, we find, they variously obtain or fail to obtain in the real world and are so far objective. Roger Trigg writes, 'The aim of any conceptual system will be to draw distinctions which already exist in nature.'[106] That 'any' is doubtful, but I applaud the rest. The relation verbally expressed as 'smaller than' is useful because everything is not exactly the same size as everything else. 'Brighton is smaller than London' then holds because Brighton *is* smaller than London. The relation 'smaller than' will not apply to those two places the other way round. Hume said, 'There is no object, which implies the existence of any other if we consider these objects in themselves.'[107] To think thus is to impose on the world an artificial nominalist reduction. As soon as Hume inserts the phrase 'considered in themselves' he excludes the idea of relations which might actually obtain in the world. Although it is true that there is no object which could not *conceivably* exist without other objects, the world we inhabit is intricately relational, so that practical inference is not only possible but easy. 'Merely trivial' analytic implications in terms are answered by implications *in rebus*. 'Daughter' implies 'parent'. If one meets a person properly describable as a daughter, she, the concrete person, must actually have had a real parent. This is in one sense tautological, since, as soon as I said 'properly describable as a daughter' the parent was implied, for 'having had a parent' is part of the *meaning* of 'daughter'. But at the same time a real parent will have to have been related to a real daughter for the analytic implication to apply at all in a particular case. The parent-child relation itself is a cultural product in so far as it is formulated by our society. Once formulated, however, its use is neither to weave fictions without reference to brute reality nor yet to compose an *ersatz* reality; its use is interrogative, and nature may meet or refuse its demand. Of course one can suppose with Hume that the world might lapse into incoherence; there is no guarantee of everlasting stability on the basis of practical inference. If the world became incoherent, relational language would indeed lose its utility; this fact is one more testimony to the importance of the objective. Thus far the world has exhibited enough relatedness to permit the growth of a richly syntactical language.

Second, as we have seen, semantic meanings are variously applicable, variously useful in reference, description, evocation, commanding, exhorting, persuading, demonstrating, asking, soothing, exciting and so on. When semantic meanings and syntax (*langue*) are actually used in a concrete situation (*parole*) a further kind of *meaning* emerges, and this is the kind I call 'operative'. Operative meaning is governed not only by the conventions employed but also by the objective context in which it occurs. Here perhaps is our best hope of a solution to the problem of entering, or beginning to learn, a contextual system. Children learn the highly abstract and relational term 'more' early and easily. They learn it when they have had some food but are still hungry. I said earlier in this chapter that the 'last context' was the world itself. As a way of ending an indefinite regress this may seem ill-judged, since the world itself is indefinitely rich and recedes from us. Nevertheless the objective world is immediately available in particular situations precisely because it is *not* a mere extenson of our cultural scheme, and so that scheme may either break or be rewarded as it meets that other, immense fabric. Thus any point of contact between the cultural scheme and reality may provide a genuine terminus of operative meaning for a user of the scheme.

Finally, *truth* is primarily determined by the fabric of reality. A string of *meanings* will be *true* if it composes a sentence which is satisfied by the real world. There is no need to suppose that authors or objects are fictions or that language is incapable of any relation to reality. But our fifth theorem, 'Verisimilitude is the mask in which the laws of the text are dressed up', remains. The connection of fictitious literature with reality is trickier and will, in one form or another, fill the rest of this book.

2
The dissolution of mimesis

Le concept du vraisemblable n'est plus à la mode.
(Todorov)

The 'mask of realism'

In 1921 Roman Jakobson published his essay, written in Czech, on
'Realism in art'. It is difficult to decide now whether the essay,
operating first on a few readers who could understand Czech and then
through widening circles of the European intelligentsia, actually caused
the movement which followed or whether, on the other hand, Jakobson
merely wrote down what many people in many places were in any case
beginning to think. Jakobson's thesis is that our notion of what is realistic is conventional and fluid. He makes it clear early in the essay that his
primary intention is not to address the problem of literary realism:
'While in painting and in the other visual arts the illusion of an objective and absolute faithfulness to reality is conceivable, "natural" (in
Plato's terminology), verisimilitude in a verbal expression or in a literary description obviously makes no sense whatever.'[1] The scope of this
observation shrinks abruptly, halfway through the sentence. The first
half seems indeed to promise a radical thesis, that there can be no such
thing as literary realism. But then the word 'natural' enters (with a nod
to Plato's *Cratylus*) and we receive instead the almost platitudinous

observation that literature does not sound like what it represents in the way sculpture looks like what it represents. Literary realism comes to us via the arbitrary, formal conventions of language. One senses that Jakobson may have thought that 'natural' resemblance to reality was the only sort that could have any claim to objective status and that, if he could exclude natural resemblance from literature, nothing more need be said on that front. Meanwhile he addresses the problem as it appears in the visual arts.

Jakobson was writing at a time when traditional canons of realism were being violently changed by modernists and primitivists. In the history of art a general consensus on what constituted realism, first attained in antiquity, lost in the middle ages and recovered at the Renaissance, had held firm in its broad outlines for a very long time. It appears most clearly in the writings of the sixteenth-century artist and critic Vasari, who saw realism together with other artistic virtues as rising to a new eminence in his own century: Giotto had been more realistic than Cimabue and Michelangelo had outstripped all. In the more sophisticated art history which followed there was little sense that the terms of the discussion were changing. One critic might argue, say, that certain late medieval artists, such as Van Eyck, were more realistic in certain respects than certain high Renaissance artists, such as Raphael, but the canons of demonstration were not fundamentally disturbed, until the Impressionists appeared, followed swiftly by the modernists. Jakobson, when he wrote his essay, was watching the growth of modernism and hearing it described as a mode of realism:

> A contemporary critic might detect realism in Delacroix, but not in Delaroche; in El Greco and Andrej Rublev, but not in Guido Reni, in a Scythian idol but not in the Laocoon. A directly opposite judgement, however, would have been characteristic of a pupil of the Academy in the previous century.[2]

Jakobson concludes from such extreme variation, amounting at times to contradiction, that there are several different concepts of realism and that a mature criticism must become aware of such conceptual distinctions if it is ever to avoid profitless collisions of judgement. He brilliantly observes that those who found realism an aberration from the merely conventional norm naturally welcomed primitive sculpture as providing the shock of reality, when in fact such sculptures were, as often as not, executed in docile obedience to utterly conventional canons of practice prevailing in the primitive society. The same work could be, in one place, as placid as a Guido Reni and, in another, as subversive as a Picasso.

Jakobson's preliminary attempt to map the various concepts of realism is, however, weak and confused. One of the versions is 'the sum total of the features characteristic of one specific artistic current of the nineteenth century'; another is that which 'the persons judging it' perceive as 'true to life'; a third is 'the tendency to deform given artistic norms conceived as an approximation of reality'.[3] The lack of co-ordination in these descriptions is extreme. Presumably a person may 'judge' or 'perceive' a work as true to life under *any* of the conventions, but these judgements will vary as the conventions vary. Thus, such judgement may base itself on norms or on striking deformation of norms, and is not itself an operative concept to be set alongside 'deformation'. Meanwhile the reference to the characteristics of nineteenth-century art manifestly fails to specify the *concept* in accordance with which such art is organized, which was supposedly the object of Jakobson's critical enterprise.

Though Jakobson argued for a complex conventional element in our use of the term 'realistic', he did not clearly rule out a running reference to objective reality. At the same time, the weight of his mind, so to speak, is on the conventional side of the equation. Here is the source of all our difficulties, here is the proper matter of a rational criticism.

In the years which have followed, Jakobson's insight has assumed a curiously uncritical yet metaphysically radical form: realism is itself a tissue of conventions and therefore has nothing to do with reality. Thus baldly stated, the non sequitur is glaring. Why should the presence of convention preclude reference to reality? The truth is almost exactly converse. All reference to reality (including pointing with the finger) is conventionally ordered. Language is an immensely rich system of conventions and is the best means we have of referring to the real. The error of those who suppose otherwise might be christened 'The Bellman's Fallacy', if we recall the lines from *The Hunting of the Snark*:

> 'What's the good of Mercator's North Poles and Equators,
>   Tropics, Zones and Meridian Lines?'
> So the Bellman would cry: and the crew would reply,
>   'They are merely conventional signs.'

> (Fit the Second)

The current fashion of knowing shudders at the void which yawns between words and reality is a curious survival from the seventeenth century. In fact it is because words are conventionally ordered and thus separated from other things that they can be used to refer or describe. You don't point at a cat with a cat. You use your finger, or a word. You don't describe a cat with a cat. You may illustrate the word 'cat' with a real cat and you may explain that the word for that animal over there is 'cat', but in all these cases the so-called paralysing 'gap' between word and thing is in fact indispensably necessary to the practical operation.

It is odd that so palpably inadequate an argument should have carried all before it, and yet it is so. The student who says in a seminar that Lawrence is splendidly true to life will be answered with smiles of conscious superiority as if he had committed some mild *bêtise*. The assumption behind the smiles is, quite simply, that modern literary theory has exploded the idea that literature is in any way authentically true to life.

I have cited Jakobson as one important source of the trend. It appears in a developed form in the celebrated eleventh issue of *Communications*, the issue devoted to *vraisemblance*, or 'verisimilitude'. Tzvetan Todorov in his introduction to this issue tells the story of a dispute in Sicily in the fifth century BC. The quarrel came before judges but the judges had no means of deciding which story was true. Instead they were driven back upon a somewhat different decision: which story gave the greater impression of truth? Here, says Todorov, the laws of persuasiveness became dominant over the laws of truth. The persuasive, or *vraisemblable*, has no relation to reality.[4] He refers to the laws of persuasiveness as the laws 'proper' to the work.[5] Todorov's thought, evidently, is primitive. He has a conception of factual truth and a conception of 'the pleasing'. The idea of the probable seems not to have dawned upon his mind. Relation with the real may be direct (factual truth) or it may be indirect (what is known to be likely). Those judges in ancient Sicily did not consider that, because they had no empirical evidence on the immediate issue, they were therefore restricted to making aesthetic judgements only. They thought they ought to decide which story was the more probable. So far we have heard no philosophical argument to suggest that they were mistaken in their conception of their task.

Todorov himself is no Derridian sceptic. He has a naive faith in science as involved with truth, as opposed to *vraisemblance*: 'Le concept du vraisemblable n'est plus à la mode,' he writes, 'on ne le trouve pas dans la littérature scientifique sérieuse'; 'The concept of verisimilitude is out of fashion; it is not found in serious scientific literature.'[6] The idea of a scientist who restricted himself to ascertained fact and had no truck with probability or hypothesis is simply ridiculous. With regard to literature, on the other hand, Todorov is a radical sceptic. He perceives that verisimilitude has, somehow, the look of reality, but this 'look', he roundly asserts, is unfounded. The realistic work pretends to be real and is not. This, let us note at once, is certainly a misdescription. George Eliot is a realistic novelist. She shows no signs of wishing to dupe her readers into supposing that her books are factually true (such stratagems belong to the embryonic stage of the novel in the seventeenth century). She does however implicitly claim probability for her stories. The claim on probability cannot itself be resolved into a pretence of truth. Its proper falsification is not by means of a demonstration that Gwendolen Harleth never lived but rather by showing that events of the kind shown in the novel do not occur in real life. In fact such events do occur in real life and thus George Eliot's claim to realism is, very simply, vindicated.

But Todorov pushes doggedly on with his theory of realism as mendacious pretence:

> One may ascribe verisimilitude to a work in so far as it tries to make us believe that it conforms to the real and not to its own laws; to put it another way, verisimilitude is the mask in which the laws of the text are dressed up, a mask which we are supposed to take for a relation with reality.[7]

It is as if Todorov has forgotten the central, classic statement of *mimesis*: Aristotle's observation that, while history tells us 'what Alcibiades did', poetry tells us 'the kind of thing that would happen' (*Poetics*, 1451a). The very antiquity of this pronouncement should serve as a salutary warning. It is fatally easy to view the progress of European literature as a movement from a purportedly literal truth to a mere play of arbitrary modes; after all, Dante's *Commedia* and the miracle plays tell the Great Story, the Story which is more real, more actual than the accidents of everyday life; but in the nineteenth-century novel the hero may have any name at all, the carriage may leave at whatever hour the novelist chooses. This change is important but we must not allow it to displace everything else. Even in the middle ages artists took pains to make *fictions* plausible. Even in the nineteenth century the episodes in a novel were not utterly unconstrained. They were governed by ordinary probability. Probability is the missing factor, and its importance was plain to Aristotle more than 2000 years ago.

Todorov's reference to 'the mask' of realism is our fifth 'brief theorem'. His language is oddly puritanical, both in its literalism and its moralistic tone: poets are liars, they go about in strange masks, deceiving the people, telling them things which are not true. It is mildly disturbing to think of such a man teaching literature; rather like a somewhat smoother version of William Prynne teaching drama. One is tempted to borrow the words of Blake: this man was hired to depress art.

Nevertheless the thesis is fairly stated and is ingeniously applied by other contributors to the same issue of *Communications*, most notably, perhaps, by Roland Barthes, in his marvellous essay, 'L 'Effet de réel'.[8] Barthes chooses to discuss the barometer included by Flaubert in his description of Mme Aubain's room in 'Un Coeur simple'. Barthes swiftly concedes that the barometer is not there for the usual cultural or ideological reasons; the piano, also mentioned, perhaps conveys bourgeois status, the heap of boxes may be there to convey the idea of disorder. But the barometer is merely itself. Its sole function is to suggest reality; it is 'un effet de réel'. But then Barthes makes a fine but crucial point. The barometer is not there because of truth (there is really no barometer, no Mme Aubain) but, so to speak, because of its true-ish-ness. Flaubert is not interested in the reality of the barometer, but rather in the detachable, *ideologizable* feeling of 'real-ness' which the nineteenth century attached to such things. Thus the 'real' in such a context is not an actual object (nothing is in fact denoted) but is another – very general – *signification*, just another fictional meaning for the author to play with; at the very moment when Flaubert's words seem to escape the web of cultural significations and to denote a real object, what they actually do is not to denote anything at all, but to signify the real-ness of such an object:

> Le 'réel' y revient à titre de signifié de connotation, car dans le moment même ou ces détails sont réputés dénoter directement le réel, ils ne font rien d'autre, sans le dire, que le signifier: le baromètre de Flaubert, la petite porte de Michelet ne disent finalement rien d'autre que ceci: 'nous sommes le réel'.

The very uselessness of the barometer, as judged by the systems of signification, secretly assumes a wholly literary utility and must therefore be added to the list of 'mere effects' it apparently disrupts.

Like Todorov, but with greater subtlety, Barthes misdescribes his material. The barometer does not 'signify' reality in the same manner as the piano signifies bourgeois status. The latter signal operates *within* the fiction. The point Barthes makes about the barometer is a point about its rhetorical function; it falls outside the fiction (the difference we are dealing with is the difference between 'King Lear is Cordelia's father' and 'King Lear is the hero'). So understood, the barometer in any case does not say, 'I am real'; it says, 'Am I not just the sort of thing you would find in such a house?' Barthes's formulation, no less than Todorov's, automatically invites a brisk puritan rejection; the second formulation, which is the more accurate, might even be answered with an affirmative.

Neoclassical verisimilitude: adjectival and adverbial realism

A historical survey of the literary practice of verisimilitude will quickly show that realism is a freely movable feast. In the seventh century BC Archilochus, tiring of heroic convention, wrote his 'shocking' poem about throwing his shield away in flight and became the model for various docile imitations.[9] Sidney's 'Look in thy heart and write'[10] had a similar fate. The rough realism of Donne's new voice became the artificial fustian despised by the mature Dryden, whose forensic plainness became in its turn the artificial Augustan diction rejected as artificial by Wordsworth – whose Romantic Truth became in *its* turn a 'manner', to be austerely eschewed by twentieth-century poets. It is as though the hope of reference to reality is endlessly renewed but endlessly defeated – or found out. In a very few years Pinterian dramatic dialogue, which seemed at first to catch the very accent of reality, has become a trick, at the command of second-rate television writers.

Nor, it would seem, is the *theory* of verisimilitude any less fluid. In seventeenth-century France la Mesnardière held that to bring upon the stage a judicious valet was to affront verisimilitude.[11] He felt the same way about an uncivil Frenchman and a subtle German. La Mesnardière will seem all the odder if we remember that the most classical of all English comic writers, P.G. Wodehouse, built an entire career on a judicious valet. But it is not that la Mesnardière is unaware of the New Comedy tradition of the clever servant. He simply thinks it unrealistic, *mere* convention. Dryden's Eugenius, in the *Essay of Dramatic Poesy*, similarly stigmatizes the clever servant as stock convention.[12] I would guess that most people today would tend to think both a stupid servant and a clever servant highly conventional, but would be slightly inclined to regard the second as the more realistic, precisely because it divagates from the norm. For la Mesnardière on the other hand it is precisely divagation from the norm which damns a character as unrealistic. Surely, it will be said, this man's use of the term 'realistic' is wholly governed by his literary ideology and has nothing whatever to do with our use of the term; moreover, we have no reason to suppose that our own usage will be exempt from a similar historical subversion.

But Barthes in his essay, 'L 'Effet de réel'[13] went a little further than this. In the seventeenth century, he suggested, there was no nonsense whereby verisimilitude was 'contaminated' by any relation to reality: it was all simply a matter of what was acceptable to public opinion, that is, mere ideology, confessed as such. Ultimately, in Barthes's theory, the definition of *vraisemblance*, 'that which conforms to public opinion', applies as much to Flaubert as it does to Boileau or any neoclassical writer. The only difference is in the clear-headedness and candour with which the operation is conducted. At least, he implies, our polished ancestors knew what they were about and made no pretence.

Barthes cites in support of his thesis the following passage from Pierre Nicole's *Treatise on True and False Beauty*: 'One should not regard things as they are in themselves, nor as they are known by the speaker or the writer, but only by their correspondence with the knowledge of readers and hearers.' Barthes quotes from the French translation by Richelet, published in 1698. Pierre Nicole (1625–95) was a Jansenist theologian who taught at Port Royal. He laboured long to reconcile Jansenist teaching with orthodoxy. The moral austerity of his beliefs found expression in ponderous Latin. The original version of the *Treatise on True and False Beauty* appeared in a small volume with a sesquipedalian title: *Epigrammatum Delectus ex omnibus tum veteribus tum recentioribus poetis accurate decerptus, cum dissertatione de vera pulchritudine et adumbrata, in qua, ex certis principiis, rejectionis ac selectionis Epigrammatum causae redduntur.*[14] This work was well received in Protestant England and was for many years used as a textbook at Eton College. It is somewhat surprising to be told that such a writer held the urbane, cynical view attributed to him by Barthes. Was Nicole really so contemptuous of the part played in art by truth?

In fact he was not. The passage Barthes cites comes from a special section of the treatise dealing with the best way to fit one's discourse to the needs of one's audience. Elsewhere Nicole thunders out continually the need for truth: *prima igitur sententiarum virtus veritas*, 'the first virtue of propositions is truth.'[15] Thus he echoes the sentiments so prominent in the *Logique* he wrote with Antoine Arnauld: 'cette excellente règle, Qu'il n'y a rien de beau que ce qui est vrai', 'the outstanding rule: that nothing is beautiful which is not true.'[16] Again in the *Treatise* he writes, 'Whatever is false is at variance with the things themselves, nor is there any beauty in falsehood except in so far as it feigns truth. From this you may learn that the fountain of beauty is in truth, and that of falsehood, on the contrary, is in deformity.[17]

Indeed, Nicole's heavy insistence on truth, as might have been expected in a Jansenist, borders on puritanism. Hence the momentary slippage of thought, 'except in so far as it feigns truth'. The word I translated as 'feigns' is in the original *mentitur*, of which the ordinary meaning is 'lies'. Lewis and Short's *Dictionary* allows 'feigns' as a possible sense but rightly adds that there is always an implication of falsity. One senses that Nicole, without proper preparation, has stumbled in passing on the fact that realistic passages are often not literally true. His theoretical vocabulary is so effectively simplified by his Puritan doctrine that he can scarcely express the new thought, save by the formally contradictory *veritatem mentitur*, 'lies a truth'. This is the best he can do to convey the idea of saying something which is in fact false but is nevertheless the kind of thing that happens. For Nicole is not, as one might have expected, straightforwardly in favour of factual truth and against *vraisemblance*. In his section on 'debatable and controvertible ideas' he suggests that this entire category lacks literary merit and should be studiously avoided by those who aim at beauty, which is ultimately to be found in truth alone, and in truth of such a sort that it is immediately recognized and accepted by readers. The last clause unmistakably allies itself with the frequent neoclassical insistence that the *vraisemblable* should be the sort of thing which is commonly received as really the case and at the same time he is willing to fuse this expectation with genuine truth.

Here indeed is the proper *caveat* for twentieth-century writers who quote bits of neoclassical theory out of context. Neoclassical theorists certainly say that the *vraisemblable* is that which conforms to public opinion. But 'public opinion' is not with them a covert term of abuse. Public opinion is thought of as likely to be correct. Francis Bacon, the source of so many platitudes for the age which followed, made universal consent one of the tests of truth, and carefully distinguished true and rational consent from the mere aping of authority.[18] Lord Herbert of Cherbury says more directly that what we must rest on is 'whatever is universally asserted as the truth'.[19] Of course 'opinion' was sometimes contrasted with firm and universal agreement. The seventeenth century was no more proof against variations of sense and interpretation than our own century. But a general willingness to respect common expectations is as evident in that period as is the reverse in our own democratic age. The commendation of *vraisemblance* is firmly linked to the injunction to follow nature, prominent in classical sources[20] and echoed by the moderns such as Vida,[21] Montaigne,[22] Charron[23] and hundreds more. Barthes's attempt to separate neoclassical verisimilitude from any reference to reality is fundamentally unhistorical. J.E. Spingarn, whose knowledge of seventeenth-century critical theory was profound, wrote apropos of Hobbes, 'The subject-matter of poetry is, then, the manners of men; its method is that of verisimilitude, or resemblance to the actual conditions of life.'[24] The definition he gives is stock, and quite inescapable for a reader with any respect for etymology.

The attempt to assimilate neoclassical theory to modern formalism may fail, but meanwhile the glaring difference between what counts as realistic for a neoclassicist and what counts as realistic today remains. The existence of this difference, indeed, supplied the ground on which, in Jakobson and others, the theory of modern relativistic formalism was raised. The seventeenth century may not provide fellow relativists but surely, it will be said, it provides powerful primary evidence of the fact of variation.

That variation exists is indeed unquestionable. But it is important not to let such evidence run away with one's intelligence. In order to test the degree of *conceptual* variation involved we may ask, if different ages are so divided over *vraisemblance*, should we ascribe different *lexical* senses to the word? After all, we conclude from Chaucer's saying that a lady was not 'dangerous' of her speech to him, that 'dangerous' once had a different lexical sense. Can we similarly conclude that, whereas *vraisemblable* now means 'lifelike', in the seventeenth century it meant 'decorous'? In fact we cannot. *Vraisemblable* is not changing semantically like *dangerous* (from something like 'grudging' or 'standoffish' to 'perilous'). Rather, *vraisemblable* retains a stable core-meaning, but is successively applied to very different things. Because of the core-meaning, these shifts of application can be the subject of rational debate in a way that cannot occur with merely semantic shifts; that is, one person will say, 'Real verisimilitude means in practice x', and another will reply, 'No, *real* verisimilitude means y.' But it would be silly to say to Chaucer, 'You were wrong about that woman; *real* danger is to be found in things like rock-climbing.' The word *verisimilitude* retains as its clear but open meaning, 'approximating to what is really the case'. Given this openness, it is possible to dispute at length over the examples which best satisfy the definition.

A rather clearer example than *verisimilitude* of the sort of thing I have in mind is provided by the word *tall*. Professor X is, I am told, a tall man in Belfast and is certainly a short-ish man in Brighton. Thus the word *tall* is differently applied in Belfast (because, I presume, most people are shorter there). But the word has exactly the same lexical meaning in Belfast that it has in Brighton. A rational appeal to the core-meaning, 'Higher than ordinary' will in this case instantly resolve the apparent contradiction. The case of *verisimilitude*, though less clear, is similar. As I suggested earlier, no one with any sense of etymology (and the neoclassical critics were highly conscious of such things) could long remain unaware that the core-meaning of *verisimilitude* was 'likeness to the truth'.

It is therefore not enough, when looking at an extreme neoclassical critic like la Mesnardière, to observe that he is merely using the term in a different sense. In fact, the core-meaning remains strong enough for the following dialogue to take place, across the centuries.

la M.   A judicious servant would obviously lack verisimilitude.

Modern   Why? A stupid servant on the contrary would just look conventional; a judicious servant might begin to exhibit the sort of oddity we encounter in real life.

la M.   Oh, surely not. Obviously servants are a servile species. Where does *servile* get its meaning if not from the way servants actually behave? When I see a servile, stumbling scullion lurching onto the stage, I say to myself, 'That's *exactly* what servants are like.'

Such conversations, moreover, do not have to take place across centuries. They can occur within the neoclassical period. For example, when Dr Johnson had affirmed in his Preface that Shakespeare had truly imitated the species of human nature, the term *nature* (closely linked with the idea of verisimilitude) was subjected to exactly this sort of rational dispute, for William Guthrie in the *Critical Review* for November 1765 observed against Johnson:

> Shakespeare has succeeded better in representing the oddities of nature than her general properties, which characterize a Menander, a Terence or an Addison. . . . Can a Falstaff, a Malvolio, a Benedick, a Caliban; in short can any of Shakespeare's successful characters in comedy be termed a species? Or rather, do they not please by being oddities, or, if Mr. Johnson pleases, individuals?[25]

Notice how in this passage Guthrie is able to *argue* with Johnson and does not simply shift the meaning of the terms. He appeals to the core-meaning of *nature*: 'what is'. He and Johnson are not playing separate language-games.

Of course the shift from locating realism in statistical norms to locating it in oddity is profound. I imagine that a man from Mars would find the second position (the one which comes more naturally to us) initially the less credible. I take it that the later feeling becomes strong when a certain suspicion has arisen: namely, that a given passage is written in conformity with a general rule rather than with the real. *The fact that the general rule may itself be founded on reality becomes immaterial.* The mere availability of a rule providing the writer with a 'short cut' renders the passage suspect. In these circumstances it becomes the specifying mark of the real to divagate from the rule. Thus 'quirkiness' becomes a paradigm of realism. Then, later still, since all linguistic operations, as I said at the beginning, have a conventional aspect, this shift also, to the aberrant as typically realistic, can be reduced to its increasingly perceptible convention and – if you are that way inclined – relegated to the category of the unreal (by way of the ubiquitous fallacy, 'Whatever is conventional is unreal'). This is what Barthes in effect sought to do to Flaubert.

All sorts of shifts in what constitutes for the time the most useful application of 'realist' are possible. They are licensed by the actual richness and complexity of the objective universe. Please note, there are no apologetic inverted commas round the words *objective universe*. One may, for example, regress from an 'adjectival' to an 'adverbial' realism. We have the adjective 'real' and the adverb 'really'. If we ask whether something is real (adjective) we are simply asking whether something is found in nature or not. If on the other hand we employ the adverb – 'What is such-and-such really like?' – we find that the term naturally attaches itself to hypothetical events which are unfamiliar yet possible. Reference to reality is involved in both cases, but in the second (the adverbial) the possible reality treated may be far from commonplace. In fiction, adjectival realism simply uses the sort of objects which are found in reality, events of the kind which happen. Adverbial realism, on the other hand, proposes an inherently improbable event (such as a voyage to the moon was in the time of H.G. Wells) and assumes the burden of showing, in circumstantial detail, what it would *really* (adverb) be like if it were to happen. *The History of Mr Polly* is adjectival realism, *The War of the Worlds* is adverbial realism.

Oddly enough, H.G. Wells has to show a more than neoclassical reverence for norms of probability, postponed to the level of Newtonian physics, in order to corroborate as realistic the superficially bizarre situation he presents. Thus all the old apparatus of corroborative norms is still involved, in a somewhat different form, at a secondary level. As soon as the writer turns from showing the initial strangeness of his material and embarks on the secondary task of showing how such events may nevertheless be possible, he must invoke norms. The norms are scientific or physical rather than patterns of customary human behaviour for the simple reason that science-fiction writers (I intend of course the older realistic kind of science fiction) do not restrict themselves in their initial unfamiliar hypotheses to human beings. Adjectival realism cannot embrace *le merveilleux* but adverbial realism, with certain safeguards, can, whereupon *le merveilleux* reappears precisely as Wellsian science fiction. Thus, although we have two *concepts* of realism, they are not utterly distinct, arbitrary coexistents, such as Jakobson envisaged. They are branches from a single stem given in the concept, 'reality'. Each proposes an alternative use of what is, at the most fundamental level, a single notion.

Again, a neo-Platonist who thinks that what is truly real lies beyond this world may claim that an idealized statue is more realistic than a naturalistic one. Note that the neo-Platonist uses the word 'real' in exactly the same lexical sense as his opponent, who maintains that on the contrary only sensible particulars are truly real; otherwise there would be no *philosophical* disagreement between them.

Occasionally the neoclassical taste for generality as good in itself could lead to a real wobble in the core-meaning of *vraisemblable*, so that it crossed temporarily over to its proper antithesis, from 'like what is' to 'like what ought to be', from 'Nature' to 'the rules' (and of course the same thing occasionally happened to 'Nature' itself, by way of the concept 'regulated Nature'. Thus Rapin writes (1674) 'Truth gives things only as they are; *vraisemblance* gives them as they ought to be. Truth is almost always defective, because it consists of a mingling of specific conditions.'[26] Rapin's opening ploy here strains the core-meaning, perhaps to breaking point. This happens because he is exaggerating the difference between truth and lifelikeness in order to make a point which even then must have been felt as mildly paradoxical. For the moment at least he is as complete a conventionalist as Barthes could have wished. But it would be unwise to assume that Rapin's celebrated definition, 'Le vraisemblable est ce qui est conforme à l'opinion du publique',[27] is similarly conventionalist. For him as for other neo-classical thinkers public opinion is likely to be correct. In context this is clear, for Rapin is contrasting *le vraisemblable* with *le merveilleux*, with Niobe turned to stone. In Section xii he says roundly that *vraisemblance* is based on probability. The normal position, in which etymology and core-meaning are fully preserved, acknowledges easily that realistic fictions do not convey literal truth about individuals but insists that they are constrained by probability and in this way satisfy the requirement that they should 'approximate to what happens'. 'What happens', notice, is itself an open generalization.

Thus Boileau's famous line, 'Le vrai peut quelquefois n'être pas vraisemblable',[28] 'What is true can sometimes be unrealistic', does not license us to separate realism from what happens. The whole thrust of his argument is that the realistic must be founded on what happens most of the time. Freak events do occur but they will hardly give the force of reality to a line of poetry, since they will rarely have figured in the experience of the listener or reader. This is made quite clear by the preceding line, 'Jamais au Spectateur n'offrez rien d'incroyable', 'Never offer your audience something they cannot believe.'

There remains Aristotle's observation (wittier than anything in Rapin) that a believable impossibility is preferable to an unbelievable possibility (*Poetics*, 1461b). Aristotle pushes the thought to an extreme conclusion. Yet it is still, I submit, fully consonant with the core meaning of *vraisemblable* and represents one extreme but tenable position within that constraint. Of course no impossibility can really be probable, though it may be credible. Aristotle is commenting on the imperfect apprehension of the audience. So far, so cynical. But an episode will not be believable if it does not reproduce features which are seen to operate powerfully in the real world. Reference to reality remains not merely a vestigial factor but a crucial one in the success of the deception. Only an improbability with pretensions to probability, so to speak, will succeed, and probability means, as always, approximation to the real. It is important to remember that all these aphorisms, from Aristotle's πιθανὸν ἀδύνατον ('believable impossibility') to Bussy's 'L'extravagance est un privilège du réel',[29] are, to a greater or lesser extent, *jokes*. When these jokes are taken literally they produce self-consuming systems of sceptical metaphysics. One is reminded of C.S. Lewis's formula for the mystique of courtly love, which he deemed to have arisen partly from a laborious misreading of a flippantly urbane Roman poet: 'Ovid misunderstood.'[30]

I have said that the neo-Platonist who locates reality in an ulterior world of forms and the naturalist who locates reality in the here and now are both using 'reality' in the same sense, since otherwise there would be no philosophical disagreement as to the nature of reality itself. The aristocrat may really believe that well-born people have finer natures and the liberal democrat may believe equally that ordinary people are of sterling worth. Each may then write a novel exemplifying his judgement. The aristocrat A depicts life in a great house as a compound of chivalry, intelligence and honour; the democrat B shows his readers a city stricken by unemployment but sustained by common kindliness, good humour and stoic endurance. My example is simplified, since in practice any writer worth his salt will defend his central thesis with a thousand stratagems, including episodes which purport to show his pre-emptive understanding of the opposite view. But, for all that, two novels such as I have described are conceivable. Now, what happens if A reads B's novel, and vice versa? In either case, the answer is the same: each finds the other's book hopelessly artificial. Each will say that what purports to reflect the character of reality itself merely reflects the unfounded ideology of the author. The structuralist critic, looking on, will say that each party is correct in his negative criticism of the other and was deluded in his original positive thesis. Both the courteous aristocrat and the stirling working man are ideological confections. This structuralist response is very elegant and, incidentally, gains a certain support from the running (ideological?) presumption that unbelievers are shrewder than believers. It is in this manner that the essentially literary law that works are governed by convention naturally extends itself until it becomes the metaphysical claim that our conceptions of reality are themselves ideologically determined. Nevertheless there is a profound difference between the two positions.

We may consider the above structural judgement on our two novelists under either heading. The modest, 'merely literary' structuralist will point out that in both books there is a powerful vein of convention, the convention that the hero should be in either case a certain sort of person, and this determines the character of the book. The unreal, conventional nature of this weighting of the material can be seen at once if we compare it with appropriate sectors of real life, where an ethically mixed situation will at once present itself. The metaphysical structuralist, on the other hand, will have no neutral conception of reality which he can employ as a corrective. Neither writer is right but then, equally, he cannot say that either writer is wrong, since there is no longer any means of corrective reference to the real. But he can and must claim that the writers do not disagree, since disagreement implies reference to a common subject matter. Each merely deploys his vacuous categories.

It is clear that the initial promise of a brisk resolution of all our difficulties is not fulfilled in either case. The 'merely literary' structuralist has to strain a little to suggest that the conventions involved are merely literary (conventions governing hero status and the like). In fact conventions of what is proper to a work of fiction merge with conventions of what may be expected of the real world. In a few moves the structuralist can be manoeuvred into confessing that he really thinks novelists A and B have simply failed in their attempts to convey reality. This, we note, is utterly commonplace criticism in the immemorial tradition of realism. For no one ever pretended that realism was easy, that reality was never misdescribed. Instead of being liberated into a new world of easy critical dismissal, we find that we are confronted by the ancient task of deciding, in every case, how successful the writer has been in his or her mimetic enterprise for where there are degrees of failure there are likewise degrees of success.

The metaphysical structuralist, on the other hand, can say nothing about the question which naturally engrosses the attention of ordinary literary readers: 'Is *this* successfully realistic or not?' I take it that all literature which *purports* to be probable can be called 'realistic' and that which *is* probable can be called 'successfully realistic'. The metaphysical structuralist must say that in either case, as in all cases, the 'purport' was empty and by this blanket judgement forthwith disclaims interest in the literary phenomenon as it appears to most readers, i.e. an exciting claim which may or may not be justified. For, to the metaphysical structuralist, neither of our novels is *strikingly* or *distinctively* empty. Once corrective reality is jettisoned, there is no ground for discriminating between our two naive ideologists and, say, Tolstoy, or even the author of a scientific paper on metallurgy (or a structuralist paper on reference). When everything is unreal a particular charge of falsehood can carry little interest.

I suggest, then, that the structuralist emphasis on convention, as soon as it offers to account exhaustively for a specimen of realism in conventionalist terms, must either be driven to a self-destructive metaphysical extreme or else collapse into orthodox criticism (where it may indeed display an exceptional skill in eliciting conventional factors).

Eighteenth-century perceptions of Shakespeare

I have argued that in all the various applications of 'realistic', the single aim of referring to reality persists. But I do not wish to deny that critics or theorists were ever confused or shifty in their use of terms. In English criticism of Shakespeare in the eighteenth century, the idea of 'nature' and 'the natural' (our nearest equivalent to *vraisemblable*) is repeatedly set against the notion of 'the rules'. The two concepts then perform a giddy dance.

The basic contention is that Shakespeare's plays are not founded on artificial rules of dramatic composition but simply on the world itself. This thought, now tedious and stock, seemed then to blaze with meaning. The sudden sense that a writer might be capable of raising his head from books and looking at the world itself, full of colours, objects and above all richly various people, was intoxicating. As a critical theorem, it combined a marvellous simplicity with an unlimited capacity for subversive elaboration. The same thing is said again and again, yet the note of excitement is unmistakable. 'He had no written precepts,' writes Arthur Murphy in the *Gray's Inn Journal* for 1753–4 'and he wanted none: the light of Nature was his guide.'[31]

Even those who retained a respect for 'the rules' felt that Shakespeare somehow shattered the normal canons of aesthetic preference. John Armstrong (using the pseudonym, 'Lionel Temple') wrote in his *Sketches: or Essays on Various Subjects* (1770),

> The three great French dramatic poets, Corneille, Racine and Molière, have . . . been much more successful than the English: amongst whom . . . we shall find very few who have built upon a regular plan. . . . Shakespeare indeed without one perfect plan has excelled all other dramatic poets as to detached scenes. But he was a wonder! – His deep knowledge of human nature, his prodigious variety of fancy and invention, and of characters drawn with the strongest, truest, and most exquisite strokes, oblige you to forget his most violent irregularities.[32]

Elizabeth Montagu wrote in her *Essay on the Writings and Genius of Shakespeare, Compared with the French and Greek Dramatic Poets, with Some Remarks Upon the Misrepresentations of Mons. le Voltaire* (1769),

> The dramatis personae of Shakespear are men, frail by constitution, hurt by ill habits, faulty and unequal. But they speak with human voices, are actuated by human passions, and are engaged in the common affairs of human life. We are interested in what they do, or say,

by feeling every moment, that they are of the same nature as ourselves.[33]

Elizabeth Montagu's trumpeting title shows that the bias of her argument may be partly nationalistic. On that side stand Greeks and Frenchman, consumed with convention, and on this stand the English, with a bluff loyalty to nature as their guide. It is an early version of a national tension which can still be sensed today in philosophical and literary disputes. But Elizabeth Montagu makes a great point of audience identification and so implicitly universalizes the natural truths set down by Shakespeare. All of this, of course, is in line with the classical theory of verisimilitude which never insisted on historical actuality. But in preferring, or deeming 'most natural' those elements which most easily admit of audience identification, Elizabeth Montagu has admitted a covert ground of *prescription* into what had seemed to be an antiprescriptive, squarely descriptive stance. All are natural but some are more natural than others.

Evidently nature itself may be conceived as more or less extravagant, more or less rule-governed. Its being the natural antithesis of 'rules' leads to the definition of nature in descriptive terms. Various pressures, to do with the question of universal appeal and relevance, enforce the second, prescriptive conception. Before the eighteenth century began Charles Gildon was stung by Rymer's bone-headed neoclassicism into a professed preference for irregularity, at least as practised by Shakespeare. He wrote in 'Some Reflections on Mr. Rymer's *Short View of Tragedy*, and an Attempt at a Vindication of Shakespeare', published in his *Miscellaneous Letters and Essays on Several Subjects in Prose and Verse* (1694): 'A nice Observation of Rules, is a Confinement a great *Genius* cannot bear, which naturally covets Liberty. . . . 'Tis not govern'd by Common Rules and Methods but glories in a Noble Irregularity.'[34] But when Samuel Johnson came to write his Preface to the eight-volume edition which appeared in 1765, he finds in Shakespeare's very adherence to nature a profound and ordered uniformity:

Shakespeare is, above all writers, at least above all modern writers, the poet of nature; the poet that holds up to his readers a faithful mirror of manners and of life. His characters are not modified by the customs of particular places, unpractised by the rest of the world; by the peculiarities of studies or professions, which can operate but upon small numbers; or by the accidents of transient fashions or temporary opinions: they are the genuine progeny of common humanity, such as the world will always supply, and observation will always find. His persons act and speak by the influence of those general passions and principles by which all minds are agitated, and the whole system of life is continued in motion. In the writings of other poets a character is too often an individual; in those of Shakespeare it is commonly a species.[35]

It is a curious conception of nature, as that which is opposed to individuality and accident, but for Johnson it is so. Here is 'nature methodized' with a vengeance. Yet, although he might be thought of as edging his author in the direction of prescription rather than description, it is quite clear that Johnson will not relinquish his hold on what really happens as the ultimate governing conception. Accidents and individuals are rejected because they *happen less* than the great primary movements of love, valour, greed and terror. For Johnson there is *more of reality* in such things. His preference for the species over the aberrant and uninformative individual no more implies contempt for reality in him than it would in a biologist.

The English critic who really had transformed Aristotle's 'what would happen' into a moral, prescriptive doctrine was Sidney. David Daiches has observed that in Sidney imitation by the artist of the world becomes imitation by the reader of models of excellence proposed in the work. Mimesis is transferred to the reader, and the artist's task in providing material for such imitative emulation is precisely *not* to render this leaden world as it is, but to deliver a golden world of regal kings and heroic heroes. Aristotle's probable 'would' becomes in Sidney a moral 'should'.[36] Sidney's doctrine found adherents: Voltaire in particular argued that Shakespeare erred against the proper kingliness of kings in showing Claudius drunk.[37] Voltaire's position admittedly can be put in terms conformable to the doctrine of nature: 'Most kings are regal (hence, indeed, the meaning of the word "regal"); an un-regal king is an aberrant accident.' Johnson, one might have thought, could easily have agreed with this. Yet he resists, and it is hard to avoid the inference that he finds Voltaire's view priggishly prescriptive.

But notice the form of his resistance. He does not answer by saying, 'A real human king might happen to love wine' (that, as we have seen, was Guthrie's answer to Johnson). Instead, he appeals to a level of *generality* higher than Voltaire's. Shakespeare's story, he explains, 'requires Romans or Kings, but he thinks only of Men . . . he therefore added drunkenness to his other qualities, knowing that Kings love wine like other men.'[38] This ultimate meeting of the highly abstract and the fully concrete is very characteristic of Johnson.

Difficulties can arise from the varying ways in which we take the measure of the real world. Sometimes, if we have had more rules than we want thrust down our throats, we rejoice in the myriad accidents and eccentricities of nature; at other times, when we wish to strengthen our grip, to predict developments or sift the important from the unimportant, we want to exclude accidents as far as possible. The root sense of 'unnatural' is always 'not occurring in nature', but, because of the powerful exigencies of the second approach, 'unnatural' can easily come to mean, 'not fitting in with what we know from other sources'. And, of course, latent in the idea of 'not fitting in' is 'contrary to the rules'. Follow that path and, with the word 'unnatural' still upon your lips, you will find yourself on the other side of our original antithesis between 'What is' and 'the rules'.

We saw something of this sort happen to Rapin. One can see it happening in England to the ingenious Guthrie, in his *Essay upon English Tragedy* (undated, but probably 1747):

> NATURE never designed that a complication of the meanest, the most infamous, the most execrable qualities should form so agreeable a composition, that we think Henry the fifth makes a conquest of himself when he discards Jack Falstaff. Yet Shakespeare has struck out this moral contradiction, and reconciled it to nature.[39]

Of course a Nature who 'designs' may well be a little affronted, not only by Shakespeare, but by certain features of the real world. Guthrie supposes her seriously disconcerted by Desdemona's falling in love with the Moor.[40] This means that he would be obliged to describe such an affair in real life as 'unnatural', and, oddly enough, usage permits the application of the word to real-life events, despite the fact that, by our radical definition, this generates the contradiction 'What is, is not according to what is'. In the passage quoted, Guthrie has embarked on his sentence with a quasi-prescriptive conception of nature in his head. The sense 'unfitting' may be subliminally enforced by a feeling that it is not natural *to good drama* (for dramas have their proper natures no less than human beings) to align human characteristics in this way. But then part of his mind begins to clamour in opposition, 'This is really very natural!' The root sense of nature, 'What is', flows back (*tamen usque recurrit*). He covers the awkward transition in his thought with the diplomatic word, 'reconciled', as if, paradox of paradoxes, Shakespeare achieved his end by a feat of artificial cunning. But the reader knows that 'moral contradictions' of this sort do not really have to be reconciled with nature. They happen all the time.

Charles Gildon, similarly, was harassed by varying uses of 'natural'. Just as Jacques Scherer in the twentieth century helplessly contemplated 'le domaine mouvant des vraisemblances'[41] so Gildon finds 'nature' unmanageably fluid:

> *Nature, Nature* is the great Cry against the Rules. We must be judg'd by
> *Nature*, say they; not all considering, that *Nature* is an equivocal Word,
> whose Sense is too various and Extensive ever to be able to appeal to;
> since it leaves to the Fancy and Capacity of every one, to decide what is
> according to Nature and what not.

But, having decided that the word is unusable, he goes on to use it:

> the Droll-Pieces of the *Dutch* are all very natural; yet I dare believe there
> is no Man so very ignorant of the Decorum of History-Painting, as to
> think, that in the Tent of *Darius*, by Monsieur *le Brun* or the *Jephtha's
> Sacrifice* it would be natural or proper to introduce one of those Droll-
> Pieces, either of Drinking, dancing, snick-or-snee, or the like.[42]

It will be said that he proceeds to use the word 'natural' precisely in order
to show that it is unusable. But the reader who has grasped that *natural*,
like *verisimilitude*, is a complex branching from a single centre and not a
mere congeries of meanings will have no difficulty with Gildon's
sentence. The humorous pictures of the Dutch are natural because, in
accordance with the root sense of the word, they show what happens.
The second use, which appears to have crossed wildly over to the opposed
sense, 'decorous', arises perfectly rationally from the application of
'natural' to the relation between a work and its contents, rather than to
the relation between the contents of a work and the outside world. With
Guthrie we began to suspect that the thought 'natural *to the drama*'
might have begun to rise in his mind. With Gildon it is quite obvious that
this has happened. Thus his attempt to bombard us with intractable contradictions fails. The collision is resolvable. Dancing, drinking and
rowdy cut-and-thrust are elements natural to contemporary Dutch
society. Dignified personages are elements natural to dignified Biblical
pictures.

   Gildon was philosophically minded and looked hard for some means of
resolving what seemed to him a messy state of affairs. In the *Complete
Art of Poetry* he strives to annihilate the very distinction between art and
nature, urging that art is 'no more than *Nature reduc'd to Form*'.[43] Yet in
that one word 'reduc'd' lies a world of more or less wanton transforma-
tions. When (a few months later) Pope adopted the thought, so that like
an earlier Alexander he might be seen to slash through the Gordian knot,
he prudently confined the identity of art and nature to a single source, of
primeval purity:

> Nature and Homer were, he found, the same.
>
>   (*An Essay on Criticism*, 135)[44]

   It is indeed rapidly obvious that some literary conventions can plausibly be presented as formulations of reality while others cannot. Neither metre nor the celebrated 'unities' of time, place and action can be regarded as answering to reality. If metre 'methodizes' speech, it does so by changing it fundamentally. On the other hand, Virgil's use of declamatory repetition, say, reflects and formalizes something which happens in real life.

There is no short way out of our difficulties as readers and critics. Art cannot be reduced to convention or redistributed in nature. Some conventions are susceptible of realistic use, some not. In all the twists and turns of the long eighteenth-century conversation about Shakespeare, which took place in periodicals, weighty folios and coffee houses, the intuition that Shakespeare more than any poet except perhaps Homer really conveyed the nature of reality is never lost. The notion that readers trained on neoclassical conceptions would never commit the philistine error of supposing that art might convey reality breaks upon this great rock. These people looked at Shakespeare, and that is *exactly* what they thought.

Attempts to redefine *verisimilitude* as 'conventional acceptability' always fail. One may show that a given writer's use of the notion *comes down to* that in practice, but this is simply to say that this writer failed to do what he hoped to do. Certainly 'conventional acceptability' will not represent what he intended by the term, and to reduce meanings to their 'cash results' would make nonsense of all lexicography. One can perhaps imagine a Thrasymachean dictionary, in which justice is defined as 'the interest of the stronger' but it will be of little use to someone who wants to know what words actually mean. Philosophers occasionally produce such dictionaries. They are, of course, jokes.

The very withdrawal of current structuralists and poststructuralists from the term 'verisimilitude' shows that they well know what it means. If it really meant 'ideological acceptability' it would be the commonest term in their critical vocabulary. Its banishment is eloquent. In exile it continues to press the other side of the great equation of literature – in commerce with which many, though not all, literary conventions acquire their life and force.

In the neoclassical period whatever strength formalism possessed broke on the example of Shakespeare. But in our own century first E.E. Stoll and then the structuralists have attempted to sever Shakespeare from the real world. It is almost time to look at him again. But one more theoretical round remains to be fought.

Soft formalism

Hard formalism says that everything in literature is formal. Soft formalism flinches from such absolute assertions and contents itself with a more modest claim. It permits (in passing) reference to the real but denies that such reference can play any part in determining the aesthetic character of a work of art or in providing the ground for aesthetic approval. Soft formalism, it will be observed, is a much tougher and more formidable affair than the hard formalism we have so far been discussing. Hard formalism appears only intermittently in the history of criticism, as an occasional convulsion. Soft formalism is perennial, and deserves to be so, because it is highly plausible.

A soft formalist might reply to everything I have said in this book in the following way:

> I grant that reference to the world is ubiquitous in literature, by the mere use, if you like, of ordinary language. Even fairy stories, in so far as they say 'the widow' or 'the youngest son' employ terms which apply outside the story, to the old lady down the road and to the Queen of Carthage, to James Donagh and Prince Edward, and this forms an inescapable groundbass. I further concede that George Eliot works with palpable probabilities. Which is as much as to say, I concede the mimetic dimension of literature. But – if I may speak for a moment in Aristotelian terms – to designate the mimetic element is to designate the mere matter of literature and not its form, by which alone it is what it is. Artists indeed use the real and the probable, but the verb is all-important: they *use* the real, and do not *serve* it. Their art consists in the varying modes of use, and these in their turn are governed entirely by formal considerations and not at all by truth. Therefore, as literary critics we are never concerned with the degree to which a work reflects reality but always with the varying formal modifications.

All this I can almost believe. Almost, but not quite.

Certainly, if accurate representation of the world were what we chiefly needed from art, we should in general prefer photography to painting. Of course photographs employ conventional equivalents, but the equivalence is more smoothly systematic, more easily read off than that of almost any painting. The great soft formalist, E.H. Gombrich, when demonstrating the half-inadvertent formal distortions of art, will use a photograph to tell his readers what the West Front of Chartres Cathedral is really like.[45] Moreover, when art historians wish to represent a *painting* in a book they do not ask a draughtsman to *draw* the painting; they employ a photographer. In either case distortions occur, but in the photograph they can for the most part be automatically adjusted or set aside by the viewer. If we want to know what Richard II was really like, we consult not Shakespeare's play but history books. The play we use in quite another manner. To admire Milton's lines on the leaf-strewn brooks in Vallombrosa on the ground that one has visited Vallombrosa and checked that the brooks are indeed strewn with leaves is mere a-critical sentimentalism. And exactly the same strictures apply to general or probable truths. We do not read *King Lear* in order to satisfy ourselves that abdication of power may be incompatible with the retention of love and allegiance; this sentence is not art, does not engage us aesthetically as *King Lear* does.

But what, I cannot but ask, of that catch at the heart when we look at a Vermeer painting of a brick wall, or watch the formal, fairy-tale opening of *King Lear* (an old King and three daughters, two evil but the third and youngest good) splinter into something which can be understood only because it conveys so piercingly the real inept demonstrativeness of the old and the gauche inhibitions of the truthful young? Lear tries to play the old game, as if Cordelia were 3 years old and bouncing on his knee: 'Who loves Daddy best?' Cordelia really does love her father best, and the sweets are waiting (the best third of the kingdom for her alone), but she has grown up, the reward has assumed political dimensions and was implicitly proposed before the game began; in these circumstances she cannot play Lear's still genuinely loving game. Instead, her own love for her father is shocked and impeded, and she cannot tell him warmly how much she loves him but is driven upon a cheese-paring quantification of her love for him as a subtraction from her love of husband, which would be either absurd or repellent were it not for the circumstances. The audience is moved, not by triumphant fulfilment of, or brilliant divagation from a dramatic norm, but by what could be summed up, barbarously enough, as the parent-child-ness of it all. If parent-child-ness were not found in the world the scene would be empty. If the representation were less accurate it would be less moving. It pierces by its truth.

Even if the brief critical sketch I have given of the beginning of *King Lear* were disputed, it can hardly be denied that this *kind* of criticism is virtually inescapable when we deal with Shakespeare. We find that we must write not only about artistic conventions but also – and with real engagement of mind – about people, as such. We may think also of those countless moments of private applause which come upon the reader of George Eliot and spontaneously assume a cognitivist form: 'That's *very* true!' 'That's *just* right!' It seems bizarre to claim that something so dynamic, so energized, should be mere matter, should play no active part in the aesthetic economy of the work.

Meanwhile, the question 'Why, then, do we not check in *King Lear* to see whether parents and children really have such difficulties?' is easily answered. We do not use literature in this way because so many things are going on in literature *in addition to* the presentation of reality that we could never conclude from a given feature of the work that an equivalent feature existed in the world. With photography, while we cannot quite say, 'Nothing appears in the photograph which is not founded securely and intelligibly on features present in the scene photographed', we know nevertheless that the odds are heavily loaded in that direction. Thus, although photographs do not invariably provide conclusive evidence, they are usable and are commonly used as sources of evidence. I plead for the inclusion of veracity or probability as *part* of the aesthetic whole.

Nevertheless, we are committed to the thesis that the artist, as artist, deals occasionally in realities and therefore is concerned with knowledge. This does not mean, however, that good mimetic art must present us with fresh knowledge, should teach us things we did not know before. From antiquity the commonest praise of the mimetic artist is that he has truly rendered some readily available, known subject. We praise a work of scholarship when it adds to our stock of information, but that has never been important in the mimetic tradition. That is why the claim, 'We do not go to *King Lear* to satisfy ourselves that abdication may be incompatible with the retention of love and allegiance', though obviously correct, 'feels irrelevant' to the orthodox lover of realistic art. Even in the heyday of mimesis, no one ever used plays in that way. This difference between the scholar and the artist is at first sight puzzling, since it is assumed in the case of the scholar that the mere retailing of knowledge which is already commonplace is too easy to merit praise, but in the case of the artist it suddenly seems that the mere conveying of the familiar is some kind of feat. This is not so hard to account for in the case of visual representation, where anyone can find out by personal experiment how hard it is to produce an adequate drawing of something as intimately known as one's own hand. But with literature the case is much less clear. Literature operates with words and there is a sense in which we are all masters of language. We therefore bestow no especial praise on the person who merely states a known truth accurately. We reserve praise for such things as minute, highly detailed or unexpectedly pointed accuracy of description and the power to 'realize' or 'give life' to the object of the mimesis. Thus we find that there are two ways of using words (two ways which are frequently mingled but are nevertheless distinguishable). We can use words merely to summarize or refer to known material. Or we can use words to elicit an imaginative awareness of the known material. In either case it is language – an utterly conventional system – which is used, but the difference in pace, ordonnance and the governing principle of relevance is very great. Language designed to enlist the imagination will track to and fro over the same area and will concentrate on features which energize perception rather than on logical markers.

Remember that I am not speaking of literary language as such, but only of mimetic realism. Nothing in my remarks leads us into that prominent feature of poetic language commonly known as the 'foregrounding' of the means of expression. Where such foregrounding occurs, we are more than ordinarily aware of the expressions used and derive pleasure from the awareness. This feature, immensely important though it is in the history of poetry, is not essentially involved in mimesis. In the house of literature there are many mansions. Mimesis successfully conveys the real object in a manner which deepens our experiential knowledge of that object or of like objects (we have no difficulty in praising the realism of portraits of people long dead, although we cannot check the specific likenesses). By 'experimental knowledge' I mean *connaître* rather than *savoir*, *Erleben* rather than *Wissen*, the way you know your sister rather than the way you know DNA theory. Most of literature is concerned with fictitious persons. Even where, as in Shakespeare's Roman plays, the characters are drawn from history, we do not claim, in calling them realistic, that they closely resemble their specific originals; we mean only that they behave as such people would in real life.

It may therefore be objected that, whatever art deals in, it cannot be *experiential* knowledge. Experience is of actual existents and art, since it is fictitious, has few or none of these to offer. The real Brutus doubtless had experiential knowledge of Julius Caesar, but Shakespeare can offer his audience nothing better than a pseudo-experience of both of them. This is true, but is less disabling than it seems to be. The realistic artist, as Aristotle saw, gives hypothetical cases, things that would or could happen. The notion of an *experiential* hypothesis must seem strange to those who believe that experience is always of concrete particulars, but in fact this is a pretty exact description of what happens in realistic literature. The fiction evokes from us, as we entertain the hypothesis, all the human energies and powers, the incipient commitments and defences which occur in experiential knowing, but are absent from cool, conceptual knowing.

But here my imagined sceptic may persist in his objection, 'But it is still *ex hypothesi*, a pseudo-experience, not real at all.' My answer is the traditional answer from the ancient theory of verisimilitude: 'No, indeed, but the object must be probable, that is to say, experientially probable.' In order to elicit the right energies and responses, the artist must accurately pinpoint, in his hypothesis, the features which in the real-life equivalent engage our active cognition. This indeed may fairly be termed 'truth-using' rather than 'truth-telling'.

Thus Rembrandt, in a portrait, will seize on a certain compassionate moistening of the eye which in real life would instantly produce a felt advance in personal knowledge. To possess this art is to be master of mimetic truth. Since experiential knowledge, in ordinary life, involves on a minute scale the endless testing of hypotheses and Gestalten, it permits the abstraction of potent, repeating features, which can then stand, with all the rising colour of life, in the *wholly* hypothetical world of a fiction. Conceptual knowledge is increased by the addition and elaboration of propositions. Experiential knowledge is increased by deepening, by intensification. The historian, who may serve here as a proponent of conceptual knowledge, does not merely record our present knowledge of the past; he extends it by research and reports his results in fresh narratives. The realistic artist, on the other hand, works by deepening our experience of the possible reality he presents. But that is not the whole story. Because the object is probable and the manner of our induction into deeper acquaintance with it is rooted in the way we know real people and places, there is sometimes an overspill of deepened awareness into our experiential knowledge of the real world. Rembrandt in his self-portraits profoundly enhances our knowledge of a possible face, but he does more than that. When we leave the gallery we look with greater insight into the first face we encounter. He thereby directly deepens our experiential knowledge of the real human face. The greatest realistic artist takes, and then gives largely. He does not merely exploit human cognitive responses, but, injecting fresh life into Gestalten which are in turn used in ordinary perception, he deepens our knowledge of the world we live in. I am saying that Gestalten, or hypothetical forms, play a part in the way one gets to know a real place, just as surely as they do in the formation of descriptive theories. He who gazes with understanding at a Rembrandt self-portrait cannot be said, verifiably, to have learned more facts about Rembrandt (though I would not wish, absolutely, to exclude even that). What he learns is the strange twofold truth, a possible face from the seventeenth century and, at the same time, Human Face. If you say, 'Well, he knew that before,' I answer, 'Now he knows it *more*, or *better*.'

Although experiential knowledge may be evoked by literary narrative, it is not normally expressed in subject-predicate propositions. Instead we use simple nouns. Experientially you do not know 'that x is p', rather, you just know x. Thus, although, in *Middlemarch*, we are told that Dorothea married Casaubon, that is not the *knowledge* which the book confers. Rather, the book leads us to know a possible nineteenth-century person and Aspiring Woman, as a concrete universal, with much of the possible detail and complexity of a real-life instance, but held at the level of hypothesis. It naturally 'feeds into' our experiential knowledge of real individuals, much as experiential knowledge of one real individual can 'feed into' our knowledge of another. This is not to say that the chronological action of the novel is superficial or inessential. But in order to understand the hypothetical/experiential character of the knowledge involved, we need to cast this too in the form of a noun, not a proposition. *Middlemarch* does not convey the information that Dorothea married Casaubon (for, after all, she never did) but it does convey, with great depth, the possible marriage of such as they.

It may be said, however, that since truth is a property of propositions, it cannot be applied to an art which deals primarily in experiential knowledge of substances. But, as we have seen, realistic art does not merely transcribe actualities; it offers variously quickening hypothetical cases. And these must be answerable to reality or they will not succeed. Truth and probability inhere inexpugnably in the requirement of 'answerability'. Experiential knowledge is not knowledge unless it relates – I will not say, to what is really the case, since that suggests a universe of propositions – but to people and things. Just as propositional knowledge can be found out or falsified, so experiential knowledge can stumble, can be shocked to find itself astray. When Troilus saw his love doing things which were no part of the woman he had known before, he cried out,

> This is and is not Cressid.
>
> (*Troilus and Cressida*, V. ii. 144)

Because experiential and propositional knowledge do not exist in hermetic separation, translation is possible from one mode to the other. Thus we may express Troilus's shock with ' ''that''-clauses'; he thought *that* Cressida was true and found *that* she was false. But that is not the form of *his* knowing, which is accurately expressed by Shakespeare with a single proper noun, advanced and then destroyed by mere negation: 'This is and is not Cressid.' Here Shakespeare includes, with great brilliance, an experiential faltering of knowledge *within* his own great feat of hypothetical/experiential knowing, called *Troilus and Cressida*. In this play Shakespeare *knows*, experientially, the possible failure of experiential knowing, and that is what he teaches us, his audience.

The switch of emphasis from propositional to experiential knowledge immediately disposes of certain hoary objections to the view that literature conveys reality. For example, it was said with obvious truth that we do not go to *King Lear* to check that abdication may be incompatible with the retention of love and allegiance. Because this is in propositional form it follows that it is a translation from Shakespeare's substantival hypothesis. Moreover, it is a brief summary. Propositions, as they are extensible 'laterally' by elaboration, are in like manner capable of being contracted into a summary form. But experiential knowledge cannot be summarized without a far more urgent sense of loss. Bernard Mandeville's argument in his *Fable of the Bees* (to take a propositional work) really can be represented by the phrase, 'Private vices are public benefits.' We know that further details are available on demand, that supportive arguments and explanations are needed, but at the same time we do not feel that the summary is a violation of the book. Yet this feeling almost always arises when literary works are paraphrased. The proper conclusion is not that literary works have nothing to do with knowledge but rather that they have to do with experiential knowledge. After all, human beings are just as indignant when someone 'summarizes' the people they love, or know well.

Again, if we think of experiential rather than propositional knowledge, we shall be less embarrassed by the persistent tendency of literary works, even those which lodge a claim to be realistic, to blur outlines, to bury information and to withhold clues. Experiential knowledge is naturally involved with emotional commitment and withdrawal, is naturally dynamic. It is deepened or intensified by the overcoming of difficulties. Thus a work which stimulates (even by temporarily frustrating) the faculty of apprehension will engage us more fully than one which blandly displays its material. It is important to remember that these remarks apply only to those artists who, for all their varying stratagems of obfuscation, are perceived or read as realists. Certain artists make such obfuscation the central principle of their art and offer no ultimate mimesis whatever. Such art is partly parasitic on the expectations created by earlier, mimetic art and easily becomes purely formal. The difference between obfuscation concretely applied as a means of sharpening one's sense of reality and an abstract obfuscation is crucial, though it is not always easy to decide in practice to which category a given work belongs. Even severely abstract works by Mondrian can be fleetingly construed as strange cities, but it is generally evident that the play of forms has in Mondrian ousted any promise of heightened *perception*. In visual art this process can fairly rapidly be brought to a point where the word 'obfuscation' (even 'abstract obfuscation') no longer applies. In literature this moment is indefinitely deferred, because as long as words are used some flicker of expectation will remain in the reader, some restless intuition of a possible field of reference. A modernist poet cannot reach the pitch of abstraction attained by Mondrian. To do so he must cease to be a poet and become a composer of music. To that condition, indeed, some modernist literature aspires. My own concern, however, is with the accepted monuments of realism. The notion of experiential knowledge accounts at once for our preferring a Rembrandt to a photograph. The very difficulties of 'reading' Rembrandt are made to serve a cognitive end; by such loving travail of the eye, by such arduous visual wooing, we come at last to know, not more *about* the human face, but the human face itself, better and more deeply than we ever did before.

Historians of art and literature are professionally concerned to plot formal modifications as they succeed one another in time. They find that even artists who are acclaimed in their own day as realists in fact stamp an authorial identity on their work through a series of subtle modifications of the formal tradition. These scholars are then drawn, by the very nature of the job they do, towards the fallacious conclusion that art consists *wholly* in the sequence of formal changes. They listen to poem after poem, gaze at painting after painting, and forget that Joyce, the disciple of Homer, listened to real Dubliners and Cézanne, the disciple of Poussin, stared at apples till they rotted on the cloth (Cézanne's remark that he wanted 'to do Poussin over again, from nature',[46] admirably catches the balance I am seeking). The formal changes certainly happen and are often used to create a wholly formal aesthetic effect. But the very distortions of normal visual equivalents can be used to evoke rather than to exclude reality. Impressionist paintings are commonly more blurred than the visual field of a normally sighted person, yet the more intelligent contemporary observers felt at once that these paintings were astonishingly true to visual reality. The problem is resolved when we realize that previous *paintings* were *less* blurred than the average visual field. Painting had been unnaturally clear. This generated the sense that sustained clarity of outline is characteristic of painting and that blurring belongs with real vision. With this expectation feeding perception, the paintings of Pissarro could at once be understood as 'exaggerative realism', where the words no longer connote a contradiction but become once more intelligible. Just as a caricature can be 'more like Margaret than Margaret herself', so an Impressionist painter could harness his departures from previous art to the task of conveying a heightened sense of what it is really like to see.

In one sense Gombrich was entirely right. To understand pictures we need to know what earlier pictures were like. If we consider the formal distortions in Impressionist painting, the departures from received artistic form are at least as significant as the departures from *visual* norms. But the effect of this analysis is not to show that nature lies to one side, in mere irrelevance to the formal march of European painting. On the contrary, the analysis reveals what excessive familiarity is beginning to conceal from us, the fact that nature was one of the fundamental principles of Impressionism. The Impressionists departed from the practice of their predecessors *in order to recover the world of nature.* Their formal distortions were a kind of reverse discrimination, practised in deference to an ultimate egalitarianism. Their painting is clamorous of reality. Today the theorists minutely analyse this clamour and never hear the words that are being shouted.

The two languages of criticism

There are two languages of citicism, the first 'opaque', external, formalist, operating outside the mechanisms of art and taking those mechanisms as its object, the second 'transparent', internal, realist, operating within the 'world' presented in the work. The first language throws upon the screen of critical consciousness all the formal devices of a work in such a way that the eye is arrested by them. Formal characters, in order that they should be the more visible, are deliberately made opaque. In the second language, formal devices are, like windows, transparent. We shall refer to the first mode, shortly, as the Opaque language and the second as the Transparent language. 'Opaque' and 'Transparent' are morally neutral terms. The initial capitals mark these words as technical terms.

The following sentences are all in the Opaque language:

1 In the opening of *King Lear* folk-tale elements proper to narrative are infiltrated by a finer-grained dramatic mode.

2 In Brueghel's *Fall of Icarus*, as the eye travels from the top of the picture, the shapes become increasingly curved; the bottom third of the painting is a sort of rollicking march of swooping, overlapping loops.

3 In *Portrait of a Lady* James applies to human figures language normally reserved for artefacts; Isabel Archer is 'written in a foreign tongue'; Daniel Touchett presents 'a fine, ivory surface'; Henrietta Stackpole 'has no misprints'.

4 In *Hamlet* Shakespeare contrives that the delay should be unintelligible, because the principal figure functions not as an explanatory device but as a source of intellectual frustration.

These sentences on the other hand, are in the Transparent language:

1 Cordelia cannot bear to have her love for her father made the subject of a partly mercenary game.

2   The ploughman may
Have heard the splash, the forsaken cry,
But for him it was not an important failure; the sun shone
As it had to on the white legs disappearing into the green
Water; and the expensive delicate ship that must have seen
Something amazing, a boy falling out of the sky,
Had somewhere to get to and sailed calmly on.

(W.H. Auden, 'Musée des Beaux Arts')[47]

3 Isabel Archer is innocent, but in quite a different way from Henrietta Stackpole.
4 Hamlet delays because, once he has cut himself off from the psychic support of human society, the central structure of his original motivation decays.

It is highly likely that to many readers of this book the first list will automatically look like 'real criticism' and the second like 'self-indulgent pseudo-criticism'. Yet sentences of the second type have always figured in critical writing.

Each sentence in the first list makes explicit reference to the artifice of the work; it takes as its province the artist's distinctive disposition of forms, the mechanisms of representation, evocation, enchantment. There is a mild presumption that to move from such formal scrutiny into a freer discussion of that which is represented would be to leave criticism altogether. Each sentence from the second set, on the other hand, passes shamelessly into the world mimetically proposed in the work of art, and discusses elements of that world as though they were people or physical objects. Cordelia is considered, not as a sequence of harsh yet appealing chords cutting across the sombre confusion created by the Lear figure, but as a young woman in great distress. In the Opaque group explanation is generally sought in terms of what happens in other works of art, or elsewhere in the present work. In the Transparent group no tabu exists against explaining fictitious behaviour by analogy with real-life equivalents.

Latent in the Opaque approach is a severe separation of critic and reader (or spectator). The critic knows how the conjuror does the tricks, or how the tricks fool the audience, and is thereby excluded, by his very knowingness, from the innocent delight of those who marvel and applaud. Such criticism can never submit to mimetic enchantment because to do so would be to forfeit critical understanding of the means employed. The Transparent party, on the other hand, is less afraid of submission, feeling that enchantment need involve no submersion of critical faculties, but that on the contrary without such a willingness to enter the proffered dream a great many factors essential to a just appreciation may be artificially excluded from discussion. After all its members are not in any fundamental sense fooled by the conjuror. They know perfectly well that all is done by artificial means. But at the same time they can perceive the magic as magic. They know that Ophelia is not a real woman but are willing to think of her as a possible woman. They note that Shakespeare implicitly asks them to do this, but they do more than note the request; they comply with it. They are much less aware than the Opaque party of restrictions on what they are allowed to discuss. For example, they are free to explore all the formal features which in Opaque criticism expand to fill the picture. A statement like 'The ideas of women presented in this novel are inadequate', though it refers externally to the artifice of the work, is thoroughly Transparent in its acceptance of mimetic reference. Adverse criticism of the values implied by texts is normally thus. Without a prior submission to the sovereign force of mimesis, no injustice could ever have been perceived. The Opaque critic, on the other hand, can be displeased by a work, but can never dissent from it. An Opaque critic would censor all the statements in the second group; a Transparent critic would pass all the statements in the first. The Transparent critic can and will do all the things done by the Opaque critic but is willing to do other things as well.

The main thrust of the case against Transparent criticism is that it confounds art and reality. Such was the case put in L.C. Knights's celebrated essay, 'How many children had Lady Macbeth?'[48] Knights damned Bradleian character-critics for speculating about Hamlet as if he were a real person; 'Hamlet' is not a real man at all, but a string of poetic expressions, a constellation of images. With human beings we may legitimately indulge in inference and supposition; we may say, 'She must have lived in India' or 'He must have been very religious at one time'; but with dramatic characters such inference is manifestly absurd; we cannot guess at Lady Macbeth's previous life for the simple reason that she has no previous life; her being begins and ends with what Shakespeare sets down for her to say.

It is strange that so coarse a piece of reasoning should have passed for a great stroke of destructive theory. Knights's singular presumption that humane inference is inapplicable to drama is simply mistaken. When a character sits up and yawns we infer that he has been sleeping. When another character gives a certain sort of start we infer that he is guilty (readers of *Macbeth*, especially, should be aware of this). If no inferences whatever are allowed, certain negative conclusions, on the other hand, can be drawn about Hamlet. For example he has no legs. For Shakespeare never mentions them – or may we infer (*infer?*) one leg from a down-gyved stocking? This may be thought merely silly, but a large part of Knights's case really does depend on the absolute exclusion of inference. Moreover, in a curious manner, Knights's criticism suggests that he really was more than half-willing to draw the conclusion that Hamlet is not a man. Here too one is drawn to offer a consciously philistine reply, 'Hamlet is a funny name for a sequence of images – sounds more like a person, a sort of Danish prince.' A dramatist faced with an entire audience who austerely repressed all inferences and bayed for image-patterns might well despair. Of course Bradley never supposed for a moment that Hamlet was a real man.

Knights's ill-made shaft misses both Shakespeare and Bradley, and falls on stony ground. But the stony ground, it must be confessed, received it with joy.

What remains strong in Knights's attack is his intuition that Bradleian critics occasionally carried their unverifiable surmises to ludicrous lengths. I cannot agree that the question about Lady Macbeth's children is as absurd as Knights would have had us believe, but certain of Maurice Morgann's observations on the military career of Falstaff (see chapter 4) are truly foolish. But the simple test of verifiability will not serve to distinguish an absurd from a reasonable surmise. All our inferences and suppositions with regard to fictitious persons are in terms of probability, not fact. The objection to Morgann's speculations is not that Falstaff has no previous life but that Shakespeare does not give us enough clues to render Morgann's more detailed inferences probable. Knights's logical universe (like Todorov's later) was Puritan. There are facts and there are images. He is a logical Calvinist, forbidding all intercourse with the hypothetical, the merely probable.

The Transparent critic, who wonders why Cordelia cannot answer more warmly and thinks of other daughters, some of whom have lived outside the pages of books, is charged with confusing art and reality, but the charge is simply false. Where is the confusion? When Balzac sent for Dr Bianchon (a character in one of his books) to come to his bedside, he really did confuse art and reality. If he had merely asked 'What would Bianchon have said about a case like this?' no eyebrow would have been raised. The question is perfectly rational.

A whole generation was taught by Herbert Read to repress its natural engagement with mimetic painting. Delighted gazers at Edvard Munch's *House under Trees* (1905) had allowed their eyes to linger on the group of women in the foreground, so close to one another, so enigmatic, and then to be drawn into the further space, the pale wall and the trees, wintry yet with a bloom of spring in their soft extremities, and then beyond again to someone else's house, darker in the distance. Herbert Read, on the other hand, taught them, perfectly correctly, that Munch 'sacrificed tone to line' and that his lines enclosed definite, powerful planes.[49] The error was to suppose that such formal analysis somehow prohibited the other way of looking and this error was repeated again and again. It became fashionable to laugh at Walter Pater's rhapsodic musings on the *Mona Lisa*[50] and John Addington Symonds's prose poem on Lorenzo de' Medici.[51]

An early consequence of this severe separation of technical ('critical') appreciation and ordinary 'entranced' appreciation is an impoverishment of criticism itself. If the critic never enters the dream he remains ignorant about too much of the work. The final result may be a kind of literary teaching which crushes literary enjoyment, the natural *coitus* of reader and work endlessly *interruptus*. The student who begins to talk excitedly about Becky Sharp will suddenly find himself isolated in the seminar. Another cooler student who is careful to speak of 'the Becky Sharp motif' tactfully assumes the central role in the discussion and covers the first student's confusion.

There is one other characteristic of the Opaque set of criticisms which should be noticed. They can never quite attain to pure formalism. Language has accepted (one suspects by Darwinian principle) the convenience of referring to characters in books by their fictitious names. We may remorselessly prefix such allusions with formal specifiers – 'the character, Hamlet', 'the motif, Becky Sharp' and so on – but there is something ponderously redundant about such scrupulousness. Language permits the bare use of the name because context renders the meaning sufficiently unambiguous. As we have seen, old-fashioned readers are in no way confused by this way of discussing fictional persons. Meanwhile the mere use of the proper name, 'Becky Sharp', however we fence it about with formal impediments, propels us into the world mimetically proposed, sets our thought in terms of people rather than artistic conventions. It is very hard indeed to describe a novel without referring to the things which are described as happening in it. It is similarly hard to describe a picture without occasionally looking through the arrangement of colour as if it were a window and allowing ourselves to notice, as it might be, the face, the raised hand, the distant tower.

The most determined effort to isolate 'the aesthetic emotion' was Clive Bell's *Art* (1914) with its immensely influential conception of 'significant form'. It was a time of violent reaction from Victorian 'story pictures', like *When Did You Last See Your Father?*, and Bell had no difficulty in rejecting, as irrelevant to the aesthetic emotion, all narrative features. Symbolic and representational features soon followed, leaving the purist formulation, 'lines and colours combined in a particular way, certain forms and relations of forms'.[52] Here the mimetic dimension itself becomes aesthetically tabu. Most intelligent people agreed, but not all. In the first chapter of Evelyn Waugh's *Brideshead Revisited* (1945) there is a fragmentary paragraph of remembered conversation, set in 1923, which perfectly encapsulates the resistance of the unregenerate few.

Collins had exposed the fallacy of modern aesthetics to me: ' . . . the whole argument from Significant Form stands or falls by *volume*. If you allow Cézanne to represent a third dimension on his two-

dimensional canvas, then you must allow Landseer his gleam of loyalty in the spaniel's eye' . . . but it was not until Sebastian, idly
turning the pages of Clive Bell's *Art* read: ' "Does anyone feel the
same kind of emotion for a butterfly or a flower that he feels for a
cathedral or a picture?" Yes. *I* do', that my eyes were opened.[53]

The natural movement of mimetic sympathy can be arrested at different levels. A man looking at a Vermeer may be told, by a mild Opaque
formalist, that he may see a woman with a letter in her hand but must
not speculate on her thoughts, on what has happened or is about to
happen. A harder formalist may tell him that he must not see a woman,
but a massively rounded monumental form enclosed by rectilinear
space. A still harder formalist may forbid the inference of depth or
monumental character and restrict the viewer to coloured planes and
shapes. Each of these restrictions can be genuinely fruitful critically,
since it turns out that art is already achieving complex and important
results at all these stages. It would have been so easy to assume that all
these things merely served the mimetic end. In fact in a great work of art
each has its own separate flowering. Both Clive Bell and Herbert Read
saw this clearly and our debt to them is incalculable. But none of the
prohibitions is in order.

Similarly with literature: a certain sort of Opaque critic will simply
insist that we do not speculate about characters; a severer Opaque critic
will begin to fret at the very term 'character' (feeling that it somehow
suggests an ersatz person) and will, if he is writing in the 1930s, restrict
us to the images used or else, if he is writing in the 1980s, restrict us to
the semasiological codes. One could imagine a further degree, which
would restrict the reader to what philosophers call the actual 'token',
that is, to the black letters on the printed page (which would at last
bring formalist literary theory to the same level as formalist art theory),
but, to the literate, print is instantaneously transparent: the mind
intuits the word in the token so swiftly that the formalist has no chance
to insert his screen. And all words are windows. They are never *purely*
formal.

It is curious that the modernist opponents of mimesis have turned to
primitive art for support. In fact the primitive mask divagates from the
normal human face, not only because its maker is interested in abstract
form but because he or she is so confident of the mimetic element that it
is taken as read. The primitive tends not to use the external language,
'I am making a device', but rather runs to its opposite, Transparent
extreme ('I am making a Face'). The resultant artefact is not seen as
more or less *like* a face. It *is* a face.[54] Nor are we so far removed

culturally as to be unaware, when confronted with such a mask, that a face is looking at us. Where there are two spots side by side and a vertical line below and a horizontal line below that, there is a face. It will look at you; it will catch and hold your eye. It does so not because of its autonomous formal beauty but because the two spots work as eyes. Similarly, in Homer's *Iliad* (vi. 273), when Hector wishes his mother to lay a gift on the knees of the statue of Athene in the temple, he says nothing about a statue, but simply asks her to 'lay the robe on Athene's knees'.

This primitive level of response is always operative. Indeed it can be variously manipulated by the great masters of mimesis. Rembrandt chose in his self-portraits to blaze upon the viewer from a circum-ambient darkness, looking straight at him. If we try critically to define the principal differences between Vermeer and Rembrandt we shall be paralysed unless we are allowed to notice that in Vermeer the subject very rarely looks out of the painting. Usually his people are preoccupied, in profile or turned away, and we are like 'visual eavesdroppers'. Sometimes, as we shall see in more detail later, Vermeer flirts wth a stronger reciprocity; a chair may be turned towards the viewer, but no one is sitting in it; a frontal view of the face we see in profile may be tantalizingly half-visible in dim reflection elsewhere in the room. But most of the time – and quite systematically – he works against the grain of immediate or warm relationship with the viewer. His very use of light and shade reverses the normal practice of Rembrandt. Where Rembrandt illuminated the face and plunged the rest in shadow, Vermeer commonly makes his figures somewhat darker than the environment, as though he deliberately disdains any attempt to conciliate our attention or involvement. And he knows very well that all these things will merely make us watch with another sort of attention. The viewer of a Vermeer is admitted by stealth to the world of the picture. The viewer of a Rembrandt is merely overwhelmed. But all this talk is idle if we are not to allow Transparent 'reading' of the picture.

Neither Plato nor Aristotle, using the term 'mimesis', begins from an assumption that art of itself has nothing to do with nature and that any possible contingent link with nature must be carefully explained. Rather, like Cassirer's tribesmen, they begin from the assumption that the artist makes a man, or a war, or a bed, and then carefully point out that it is not a real man etc., but an imitation one. Both begin from the fact that the poet is a maker. Today it is only the learned who are aware that the idea of making is implicit in the word 'poet'. But for the ancient Greek the word for 'poet' is simply one and the same as the word for 'maker': ποιητής. The notion of the poet as maker is usually congenial to formalists because the question 'What does he make?' for them naturally invites an Opaque, externalist answer: he makes an epic, or he makes a song. The Greek language certainly permits this kind of answer, but it seems at least as ready to receive answers of the other kind: 'The poet makes a sack of Troy.' One can watch English translators flinching from the forthrightness of this. Jowett translates *Republic* 569E as follows: 'the painter also creates a bed. Yes, he said, but not a real bed.'[55] Where Jowett gives the august word 'creates', Plato uses the ordinary word, ποιεῖ, 'makes'. Of course Plato, by his metaphysical theory, considers both actual, physical beds and beds in pictures to be unreal imitations of the ideal Bed, and Aristotle laboured in his *Poetics* to show that poetic imitations might serve society, by channelling off violent emotion, and at the same time might also engage with genuine probability. Thus they differ deeply. But one point on which it does not occur to either of them to raise any difficulty is the assumption that when an artist paints a picture of a bed what he does bears some relation to a physical bed. Why else, they might ask, do we call it painting a *bed*?

In fact the Transparent language of the world mimetically proposed is so strong that it often overflows into the Opaque terminology. Brutus, within the mimesis of Shakespeare's *Julius Caesar*, naturally addresses Cassius as Cassius: he does not break out of the mimesis and say, 'John' (or whatever the actor was called). But stage directions obviously belong to a different logical order. They lie outside the mimesis and direct its mechanics. It would thus be wholly natural in a stage direction to say, 'John should cross the stage at this point,' or, since actors change, 'The actor playing Cassius should cross the stage at this point.' After all, *Cassius* does not cross a *stage*; *he* moves acrosss a scarred patch of ground on a battlefield. But stage directions (like ordinary critical discourse) easily dispense with such cumbrous periphrases and simply adopt the mimetic term 'Cassius'. In exactly the same way a director, in rehearsal, will often shout, 'Cassius, you're on.' This tendency extends to the use of pronouns in stage directions. The female parts in Elizabethan plays were played by boys or young men, but even something as firmly and definitely external to the mimesis as a stage direction will use the mimetic in preference to the real gender: instructing a male actor, the stage direction will say, 'She runs lunatick.'

It may be said that this continual linguistic recourse to the mimetic object at the expense of the form certainly ought to embarrass the hard formalist but need have no effect on the soft formalist. The soft formalist after all, concedes that the mimetic dimension exists. Yet even he may be surprised by the vivacity of the internal language, by its superfluous vigour.

Nevertheless, it may be countered, although both languages persist and the Transparent language is strong, it is not, somehow, as strong as it was. We have, not only in the world of theory where formalists abound (hence this book) but also in informal critical discussion, retreated a little from full mimetic confidence. In part this may be attributed to the natural pendulum swing of fashion: critical formalism has alternated with critical materialism for centuries. But this time the swing is unusually strong. Could it be that, in the present century, it is founded on a real discovery?

The present age is distinguished from all previous ages by its command of technical means of recording. For thousands of years there was no better way to convey the idea of Chartres cathedral than for a draughtsman to draw it or for a writer to describe it. The draughtsman and the writers always introduced creative formal modifications and these were appreciated aesthetically, but the coexisting element of veracity must have seemed an elementary (and highly practical) function of the work.

With the invention of the camera all this was changed. It is commonly believed that the aesthetic shock and malaise produced by the camera in the nineteenth century has now passed off; that the theory of high art had little difficulty in dissociating itself from this mean mechanical contrivance, that we have sorted ourselves out. But we have not sorted out visual realism. The easy, quick answer to the camera was Herbert Read's: art endlessly exploits and celebrates formal relationships with a free creativity which is simply unavailable to the machine. The great strength of this answer lay in the fact that its proponents could easily point to such formal characters in precamera art: it was not that the artists had betrayed their utter panic at the arrival of the machine by vacating the contested ground and falling phrenetically to work on new principles (though a cursory observer could be forgiven for thinking this had happened). Such formal creativity really had operated from the beginning and could be shown to be the source of almost everything we valued. The nightmarish forms of Francis Bacon were latent – that is, were genuinely if unobviously present – in the seated *Pope Innocent X* of Velázquez.

But this leaves the status of realistic art uncertain. This uncertainty is far from being resolved today. The Impressionists' reaction to the camera was almost the opposite of the theorists'. They chose to stand and fight. Their method we have analysed as 'exaggerative visual realism'. The photograph, once its systematically repetitive conventions of representation were understood, was unmatchable as a purveyor of information. But its command of the more private intimacies of visual perception, of colour, sheen, dazzle, humane variations of focus, was less absolute. In these circumstances, for some considerable time it appeared possible for the painter to win. To be sure, the Impressionists hedged their bets. They were not so foolish as to drop the creatively formal dimension (where victory over the camera was immediate). But they did, at the same time, fight at the level of the mimetic. And they won. Later, for a long time, the practice of painters fell into line with theory.

There is nothing in literature which corresponds exactly with the effect in art of the camera. Tape-recorders presumably can defeat all comers in the business of catching the precise character of informal, undirected chat. Critics have, perfectly correctly, drawn formalist conclusions from the way we continue to prefer Chekhov to a tape-recording. The mimetic faithfulness of Chekhov to the aimlessness of desultory conversation was always the matter of a higher art, and thus the aimlessness was only superficial; behind it lay the rule and principle of drama. It is really the old paradox of 'the entertaining bore' (Jane Austen's Mr Collins) in a slightly sharpened form. Nevertheless, the defence is formalist. A writer who had, so to speak, nothing else to offer but an ear for realistic dialogue (with no power of plotting, for example) would really be threatened by the tape-recorder. Literature in general differs from painting in that it rarely concentrates on a single object in relative isolation; it builds much more discursively complex structures, encouraged to do so by the powerfully relational character of its medium, language. Therefore there is much less chance of the tape-recorder so much as seeming to usurp the principal territory of the playwright. But it remains conceivable that a culture might exist which relished, instead of tragedies and comedies, a sort of dramatic *haiku*, an art of isolated scenes, valued for their uncanny accuracy. In such a culture the arrival of the tape-recorder would have the sort of spectacular effect the arrival of the camera had on European painting.

In the visual arts many of the difficulties originally raised by the camera are beginning to be felt once more, with the return of realistic, figurative painting. Lest we commit the usual error of mistaking wishes for facts, let us first be clear what our wishes are. We want the human artist to survive. We want him to be able to do things which the machine cannot do and we want those things to be of a higher order. Although the machines are made by human beings, serve human beings and have no will of their own, it is possible to be jealous of them. I sense relief in the air when the argument moves successfully against the camera, and anxiety when it moves back. Thus Herbert Read's formalism was welcomed because it saved the party to which, after all, we all belong, the human beings. Similarly, with the mimetic challenge of the

Impressionists, after an initial anxiety at their engaging in feats of competitive mimetic accuracy (for at this point people tend to say that such things have nothing to do with art) the unhoped-for victory over the camera is welcomed and applauded by those same people who had earlier rejected the mimetic enterprise. At the same time any attempt to praise the mimetic excellence of photography is impeded by a sort of mild, cultural repression. But, in fact, the camera is very good at mimesis. Some of the things which the very greatest artists of the past struggled to do are done better by the camera. Nevertheless, human art is naturally more interesting to us than photographic images. We rapidly lose interest in the mimetic successes of the camera as we become aware, culturally, that they are done mechanically. With the camera there is no labour, no struggle, and therefore no triumph. Nor is the camera like that rare artist who does with masterly ease what others do with labour. The camera does not do its job with ease. It just does it.

But to say that the results produced by the camera are negligible because of the way they are produced is to violate a principle of New Criticism. The New Critics argued that, of two elegies, A and B, to prefer B because its author wrote it with tears streaming down his face is absurd: one's critical responses must be based on the public work and not on (usually unverifiable) information about the circumstances of its composition. The example of the camera exposes a certain crudeness in New Critical theory of intention. Thus, while it is impermissible to say, 'I like this work because the author was sad when he wrote it', it is permissible to say, 'I like this work because it gives an impression of sadness.' Certainly, one cannot verify one's intuition that Bishop King was sad when he wrote his 'Exequy'. Moreover, since poetry involves the use of fiction, it is entirely conceivable that a poem may give the impression that its human 'source' is sad and yet turn out to have been written in high good humour. But, while all this is true, *certain expressions could not so much as 'give the impression' of sadness if they did not in some degree reflect what people say or suffer when they actually feel sad. The New Critics, in their rejection of specific authorial intention, did not sufficiently notice the persisting force of hypothetical intention*, the cogency of which is rooted in ordinary behaviour. The New Critical attack on intention is like the old formalist attack on verisimilitude, founded on what I have called 'logical Calvinism'. In Calvin's theology there is no middle ground, only the saved and the damned, the things of God and the things of the Devil. So it is claimed implicitly by the New Critics that we must either infer a specific intention or else, if that seems dubious, drop the notion of inferred intention altogether. Probable or hypothetical intention hardly enters. The reader will notice that, having begun to join up fiction and the external world, I now endeavour to knit up the ravelled sleeve between the substantial author and his work. Although a joyous speech may have been written with gravity, yet, if no one ever used joyous language when genuinely joyful, the speech would not achieve the desired, public effect. It would not sound joyous. The cultural basis would have gone.

Even in specific cases, common sense finds it *mildly* surprising when glum poets write jubilant poems. In like manner we use the language of achievement when we praise works of art. We say, *War and Peace* is an amazing feat of organized imagination. The New Critic may insist that this language says nothing whatever about the circumstances of composition and in this particular case this may be true (that is, Tolstoy may have found it very easy), but if no artist ever had to strive at all, this form of praising would never have arisen and would not survive in our language. Again, the cultural basis would have gone. Something of this sort actually happened with photography; in every case as it came along, the impression of a mechanically secured mimetic success was confirmed.

This has certain awkward consequences. It means, for example, that we would not praise Dürer for his watercolour painting of grasses (in the Albertina, Vienna) with anything like the same confidence if we thought it had been painted in 1895, because, then, he might have used a camera. This is something which, according to the severe distinction laid down by New Criticism between the public work and the circumstances of its production, ought not to occur. But there is no doubt that it does. The issue is blurred to some extent by the complexity of art. The suggestion that in 1895 any competent academician, with the help of a camera, could reduplicate the achievement of Dürer can always be challenged at the formal level. The special muted harshness of line and hue, the queer deathliness of the whole are distinctively Dürer's and likely to remain so. But the mimetic achievement could certainly be matched much more easily in the nineteenth century than it could in Dürer's own time. And in the sixteenth century the mimetic achievement was not the least important feature of the picture.

Similar tensions are discoverable within the modern period. There is a picture by David Hockney[56] which seemed to me almost miraculous for the subtle truth of a certain line in it. I know that when I learned that the line in question was obtained mechanically the picture was diminished for me. My mind (which wanted to admire Hockney) instantly made the now predictable moves; it shifted its attention to the more purely formal merits of the painting and, as these were present in abundance, all was soon (relatively) well. One conclusion which might be drawn is that my original admiration of the line as a 'feat' was subcritical, an extraneous visual sentimentalism. But such strictures are highly artificial and seem doubly so if set against the whole history of art appreciation.

But what, in that case, are we to make of Vermeer, the running example in this book of supreme mimetic mastery? The great paintings of Vermeer can almost be described as seventeenth-century photographs. The work of such scholars as Gowing, Seymour and Fink[57] has made it clear that the great impression of visual truth in Vermeer's work dates from the point at which he began to use a camera obscura. From this point, to take only a minor example, his use of perspective is unobtrusively correct. The plane of focus in a mature Vermeer, although it often intersects the human figures, does so *neutrally*. If the plane of focus is found to be 9 feet from the artist's eye (and in the case of Vermeer such things can be determined very exactly) then not just the human figures but everything 9 feet from the artist's eye will be in sharp focus. This is not quite what happens in ordinary perception – and still more, in ordinary painting – where focus will be influenced by what interests the viewer and therefore human figures will tend, as in a Rembrandt, to be more sharply focused than other objects in the same plane. All this, it seems, which surely contributed subliminally to the marvellous effect of loving neutrality, may be a mechanical consequence of the use of the camera obscura. But the point is a fine one. When all is said and done, there are no seventeenth-century photographs. Vermeer had to paint every inch of his canvas and every movement of his brush required from him some aesthetic decision. The basic shapes, the angle of the table and the wall, were indeed given to him mechanically but accurate perspective was never the essence of his mimetic feat (it is merely rather odd that he could not manage correct perspective in his youth). The feat lay rather in such things as the texture of the carpet, the fruit, the jug, the wall. Here indeed the camera obscura guided him. But his adoption of neutrality of focus is likely to have been deliberative and is therefore quite properly admired. The same principle is carried systematically into other areas where the camera obscura could not be said, by any stretch of the imagination, to rule.

I have contrasted the preoccupied, neutral subjects of Vermeer with the confronting gaze of Rembrandt and have suggested that, in relation to Vermeer's people, we are 'visual eavesdroppers'. In the picture called *Lady Reading a Letter at an Open Window* (in the Rijksmuseum, Amsterdam) painted in about 1658, the lady, as commonly, is in strict profile. She is engrossed by something which is of her world, and not of ours. Moreover she is doing something which is almost emblematic of the strange privacy of the human mind. She is reading: not reading aloud to us, but reading alone. It is likely that before the middle ages no one read silently. The Ethiopian eunuch in *Acts* (viii. 32f.), was *overheard* reading in his carriage, alone. Even as late as the fourth century A D people marvelled at St Ambrose, whose lips barely moved when he read. If Plato were to be transported in time to the twentieth century and made to watch a modern, literate person reading, utterly silent and absorbed for 2 hours on end, registering in faint succession on his intent features a variety of emotions, I suspect that the philosopher would be obscurely shocked. In his own time he was already troubled by a sense that reading might be a sort of ersatz thought. The modern, silent reader might well strike him as slightly indecent. Vermeer's lady is to be sure closer to us than to Ambrose and it is entirely likely that she is reading silently. Equally, it is possible that she is murmuring as Ambrose did. Her lips are parted in what may or may not be motion and the really important thing is that we do not know. Her reading is entirely private from us. Not only are we the unregarded spectators of the picture; we are, so to speak, deaf spectators. We cannot hear if anything is going on in the street outside that room and can only suspect (somehow the suspicion is quite powerful) that somewhere in that house a clock is ticking. This, note, is Transparent criticism in its most extreme form.

The first signal of our exclusion is indeed the simple fact that the figure is in profile. But the principle of lateral rather than frontal presentation is respected, in a less obvious fashion, throughout the picture. One might say as a sort of epigram that not only the lady but also the room is in profile. Thus the window is to one side. She, if she looked up, could see through it. We never shall.

In the earlier art of Flanders or of Italy windows are more generous things. Through them we see turbanned strangers approaching down winding roads, camelopards, castles, mountain fastnesses, blue remembered hills. Vermeer instead restricts us to the limited perspective of one who watches through a keyhole. Part of the attraction of covert observation is its promise of truth: what we are getting is not tailored to our needs; this is the way things are when we are not there. This Vermeer exploits, with deliberate creative skill, as a means of creating that almost uncanny sense of the real which marks his art. As the window is in profile, so the table with its heaped richness of carpet is again in profile, intervening between us and the lady, excluding us. The curtain is in profile and again suggests not so much a Punch and Judy show displayed for our delight as – taken together with the table – a seventeenth-century bed, past whose hangings we are, by pure chance, able to see. Only the glass casement and the empty chair are half-turned towards us, and this is perhaps the most subtle spatial device in the picture. The chair is, so to speak, half-responsive to us, but there is no one sitting on it. The glass casement, much more tantalizingly, actually contains the girl's face, and almost from in front. But indeed we see in a glass darkly. The face is there, but it is not there for us. The lady's preoccupation is not mitigated but is rather intensified by that shadowed, downcast shape in the window. Vermeer, who can when he chooses almost rival Van Eyck in detailed clarity of visual presentation, shows a master's instinct in knowing when to withhold clarity. In this picture the accidents are given as strongly as the essence – the carpet, the dull sheen on the inside of the blue bowl, the fringe of the curtain. The thing we most want to see, the full face, is withheld from us, by a visually truthful unclarity. But behind the ignoble curiosity of the eavesdropper there may perhaps lie a more philosophical interest. This, it might be said, is the room to answer Berkeley's fear: is the cow in the meadow when no one sees her? Here is a lady whose *esse* is not *percipi*. Her *esse* is merely to be, independently of us, to read her letter by the light of the window. But then (as with all philosophic art) the fear flows back with double force. For this picture, if we construe our categories differently, is all perception: not praxis, not relationship, but perception.

Thus the mimetic 'neutrality' of Vermeer is subtly played against all kinds of frustrated interventions by the viewer. This is how he achieved his distinctive feat of entrancing realism, and no camera obscura could do it for him.

Yet, once Vermeer has shown how, the composition, the characteristic disposition of chairs, curtains and the principal subject can all be reassembled and photographed. About 1900 Richard Polack did a series of photographs in close imitation of Vermeer.[58] Naturally he did not reproduce such features as Vermeer's amazing pointillist treatment of highlights and the result is lifeless. But a gap I valued has been narrowed. My very relief at the failure of Polack to capture the painterly life of the original is eloquent of an underlying fear.

Of the two languages of criticism it is the internal, Transparent one which most obviously lets in the outer world. *Enter* the work and you walk *out*, free, into the surrounding landscape. The external, Opaque language, sticking as it does to the analysis of mechanisms and formal factors, is far more narrowly confined to a single plane. It is conceived in cool, Olympian detachment but its very aloofness leads to its confinement. Moreover, just as it cannot move freely into the proposed, hypothetical events of the book, similarly it cannot move back from the public, manifest superficies of the work to the range of human activities and emotions which give force and meaning to fictions. The door to the larger world is likewise kept firmly shut. When we say (and people say such things all the time, quite incurably) that in a given novel 'the social scene is sharply observed', we break out in two directions at once: we presume that a high degree of probability is observed in the hypothesis (that is, that the characters are made to act and talk as their equivalents would in real life) and, at the same time, we imply that to secure such close correspondence is an achievement on the part of the real author: we make a loose but irreducible claim about the circumstances of composition. And, as long as we allow that the universe is not really partitioned into verified truths and free-floating fictions, but on the contrary admits such things as probability and possibility, we have no ground for legislating against such luminously normal talk.

The admission of a sense of authorial achievement, of human energy and striving, is immediately consonant with our conception of art as more concerned with *connaissance* than with *savoir*. If we think the artist is trying hard to reach us we in our turn will try. *Savoir* is expressed in propositions which are either understood or not. It can be added to or extended but its essence is homogeneous. The *connaissance* of a single person or thing, on the other hand, can be deepened or intensified without any material addition to the stock of information. Such deepening is accomplished more effectively when the entire apparatus of human prehensive emotion is involved. The effect of learning that a work to which one was beginning to respond in this profoundly personal manner was composed automatically is immediately disconcerting and has practical aesthetic consequences. The stream of personal response is abruptly curtailed. The devices of obfuscation by which, as we saw, artists can energize the responses of viewers so that they win through to an enhanced intuition, work because they are 'read' as human, and they are so read because in general they are known to be so. Particular cases will commonly be unverifiable but without the common presumption the entire enterprise fails.

Yet even this technique of obfuscation, still paradigmatically human for most observers, can now be produced mechanically. Gombrich shows in his *Meditations on a Hobby Horse*[59] two photographs of a sickly-smooth *Three Graces* painted in 1900, one clear and the other broken and blurred. The blurring process is mechanically obtained. Gombrich observes that nevertheless it activates our 'reading' of the picture. He is right, but one can sense, even as one looks at his example, how the activation is dying away to something of minor importance. We 'twig' that the blurring is inertly uniform and therefore mechanical. As soon as this happens three-quarters of the sensibility falls into quiescence. The minimal interpretation of the image goes on and for this indeed some extra energies are needed. But that is all. Thus, as an example of what happens in postimpressionist painting the photograph is oddly weak.

In *War and Peace* Tolstoy at one point describes an operatic performance:

> The floor of the stage consisted of smooth boards, at the sides was some painted cardboard representing trees, and at the back was a cloth stretched over boards. In the centre of the stage sat some girls in red bodices and white skirts. One very fat girl in a white silk dress sat apart on a low bench, to the back of which a piece of green cardboard was glued. They all sang something. When they had finished their song the girl in white went up to the prompter's box, and a man with tight silk trousers over his stout legs, and holding a plume and a dagger, went up to her and began singing, waving his arms about.[60]

This description comes at the beginning of a chapter. It feels very odd and the reader is slightly disconcerted that so 'harsh' and idiosyncratic a view should be 'backed' or rather simply given, by the author. In a novel of switching viewpoints, like Smollett's *Humphrey Clinker*, this would be the ostentatiously subjective perception of a particular character. In fact Tolstoy, within a few paragraphs, ascribes this view of the opera to Natasha, who is in the audience, but he has so ordered his chapter as to imply, quite simply, that she is right. The 'authorial status' of the opening paragraphs is not cancelled by the later ascription of this view to a character.

The passage is a classic example of 'defamiliarization', of 'making it strange' as that concept is defined in the criticism of the Russian formalists. The prime purpose of 'making it strange' is to induce an innocent vision, unmediated by preconceptions. Tolstoy, in effect, says to his readers, 'Let us, just for once, say what a stage presentation really looks like.' This enterprise is profoundly opposed, in its most immediate implications, to radical formalism. For it assumes the possibility of a 'pure' objectivity. It is a curiosity of literary history that this impulse has been overlaid by successive accretions of formalist theory. One effect of isolating the unmediated perception is to make one acutely conscious of the immense play of prior modifying categories in 'ordinary' perception. Poetic language, in particular, may be seen as 'negatively truthful' in the way it deliberately forces the means of expression on our attention, so that we cannot mistake them for realities which have, so to speak, been transcribed without any alteration. But to reason in this way is to forget one's original praise of that literature which successfully conveyed an unmediated vision. Sometimes the difficulty is merely evaded by an unobtrusive transference of 'defamiliarization' from the objects described to the means of expression, so that the poet, in stressing the autonomous richness of words in separation from their referents, is 'defamiliarizing' language itself. Thus the banner of defamiliarization is still held high and the fundamental shift of theory is suppressed.[61] Otherwise one may direct the reader's attention to the formal methods which are actually employed in the star cases of supposedly 'innocent eye' description. This is the truly formalist response (exactly analogous to what Barthes did in his essay 'L'Effet de réel'[62]) and its immediate result is the destruction of the 'innocent eye' theory. 'Making it strange' is, now, not the isolation of an unmediated, unconditioned perception, but the substitution of one set of (artistic) governing conditions for the usual set. The artist may think he is giving his reader a stark, immediate reality, but the formalist critic, by turning a similar searchlight on the artist's means of expression, by making them strange, reveals the fact that he is doing no such thing.

It is at this point that the real, obstinate resistance of the Tolstoy passage begins to be apparent. At first it seemed merely a congenial example of the original, root conception of 'making it strange'. But Tolstoy has made matters difficult for the formalist by applying *his* technique, *within* the novel, to a work of art. The passage in question is both fiction and criticism at the same time. Thus the shift of defamiliarization from the object to the means of expression has already occurred, within the novel, wholly naturally, because in this case the means of expression are the concrete features of a theatrical performance and are thus susceptible of seemingly direct, empirical description. This ought to mean that Tolstoy has become a good formalist critic. He has learned to arrest his perceptions at the level of the means.

In fact, as is made utterly clear both by the manner of writing and by the context, Tolstoy regards the entire paragraph, not as normal critical description of art, but as a *reductio ad absurdum*. The opacity of the means is for him a simple offence. This judgement he makes as a great realist, as one who believes that art really can be natural and ought to be so. His own realism in describing the theatrical display is, by his own theory, unexceptionable. The performers give an untruthful or improbable account of a love story (if that is what it is) but he gives a truthful, or probable account of a theatrical show.

If we now try to apply to Tolstoy as artist the formalist theorem whereby supposedly 'direct' accounts may themselves be resolved into formal structures, we are in danger of noticing something rather awkward, once again, for radical formalist theory. For we shall now be saying that the 'cold identification of the means of expression' does not really happen in Tolstoy at all. Rather some other sort of myth (perhaps a positivist one) replaces the common myth. This may be borne, as long as its application is restricted to Tolstoy (where, indeed, it could be argued that the savagely phenomenal description of the opera is echoed, on a larger scale, in the reductive account of military conquest, both proceeding from an essentially '*faux-naïf*' metaphysic). But the implication that other 'identifications of means of expression' must be subject to the same formalist solvent is not far to seek. And if that is true, the concrete critical enterprises of formalist theory are themselves subverted by the running metaphysic. We are back to the scientist who discovered an acid which would dissolve anything and went mad looking for something to put it in. Meanwhile Tolstoy, with his belief in direct realism, is in no danger of falling into an infinite regress.

It would be pleasant to end there, with praise of the firm sanity of the greatest of all mimetic novelists. Unfortunately, one final note of reservation is necessary. The formalists are entirely right when they allege that no vision is unconditioned by prior conceptions. Tolstoy was wrong if he thought otherwise. But, if he operated with *interrogative* conceptions, with a readiness to change if the world failed to answer them, his underlying claim to realism survives. Indeed, the point can be put more simply. If some theatrical performances are like this, the passage is realistic. They are, and it is.

3

Shakespeare's imitation of the world

'Julius Caesar' and 'Coriolanus'

The eighteenth century was profoundly excited by the then novel intuition that Shakespeare's works conveyed the nature of the real world. This excitement lasted well through the nineteenth century and still rises, unbidden, in the untheoretical reader, even today. But in the twentieth century formalism came to Shakespeare criticism before it appeared elsewhere. The origins of this formalism, indeed, lie outside the twentieth century and outside England. Gustav Rümelin's *Shakespearestudien* (Stuttgart, 1866) is an important early essay in this mode. The translation in 1922 of Levin Schücking's *Die Charakterprobleme bei Shakespeare* brought the new approach to the attention of the English-speaking world. The consequent critical enterprise, powerfully led in the 1930s by E.E. Stoll, forms a distinct movement, quite separate from structuralism, but sharing with structuralism a hostility to the idea of mimetic veracity and a correlative impulse to substitute codes and schemata for verisimilitude. The identification of schemata was a positive gain. But the presumption that they must be treated as terminal objects of aesthetic apprehension rather than as formulations of further meaning entailed a very considerable loss. Stoll and others conceived their schemata as necessarily intransitive. At an opposite pole, every ordinary speaker of English treats the schemata of the English language as transitive, as conducting the user to a reality which exists beyond the linguistic forms. Similarly, ordinary theatre-goers treat the very different stereotypes of drama as transitive, in so far as they pass through them into a world of probable inference.

L.C. Knights, following in the footsteps of Stoll,[1] would have us understand that Falstaff 'is not a man, but a choric commentary'.[2] In such statements the Opaque language of criticism rises up to condemn its former ally, the Trà\nsparent language. Knights's unguarded epigram expresses a hard formalist view and is as easily rebutted as such views always are. Falstaff is quite clearly presented, through fiction, as a human being. To strive to dislodge such fundamental and evident truths as this is a kind of critical idiocy. But the soft formalist position is a little more plausible. Falstaff, Everyman and Jack the Giant Killer are all fictional people but they are not realistic. The emphasis in realistic art is on *possible* people, but in none of these cases is any strong interest shown in the area of possibility and probability, while, conversely, a great deal of interest is lavished on story, image, motif. They are therefore only minimally mimetic and such minimal mimesis does not invite or reward critical scrutiny. Once again the 'weak thesis' is really the stronger one. Nevertheless, while they may be right about Jack and Everyman, they are wrong about Falstaff. The motifs and images are certainly there, but so is attentiveness to the world. The eighteenth–century critics were right. The poet of glorious, licentious imagination was also the poet of reverent and attentive perception. So long as we remember that fictions involve mediated truth to probabilities rather than immediate truth to specific facts, Shakespeare's plays may properly be seen as a continued feat of minute yet organized accuracy. So far in this book the literary examples have been simple illustrations, appropriate – I hope – to some twist or turn of the argument. Shakespeare's imitation of the world, on the other hand, is a complex thing and we must take it slowly.

How Roman are the Roman plays of Shakespeare? Teachers of literature used confidently to assert that Shakespeare had no sense of anachronism. Clocks chime in *Julius Caesar* (II. i. 192) and in *Coriolanus* the short-sighted wear spectacles (II. i. 196).[3] The notion that Shakespeare's Romans are really Elizabethans with specially sounding names persists. Students disparagingly observe that

Shakespeare in *Antony and Cleopatra* betrays his complete ignorance of the most obvious and familiar of all Egyptian artefacts, the pyramids. In one sense they are quite right. The most ignorant student today probably has a better idea of the *appearance* of, say, a Roman senator or of the Roman forum than Shakespeare had. The reason for this is simple. Schoolchildren now grow up with lavishly illustrated history books, with classroom walls liberally decorated with posters showing the Colosseum and the like. Shakespeare had none of these things. But he read certain ancient authors. So it comes about that, while he will blunder in the physical detail of daily life – that is, over things like clocks and spectacles – when he comes to deal with a Roman suicide, as distinct from an English suicide, he leaves the average modern student light-years behind. In the study of history Shakespeare lacked the means to walk, but he saw a way to run and seized it. The more sophisticated conceptions of later historians are easily within his reach.

For example, it is commonly believed that it takes a modern anthropologist or cultural historian to see that human nature may itself evolve in time. Previously history was a tract of battles, legislation and migration, all presumably conducted by persons fundamentally like ourselves. This was the doctrine from which C.S. Lewis at last prised away his mind in 1942, in his celebrated rejection of 'the Unchanging Human Heart'.

> How are these gulfs between the ages to be dealt with by the student of poetry? A method often recommended may be called the method of the Unchanging Human Heart. According to this method the things which separate one age from another are superficial. Just as, if we stripped the armour off a medieval knight or the lace off a Caroline courtier, we should find beneath them an anatomy identical with our own, so, it is held, if we strip off from Virgil his Roman imperialism, from Sidney his code of honour, from Lucretius his Epicurean philosophy, and from all who have it their religion, we shall find the Unchanging Human Heart, and on this we are to concentrate. I held this theory myself for many years, but I have now abandoned it. I continue, of course, to admit that if you remove from people the things that make them different, what is left must be the same, and that the Human Heart will certainly appear as Unchanging if you ignore its changes.[4]

Could Shakespeare conceivably have discerned a change in the Human Heart, dividing the Romans from the people of his own time? Surely, it will be said, we can look for no glimmer of such a conception of human nature before, say, the novels of Sir Walter Scott; indeed, even tentatively to attribute such a conception to Shakespeare is historical solecism.

Yet Pope, who lived a hundred years before Sir Walter, saw some such thing in Shakespeare:

> In *Coriolanus* and *Julius Caesar*, not only the Spirit but Manners, of the *Romans* are exactly drawn; and still a nicer distinction is shown, between the manners of the *Romans* in the time of the former and of the latter.[5]

It may be thought that Pope's emphasis on something as superficial as 'manners' impairs my case. But by 'manners' Pope intends far more than the formalized shibboleths of social intercourse. The Latin word for what he has in mind is *mores*. The modern English equivalent is likely to be polysyllabic and pseudo-technical: 'sociocultural behaviour patterns'. In any case, Pope has already taken it as read that Shakespeare captured 'the spirit' of the Romans. But it is the extra discrimination proposed in the second part of his sentence that is especially challenging. Shakespeare did not merely distinguish Romans from English, he distinguished early Romans from later Romans.

Let us look first at Brutus, Cassius and Mark Antony, not as Romans, but less narrowly, as men having a culture which is, at least, different from ours, so that they may be conceived as belonging to an earlier phase in psychic evolution.

Brutus at once involves us in a large, though fairly standard question of cultural history. For Brutus, as is conceded on all hands, is obviously presented by Shakespeare as a conscious Stoic. Real-life Roman Stoicism is rather an aggregate of intellectual and social postures than the philosophy of a single, dominant thinker. Its common opposite, Epicureanism, is indeed derived from the teachings of one man, Epicurus, but few people can even name the master of the Stoics, Zeno. For the Elizabethans Seneca and, to a lesser extent, Plutarch and Virgil are the authoritative names. J.B. Leishman offers an admirable summary of the cult (I use the word in its modern, debased sense) in his book, *Translating Horace*:

> The central doctrine of Stoicism was that nothing mattered except virtue, that it was possible to detect in the world a divine purpose, guiding all things to their perfection, and that it was man's duty to try to identify himself with this purpose, and to train himself to feel indifference towards everything else, except towards any possibility, whether public or private, of helping others to become virtuous. About Stoicism there was much metaphor, much striking of attitudes, much of what the Germans call *pathos*: life was a battle, in

which the Stoic's soul remained unconquerable and his head, though bloody, unbowed; life was a play in which each man had been given a part which he was to read and act at sight and to the best of his ability, without knowing what might happen in the last scene; the Stoic ate and drank from gold as if it were clay and from clay as if it were gold; amid the ruins of a falling world he would but involve himself the more impenetrably in his *virtus*, and his soul would finally ascend through the spheres to a region beyond the sway of fortune.[6]

Leishman catches admirably a certain duality which runs through Stoicism. There is, as he points out, much *pathos* about this philosophy of *apathia*, 'emotionless tranquillity'. The Stoics admired a condition of passionless indifference, but they also admired the heroic achievement of that condition. For the achievement to be spectacular or striking, some passion was after all required, if only as the material of moral conquest. Virgil's description, in Book iv of the *Aeneid*, of Aeneas shaken by Dido's plea that he stay with her, yet inwardly firm in his resolve, is one of the great images of Stoicism. Virgil likens his hero to a tree, tempest-torn yet firmly rooted, and ends his description with the famous, brief, enigmatic sentence:

> *lacrimae volvuntur inanes.*
> [the tears roll down in vain.]   (*Aeneid*, iv. 449)

The puzzle is: whose are the tears, Aeneas's or Dido's? Augustine, notoriously, thought the tears were Aeneas's (*City of God*, ix. 4). It is an interpretation entirely consonant with Stoicism: the suburbs of the personality rebel, but the virtuous will remains firm. Stoics are in one way like statues but it can be said with equal truth that the Stoic hero is typically wracked with strong emotions.

We must also notice that Stoicism is a 'postphilosophical philosophy'. Ancient philosophy falls roughly into two periods. The first (the only one which really deserves the name 'philosophical') is the period of Socrates, Plato, Aristotle. It is characteristic of this period that thinkers should see themselves as lovers of wisdom, as seekers after or purveyors of truth, as people trying to find the right answers to the most difficult questions. In the second period a strange alteration comes over the philosophers: they now present themselves as purveyors of mental health. It is as if some immense failure of nerve, a kind of generalized neurosis, swept through the ancient world, so that the most serious thinkers found that their most urgent task was not to inform or enlighten but to heal. They begin indeed to sound like psychiatrists. This is the period of Stoicism and Epicureanism, in which the philosophers say, again and again, 'Come to us and we will give you ἀταραξία, that is, *freedom from tumult, tranquillity*. The great Epicurean poet Lucretius sought to free his hearers from the crushing fear of death by arguing – somewhat surprisingly to modern ears – that death is total annihilation. The Romans of the first century BC were terrified of torture after death.

The Stoic commendation of *apathia*, 'absence of feeling', is similar. Seneca wrote 'consolatory epistles', to comfort people in distress (notice how it has now become natural to expect *solace* from a philosopher – very soon books will appear with such titles as *The Consolation of Philosophy*, which would have seemed strange to Aristotle). Writing to people broken by bereavement and similar misfortunes, the Roman Stoic recommends a kind of withdrawal from the world:

> *Recipe te ad haec tranquilliora, tutiora, maiora.*
> [Recollect yourself, back to these things which are more tranquil, safer, more important.]
> (Seneca, *Ad Paulinum: de brevitate vitae*, xix. 1[7])

Contempt of life (and, by implication, of all one's most demanding personal relationships) must be supplemented by a proper egoism; the mind is its own place, and, though a man be banished from his beloved country, yet he can always reflect that over his own mind he is undisputed king. Thus the rational man is a citizen of the world, true to himself, exempt from emotional commitment to particular people and places. He cannot be banished.

> *Ideoque nec exulare unquam potest animus.*
> [And so the mind can never suffer exile.]
> (Seneca, *Ad Helviam de consolatione*, xi. 7)
> *Animus quidem ipse sacer et aeternus est cui non possit inici manus.*
> [The soul itself is sacred and eternal and on it no hand can be laid.]
> (ibid. xi. 7[8])

When, however, it is rational to leave this worthless life, the philosopher does so, with a steady hand.

It is clear that Senecan Stoicism worked by a systematic introversion of psychic patterns surviving from a much older, heroic culture, something like the shame-culture analysed by E.R. Dodds in *The Greeks and the Irrational*.[9] In a shame-culture no distinction is drawn between performing an action for the sake of glory and performing it out of virtue. Virtue itself is seen in strangely public terms, coinciding with elements which we think of as 'merely external', like beauty and physical strength. The greatest literary monument of a shame-culture is the *Iliad* of Homer. But it is by no means confined to archaic Greece. Anthropologists have traced it in cultures as remote as that of eighteenth-century Japan.[10] It is also vestigially present in our own culture. In Stoic philosophy the heroic ethic of pride, of glory in the sight of others, is cut off from its reliance on social esteem and made self-sufficient in each individual. The rational man is taught to fill the silence of his own skull with clamorous self-applause, with a majestically austere approbation of his own feats. Every man his own Achilles in his own, private Trojan War. Certain behavioural tricks of the old culture survive in Stoicism – the military strut, the strenuousness – but they have been strangely dehumanized. The vivid responsiveness of man to man has been deliberately dried up at its source and instead we seem to be watching a set of obscurely threatened statues. Truly for them, as Cicero said, *vita mors est*, 'Life is a state of death.'[11]

All this, note, is about real Stoicism. How much of it is 'noticed' in Shakespeare's Roman plays? I answer: pretty well all of it. Shakespeare knows that because Stoicism is an artificially framed philosophy, deliberately and consciously adopted by its adherents, any actual Stoic Roman will have within him un-Stoic elements. Your shame-culture hero Achilles, say, simply exemplifies that culture, but Stoicism is rather something at which you aim. The theory of shame-culture is posterior to and descriptive of the practice. The theory of Stoicism is prior to and prescriptive of practice. There are therefore elements of cultural tension present in Brutus which are absent from Achilles (and, one might add, from Othello, but more of that anon).

In the second scene of the first act of *Julius Caesar* Brutus is 'sounded' by Cassius, as to his willingness to kill Caesar. Cassius brings to his task a profound knowledge of Brutus's personality. He begins with the basis of that personality, which is the inherited and very ancient notion of self as essentially that which is presented to others. Cassius says,

> Tell me, good Brutus, can you see your face?
>
> (I. ii. 51)

Brutus answers that the eye cannot see itself except by reflection, in some other object such as a mirror. Cassius swiftly offers himself as a reflector:

> I, your glass,
> Will modestly discover to yourself
> That of yourself which you yet know not of.
>
> (I. ii. 68–70)

Notice what is happening. Cassius is, in effect, teaching Brutus what to think. But he contrives to use an image which both apprises Brutus of the opinion of others (a powerful primitive incentive) and yet evokes the private, self-regarding virtue of the Stoics (since the heart of his challenge is, 'Brutus, what do you think of yourself?'). All this is done with the image, carrying a simultaneous implication of self-absorption and external reference, of the glass. Such talk, we sense, is congenial to Brutus. Moreover the language of mirrors which Cassius uses to compass his end subtly apprises the audience that there may be something narcissistic in the Stoicism of Brutus. This note is struck again a little later when Brutus opens the letter in his orchard: 'Brutus, thou sleep'st. Awake, and see thyself' (II. i. 45).

But with all this Brutus is perhaps better than Cassius thinks him. In the orchard scene (II. i) we see his mind, not as it is when it is being manipulated by Cassius, but working alone, strenuously, struggling to determine what ought to be done:

> It must be by his death; and for my part,
> I know no personal cause to spurn at him,
> But for the general: he would be crown'd.
> How that might change his nature, there's the question.
> It is the bright day that brings forth the adder,
> And that craves wary walking. Crown him – that!
> And then, I grant, we put a sting in him
> That at his will he may do danger with.
> Th' abuse of greatness is, when it disjoins
> Remorse from power; and to speak truth of Caesar,
> I have not known when his affections sway'd
> More than his reason. But 'tis a common proof
> That lowliness is young ambition's ladder,
> Whereto the climber-upward turns his face;
> But when he once attains the upmost round,
> He then unto the ladder turns his back,
> Looks in the clouds, scorning the base degrees
> By which he did ascend. So Caesar may.
> Then, lest he may, prevent. And since the quarrel
> Will bear no colour for the thing he is,
> Fashion it thus – that what he is, augmented,
> Would run to these and these extremities;
> And therefore think him as a serpent's egg,
> Which, hatch'd, would as his kind grow mischievous,
> And kill him in the shell.

(II. i. 10–34)

Brutus sets out the case with scrupulous care. He knows nothing personally, here and now, against Caesar. The alpha and omega of the case against him is that he would like to be crowned King. That crowning might change a nature at present blameless. The case is not specific to Caesar, therefore. It is just that, commonly, when men are thus incongruously elevated, those who were not proud before become so. The case as Brutus puts it is tenuous and some critics have seen in this a sign that Brutus is feebly rationalizing a dark impulse which springs from the imperfectly repressed violence in him. In fact there are signs in the play of such a side to Brutus's nature, notably the strangely exultant 'red weapons' (III. i. 110), but I cannot think that the dominant tenor of this passage is mere rationalization. After all, rationalization usually aims at giving as powerful an appearance as possible of logical completeness. When Hamlet explains his sparing of Claudius at his prayers by observing that to kill a man in a state of grace would be to send him straight to heaven and hence would be no revenge (*Hamlet*, III. iii. 72–9), we have an argument at once watertight and insane, and there is therefore an excellent case for supposing that Hamlet is rationalizing his reluctance. Brutus is fairly close in conception to Hamlet, but the tone of this soliloquy, with 'there's the question' in line 13, is closer to the beleaguered but still operative sanity of 'To be or not to be' (*Hamlet*, III. i. 56f) than to the faceless logic of 'Now might I do it, pat' (*Hamlet*, III. iii. 72). Brutus goes out of his way to stress the *tenuousness* of his case, pauses on all the weak links in the chain, and this, surely, is almost the opposite of rationalization.

I suspect that many who say that such a chain of reasoning is an inadequate basis for any major political act cannot have reflected how much political action is necessarily founded on exactly this sort of 'lest he may, prevent' basis. I imagine that most people today would say that republicanism is better than despotism. If you ask them why, they are likely to say that it is right that a people should be, as far as possible, self-governing, rather than subjected to the will of a single individual. If you then point out that in any system which stops short of the total democracy of the (adult, male) ancient Athenians (we will set aside the rigidly aristocratic character of real Roman republicanism!) the processes of government are in fact carried out by representative officers and not by the people at all, the answer is likely to be that as long as the officers remain answerable to the people they are more *likely* to act in the interest of the people – and now, notice, we have begun to speak in terms of *probability*.

Now let us make the situation concrete. Imagine yourself a citizen of France, wondering whether to vote for someone rather like General de Gaulle: a figure at the height of his power, who has, let us say, shown a genius for getting his country out of a tight spot, for running a system in trouble. What would such voters say? Well, they would of course say many different things. But the ones who were worried by the idea of autocratic genius might well say, 'The case against him is not personal; it's just that autocracy is inherently dangerous. Of course, we cannot predict with certainty that he will behave corruptly, it is just that he may, and because of that bare possibility it is our duty to stop him.' The seemingly factual character of formally indicative sentences like 'Autocracy is bad' resolves itself, in practice, into a cloud of (very serious) probabilities.

Assassination is, to be sure, somewhat more drastic than a transferred vote, but nevertheless Brutus's speech is both moving and impressive in its refusal to dress up a political rationale as something more watertight than it really is. It is curiously refreshing after reading the words of current politicians (who are under very great pressure to sound more certain than they can ever really be). The best place in Brutus's speech is the marvellously laconic

> So Caesar may.
> Then, lest he may, prevent.

(II. i. 27–8)

The lines beginning 'And since the quarrel/Will bear no colour for the thing he is,/Fashion it thus' (II. i. 28–30) have also been misinterpreted. I used to think that this was an example of what may be called 'dissociated motivation', the kind of thing which we shall see later in Iago, a man who *decides* what he will believe, what he will be moved by. This puzzled me, because it meant that, according to the scheme which was beginning to form in my mind, Brutus would have to be classified as 'overevolved'.

The underevolved archaic man includes in his ego many things we consider external. The ordinarily evolved man includes within the ego such things as feelings and beliefs but excludes physical attributes, to a greater or lesser extent. According to this sequence the overevolved man might narrow the field of the ego still further, until it was able to watch, in arrogant isolation, the inept dance of emotions and appetites, now psychically objectified. But I was wrong. Although there is a faint pre-echo of Iago here, this sentence has a different context and a different logic.

Brutus is not, in fact, proposing to feign a belief and then to execute the fiction in real life. He is saying to himself 'It is no use trying to construct this case with reference to what I know of Caesar, now. Rather, put it this way. . . .' To paraphrase thus is indeed to soften the worrying word 'fashion', which obstinately retains a suggestion of fiction (I have conceded a faint anticipation of Iago's *manner*). Nevertheless, the main tenor of the idiom is donnishly abstract rather than cynically self-manipulative. It is much closer to the philosopher's 'Let's try the argument this way . . .'

than to 'This shall be my motive.' If it is asked, 'Why, then, granting that the Iago-subaudition is only a subaudition, did Shakespeare allow it into the line?' the answer is, perhaps, because he wished to hint that the second state of mind was, in a sinister fashion, latent in the first; that the proper corruption of moral abstraction is diabolical cynicism. Brutus stands on the edge of a pit, but he has not yet fallen.

Moreover this psychic isolation of the reflective ego is not natural to Brutus as it is to Iago. It is really the product of a special moral effort, the Stoic assertion of reason against disabling emotion. For the beginning of 'overevolved' dissociation of the ego from ordinary feeling is likewise latent, or present as a potential corruption, in Stoic philosophy. Aeneas, weeping yet successfully separating his reason from his love of Dido, is great and at the same time rather weird. The panic-stricken retreat into a private area of the mind as being alone governable by the rational will can lead, almost by its own inner impetus, to forms of scepticism which would have shocked the Stoics themselves. The person who is broken-hearted is given the dangerous consolation (dangerous, because it can in the long run erode the very notion of value) 'You yourself can decide what is good and what is bad.' Hamlet's 'There is nothing either good or bad, but thinking makes it so' (II. ii. 248) is pivotal. It reaches back into Stoicism and forward into abysses of modern scepticism. But the contraction of the ego is the principal point at issue, and it is important to remember that in Stoicism this contraction always takes place in a context of moral effort. There is therefore a real difference between Brutus's straining to bring to bear reason, and reason alone, on the one hand and Iago's unblinking survey of his own motives on the other. Nevertheless there is in *Julius Caesar* a real, though faint, analogue to Iago, and that is Mark Antony.

Consider the behaviour of Mark Antony, first, when he moves into the circle of the assassins as they stand round the body of the newly slain Caesar (III. i) and, second, in his great oration (III. ii). In III. i Antony moves, with great circumspection but also with extraordinary 'nerve' within sword's length of men who may at any moment turn on him. He is their greatest potential danger, but the potentiality (as with Caesar) is fraught with doubt. These are the reasonings of a Brutus and it is on them that Antony counts. The conscientiousness of Brutus is for him a weakness to be exploited. Antony knows just how much of his grief for Caesar it is safe to express. He shakes hands with the murderers and is left alone on the stage, to plot the ruin of Rome.

Notice, in passing, that my entire account of this scene has been written in bull-bloodedly Transparent language; I have been considering Shakespeare's Brutus and Antony, not indeed as direct portraits of their historical originals, but at least as possible human beings and I have not scrupled to make inferences and even, at times, to guess. Yet, in the closing sentence of the last paragraph, I wrote, not 'left alone in the Capitol', but 'left alone on the stage'. The logical slippage from the tenor to vehicle is entirely easy and creates no difficulties for the reader, because it mirrors a movement of the mind which is habitual to play-goers and play-readers.

We may further ask, is Antony sincere? The question, oddly enough, can be answered with slightly more confidence when the reference is to a fictional person (where the clues are finite) than with reference to a real-life person (where they are indefinite and in any case liable to subversion). I think that Antony is sincere. He feels real grief for Caesar but is, so to speak, effortlessly separate from the grief even while he feels it. We therefore have something which is psychologically more disquieting than the ordinary machiavel, who pretends emotion while he coldly intrigues for power. Antony feels his emotions and then *rides* them, controls them, moderating their force as need arises.

Thus the great oration is at once artificial and an authentically passional performance. I would have the actor, if he can, go so far as to weep in the delivery of it ('his eyes are red as fire with weeping' – III. ii. 115) in order to give maximum effect to the conclusion of the oration, at which point Antony, his own emotion ebbing from its licensed height, watches the mob run screaming from him and says, like one who has administered a mass injection, 'Now let it work. Mischief, thou art afoot' (III. iii. 261). Naturally it is Brutus who is the man of the past, the doomed order of things, and Antony who is the man of the future. When Brutus patiently explained, with lucid logic, how he had killed his friend to save Rome from the rule of an individual, the crowd applauds him with the dreadful 'Let him be Caesar' (III. ii. 50). They do not understand the rigorous, tormented morality of his action and he, in his turn, does not understand the place in history to which he has come.

The Roman-ness, the un-English-ness, of all this is evident. Moreover, within that powerfully imagined Roman-ness we have, not only contrasts of individual with individual, but prior contrasts, operating in the region intermediate between individuals and the cultural remoteness of Rome. I mean a contrast between different degrees of psychic and political evolution within a Roman setting. Brutus, the Republican, addresses a populace which spontaneously embraces monarchy, thus exemplifying one of the paradoxes of liberalism identified by Sir Karl Popper (though Plato was there before him): what happens when a democracy decides in favour of tyranny?[12] Brutus, the aristocrat, his theoretic Stoicism borne on a foundation of shame-culture, on ancient heroic dignity, belongs to the Roman past. He can do the Stoic trick (rather like 'isolating' a muscle) of separating his reason from his passions but he cannot exploit his own motivating passions with the coolness of an Antony. With all his fondness for statuesque postures Brutus remains morally more spontaneous than Antony.

In IV. iii there is a notorious textual crux. Brutus and Cassius quarrel and are uneasily reconciled. Shakespeare presents the quarrel with great realism and elicits from his audience a high degree of sympathy with both figures. At IV. iii. 141 Cassius observes, wonderingly, 'I did not think you could have been so angry', and, a moment later, with a hint of a taunt so that we fear the quarrel may break out again, he adds,

> Of your philosophy you make no use,
> If you give place to accidental evils.
>
> (IV. iii. 143–4)

Brutus answers, bleakly, that Portia, his wife, is dead. Cassius is at once overwhelmed with contrition at his own coarse hostility. Brutus tells, shortly, the horrible story of Portia's suicide by swallowing fire and calls for wine, to 'bury all unkindness' (IV. iii. 152). Titinius and Messala then enter. Brutus welcomes them, volubly, and the talk is all of military movements and public events in Rome. Then the spate of talk dries up and the following dialogue takes place:

Messala	Had you your letters from your wife, lord?
Brutus	No, Messala.
Messala	Nor nothing in your letters writ of her?
Brutus	Nothing, Messala.
Messala	That, methinks, is strange.
Brutus	Why ask you? Hear you aught of her in yours?
Messala	No, my lord.
Brutus	Now as you are a Roman, tell me true.
Messala	Then like a Roman bear the truth I tell:
	For certain she is dead, and by strange manner.
Brutus	Why, farewell, Portia. We must die, Messala.
	With meditating that she must die once,
	I have the patience to endure it now.
Messala	Even so great men great losses should endure.
Cassius	I have as much of this in art as you,
	But yet my nature could not bear it so. (IV. iii. 179–93)

Brutus receives the news from Messala as if for the first time, although he has just confided to Cassius that he knows, and Cassius is still there, listening to every word. To make matters worse, Brutus's self-control is applauded as a Stoic feat and Brutus accepts the applause. And still

Cassius is there, watching and listening.

The easiest way out of these difficulties is to suppose that Shakespeare wrote two alternative versions and that both have somehow survived, in incongruous juxtaposition, in the 1632 Folio text (the sole authority for this play). To take this course at one stroke removes both the difficulties and the tense excitement of the scene. Brents Stirling, in a article which may serve as a model of the proper marriage of literary criticism and textual scholarship,[13] argued for the retention of both versions. He observes that Brutus is in a state of nervous excitement after the quarrel with Cassius (notice his extreme irritation with the sententious poet who enters at IV. iii. 122). In this state, bordering on exhaustion, Brutus attempts to put Messala aside with his blankly mendacious 'Nothing' at line 182. But Messala will not be put off and Brutus is forced to question him. Thereupon *Messala* 'turns witless in the crisis' and answers 'No, my lord' at 184. Brutus tries to resolve the impossible situation with 'Now, as you are a Roman, tell me true.' Messala catches the manner, is freed from his petrified immobility by the familiar *style*, and from here on forces Brutus to play out the episode in the full Stoic manner. At its conclusion Brutus's head is bowed at the humiliating praise he has received from Messala.

Given this reading, the comment of Cassius is immediately luminous. He has watched his fellow commander, in a state of near-collapse, lie and then reassert, artificially, his command over himself and his subordinates. Brutus's 'Nothing' was pure nature. It is the kind of speech which in life is wholly probable and becomes 'impossible' only when challenged by the customary canons of art. Brutus then pulled himself back and this too was nature. From the recovered ground he framed his formal response to Messala and secured the required result. Cassius who has seen the 'nature' of Brutus humiliated in the lie also perceives in the very recovery of will a feat of natural endurance. His comment is almost ironic but is at the same time movingly generous and intelligent; he observes that he could just about match Brutus's rhetoric, but he could never be so strong and brave.

This is not to say that there are no rough edges in the text as we have it. There is formal evidence in the Folio of revision. This has been investigated by Brents Stirling in a second article.[14] The speech headings give *'Cassi'* until *'Enter a Poet'*. Then, in the lines which report the death of Portia we get *Cas*. At line 164, 'Portia, art thou gone?' (which may be a single-line insertion), we get *'Cass'*. The passage containing suspected additions has different prefix forms and the passages both before and after it have standard forms. Admittedly there is considerable variation of *'Cassi'* and *'Cas'* throughout the play and this must weaken the presumption of interpolation in so far as it is founded on speech headings. But the changes are so timed (in conjunction with the obvious oddity of the presentation) as to suggest some sort of process of revision, which has not been satisfactorily completed. What is not shown at all is that the revision was intended as a replacement of one version by another. It remains entirely possible that Shakespeare, revising, determined to show us a Brutus reacting twice to the same event and merely failed to complete the 'joinery'. Brutus's lie might then have been more carefully 'framed'. We need not infer that it would have been removed.

Thus, even when Brutus's Stoicism is most artificial, most plainly exerted by will, we sense not only what is exerted but the human will which exerts; we sense a person with an emotional life. That indeed is why the artificiality is so excruciating. In Antony it would scarcely be noticed.

Brutus is presented by Shakespeare as an interplay of nature and art; the art, to be sure, is Brutus's. If we step back and view the whole, both the art and the nature of Brutus are equally formed by the art of Shakespeare. Brutus's nature is Shakespeare's art. But in conveying something which the audience will receive as nature, Shakespeare must (and does) consult and defer to reality. Therefore among the many excellencies of *Julius Caesar* we may include a specific success in realism.

Coriolanus shows us an older Rome, a city which has just become something more than a strangely warlike country town. Pope wrote that Shakespeare not only noticed the difference between Romans and English people but also saw the difference between different stages of Roman development. In *Coriolanus* the populace is only a little less contemptible than the mob in *Julius Caesar*, but at least it is interested in its political rights. Rome is firmly and consciously republican. The day of the autocrat has not yet come. The play even exhibits some awareness of economic factors. The populace in *Coriolanus* is not a Marxian proletariat of first-order producers, nor is Coriolanus himself an economic parasite. The city lives by military conquest; conquest produces tribute and the citizens are sustained by a gratuitous dole. In warfare it appears that they have been of little use (though one itches to step outside the data of the play and dispute this). Coriolanus, because he is a great killer, is in this society a great provider.

Coriolanus is at one and same time a sort of Titan and a baby. Modern critical accounts of him perhaps stress the second too much at the expense of the first. We should not forget that if any of us were to meet him on a battle field the patronizing critical smile would be wiped away very quickly. As a warrior he is almost superhuman. But at the same time he is like a 2 year old in his tantrums, his stubbornness, his tendency to stamp or hide his face.

And then there is his pride. Here, as usual, Shakespeare refuses to give the sentimentalist an easy ride. It would be nice to think that Coriolanus's contempt for the people is unmixed folly. Shakespeare keeps the situation uncomfortable by insinuating on the one hand that Coriolanus's pride has something pathological in it and on the other hand that the people are in fact much as he describes them. Strange world, where only the egomaniac speaks the truth!

In *Julius Caesar* we saw a fundamental problem of democracy broached; what happens when the people choose tyranny? In *Coriolanus* we have another, still more fundamental problem, one so uncomfortable that people prefer to set it aside as 'ludicrously abstract': what happens when it can be predicted that the people, through vice or folly will choose corruptly? Is democracy right if the *demos* is bad? What does the good man do, placed in such a society? If you make liberty a terminal value of democracy (that is, if you believe that liberty is not only good because it promotes happiness but is also good in itself and moreover is the most important good of all) then you have no difficulty in answering this question. You will oppose Coriolanus. Perhaps older Americans will do this more confidently than other people. W.H. Auden wrote in an introduction to Henry James's *The American Scene*[15] that many Americans have given up *Romanitas*. *Romanitas*, for Auden, means making virtue prior to freedom. People who give up *Romanitas* are people who would rather do wrong freely than do right under compulsion. It is interesting in view of the applicability of this conception to *Coriolanus* that Auden chose to express his idea with a word which literally means 'Roman-ness'.

Of course the Rome shown by Shakespeare is not a democracy but a republic. Nevertheless, there are moments in both *Julius Caesar* and *Coriolanus* when the political wishes of the people make themselves felt. In the tribunician elections of *Coriolanus* one has an actual specimen of rudimentary democratic machinery.

In III. i Coriolanus is therefore in an odd position. He is standing for election and he despises the electors. Falsehood is beneath him. His open electoral programme is therefore to strip the people of the very rights they exercise in electing him. It is almost a logical paradox, and equally close to being a joke. For if the people elect him, by their shrewdness they disprove his theory. Coriolanus would then be like Groucho Marx, who resigned from a golf club because it proved itself – through electing him – insufficiently exclusive. At this stage in Shakespeare's play I suppose most of the spectators have begun to feel that Coriolanus is a little mad. Yet a strand of moral integrity persists in him. He had said at the beginning of the play that he believed the populace to be in truth so cowardly and stupid that they could not even pursue their own interest:

> Your affections are
> As a sick man's appetite, who desires most that
> Which would increase his evil.

(I. i. 175–7)

By the beginning of Act III Coriolanus's contempt for the people has reached such a pitch that he can scarcely be expected even to think about their interests. But, if he did, he would maintain his course. He plainly believes that it would be to the advantage of the people if those rights which they exercise with so little intelligence were taken from them. And the strangely pitiless dramatist, who has not a grain of compassion for the hunger of the starving in this play, inserts not a line to show that Coriolanus is wrong.

Can Coriolanus ask the people to sign away their privileges by electing him? He might answer that a populace capable of self-knowledge could and should do so. But, as we saw, a populace capable of self-knowledge would be utterly unlike this populace. Self-knowledge would in *its* case disclose intelligence and, given this intelligence, it would actually be wrong to sign away political rights. Coriolanus really is in a logical prison. There is, seemingly, a fundamental discrepancy between his warrior nature and the very institutions of a civil polity.

This brings us to the central pathos of Coriolanus's nature and the central tension of the play. Coriolanus has been made, by his overwhelming mother, Volumnia, into an instrument of war. We know roughly how it was done from the episode in I. iii, where we are told how Coriolanus's son, little Marcius, a miniature replica of his father, chased 'a gilded butterfly', caught it and let it go over and over again until he fell in the chase and then seized the butterfly and '*mammocked*' it – that is, tore at it with his teeth (I. iii. 64). Volumnia greets the story with an indulgent, reminiscent smile: 'One on's father's moods.' Plainly, Coriolanus was rewarded with love for displays of aggression.

Notice how odd bits and pieces of *King Lear* are floating in this play. Shakespeare, who is full of recyclings, never merely repeats himself. In *King Lear* there are two especially powerful images. The first occurs in Gloucester's line:

> As flies to wanton boys are we to th' gods –
> They kill us for their sport.

(IV. i. 37–8)

The second comes when Lear, restored to sanity after his ordeal in the storm, is reunited with Cordelia. He says to her,

> So we'll live,

And pray, and sing, and tell old tales, and laugh
At gilded butterflies.

(V. iii. 11–13)

When he was writing *King Lear* Shakespeare had a vision compounded,
one suspects, of memory and imagination. The memory was of cruel vil-
lage boys tormenting insects. Imagination showed him gods who, while
possessed of superhuman power, were morally identical with those
remembered boys. In *Coriolanus*, which is about a hero-god who is himself like a violent child, the images naturally rose again in his mind – not
only in the picture of little Marcius teasing and tearing the gilded butterfly but also later, when Coriolanus's army is described as coming on with
no less confidence

Than boys pursuing summer butterflies,
Or butchers killing flies.

(IV. vi. 94–6)

Volumnia, then, has forged Coriolanus as an instrument of war. But
then she encounters a problem. She needs an instrument to achieve her
political ends within the city and she has built her son in a way which
does not serve her purpose. It is like trying to saw with a sword. At a word
he will hack and kill, but he is set to shy away from the very idea of compromise or conciliation. Yet his mother's power over him remains the
strongest force in his life. In III. ii Volumnia tries in vain to get Coriolanus
to sue for office and only succeeds when she gives up rational persuasion
and instead remarks – quite lightly – that she will be very pleased with
him if he does it (III. ii. 109). At once he does what she wants.

I have said that Coriolanus's character is one of great pathos. The pathos lies in the fact that he has no inside. All he has was given him by his
mother and confirmed in him in the physical stress of battle. What existentialists say is true of man in general is certainly true of Coriolanus in
particular – namely, that in himself he is a kind of nothing and acquires
what positive nature he possesses by adventitious role-adoption. It may
be thought that in asserting this I go too far for sane historical scholarship – for everyone knows that in the sixteenth and seventeenth
centuries men had a very strong and firm sense of the real nature of man,
and his place in the great chain of being. But the Elizabethan world picture, as unified and frozen by scholars, is a retrospective historical myth.
The existentialist idea that man's original nature lies in the negation of
all essence is anticipated by Pico della Mirandola, in his *De hominis
dignitate*. There the philosopher tells how God created the world, and
framed it as a great ladder, blazing with light and colour, every rung
loaded with being, all disposed in hierarchical splendour; and how God,

having completed his immense cosmos, paused, and then resolved to make something quite different. And so he made man, a creature with no given nature at all, and unleashed this little darkness into his glittering creation, a flickering total freedom among all the splendid certainties, and bade it *take on* any nature it chose, be it God, beast or devil.[16] The idea belongs clearly with that immensely influential body of thought known as Hermetism.[17] If one must look for a single cosmology appropriate to Shakespeare surely this fits better than the bland system expounded by E.M.W. Tillyard?[18] Certainly it was current in Shakespeare's time. John Donne wrote in a 'Letter to a Lord' (1624) that, 'to make myself believe that our life is something, I use in my thoughts to compare it to something; if it be like anything that is something'[19] and lyrically explored the idea of a constitutive negation in his 'Nocturnall upon St. Lucies Day'.[20] A similar way of speaking and thinking appears in Shakespeare's play, when Cominius says of Coriolanus,

> He was a kind of nothing, title-less,
> Till he had forg'd himself a name i' th' fire
> Of burning Rome.
>
> (V. i. 13–15)

From being a kind of nothing he became – never a person, but rather a *thing*, insentient, an instrument, a machine. He is repeatedly spoken of in these terms. Cominius calls him 'a thing of blood' (II. ii. 107). Coriolanus himself, in strange exultation, cries out to his men, 'O, me alone! Make you a sword of me?' (I. vi. 76). Cominius later says of him,

> He leads them like a thing
> Made by some other deity than Nature.
>
> (IV. vi. 91–2)

and Menenius calls him both 'engine' and 'thing' (V. iv. 20, 24). There is something very sad in the way this artfully brutalized piece of nothingness is at last brought to deny its own conditioning. In V. iii Coriolanus has returned to destroy Rome and his mother goes out to dissuade him, just once more, from his natural course. As he sees her coming he says, feeling himself weakening,

> I'll never
> Be such a gosling to obey instinct, but stand
> As if a man were author of himself
> And knew no other kin.
>
> (V. iii. 34–7)

Here Coriolanus clutches at a Stoic attitude for the support it gives to the isolated self. Yet the speech expresses a wish, not an achievement. Here, surely, was one who existed as a mere relation before he existed substantially as himself; he is, timelessly, a son before he is a man.

Again I have written in a freely Transparent language, treating the character of Coriolanus as a study in possible psychology. To write and think in this way is to find oneself engaged in a dialogue with a text which proves richly responsive. A rigorously formal approach might easily prevent a reader or spectator from noticing the wholly remarkable sense Shakespeare displays of the possible formative tyranny of the parent. This alone is sufficiently astonishing in a pre-Freudian writer and yet it is certainly there, in the text. The curious and the historically sceptical can discover how Shakespeare found hints of his conception in Plutarch. But *Coriolanus* like *Julius Caesar* is at the same time a study of cultural change. This time, the conception we have labelled 'shame-culture' is a little closer than it was with Brutus.

There is no contradiction in saying both that Coriolanus exemplifies a particular cultural pattern and that his personality was formed for him by another individual, his mother. Volumnia made her son according to a still available cultural model, that of the warrior. Coriolanus is therefore an artificial, but therefore especially pure, specimen of the type. Certainly he has the entire courage, the big language and perhaps the unreadiness for marriage (think of Othello) which Shakespeare seems to associate with the kind. Moreover, Shakespeare, in setting forth the growing civic institutions of Rome as existing in tension with the warlike mode is working with almost the same subject matter as a modern cultural historian. A.W.H. Adkins, for example, in his *Merit and Responsibility*[21] traces the process by which what he calls 'the co-operative values' gradually came to replace the 'competitive values', as Greek society gradually settled into relatively stable city states. Terms like 'temperate' came to carry more ethical weight than terms like 'brave'. The level of historical abstraction we find in Adkins's book seems quintessentially modern. But Shakespeare picked up from Plutarch the fact that the early Romans made much of *virtus* in its etymological sense, 'manliness', 'virile heroism'. He chose to exhibit this virile courage in a civic context to which it is not suited. The audience can quite simply watch 'the co-operative virtues' gathering power in the forum. Shakespeare shows with great clarity, first, how useful Coriolanus is to Rome in time of war and, second, how much happier the city is without him once peace has been attained. The second observation is emphasized in IV. vi where the citizens greet each other courteously and Sicinius says,

This is a happier and more comely time
Than when these fellows ran about the streets
Crying confusion.

(IV. vi. 27-9)

It is perhaps impossible to say with precision to what extent the shame-culture of Coriolanus has assumed the introverted form given to it by Stoicism. It might be said that the true shame-culture figure rejoices above all in glory, in reputation, and that Coriolanus's refusal to court the people shows in him the egoistic withdrawal of the Stoic. But we must remember that when Coriolanus goes among the people he is with men who to him are little better than slaves. Even Homer's Achilles or Ajax, the purest examples we have of archaic shame-culture, would balk at seeking the favour of such base people. Certainly there should be no suggestion in production that Coriolanus is here displaying the 'co-operative' virtue of modesty. Coriolanus wishes to hide his scars from the populace, not because he thinks them insignificant, but because he thinks them too glorious. He says,

To brag unto them 'Thus I did, and thus!'
Show them th'unaching scars which I should hide,
As if I had received them for the hire
Of their breath only!

(II. ii. 144-8)

The people correctly identify his reluctance as springing from aristocratic pride.

It is true that when we see Coriolanus amid his fellow warriors, flushed with victory in I. ix, he keeps up a certain social opposition to praise and it must be conceded that this alone places him in a post-shame-culture period. But his resistance is shallow compared with his violent revulsion in Rome. Indeed, it is little more than a half-embarrassed shrugging of the shoulders:

I will go wash;
And when my face is fair you shall perceive
Whether I blush or no. Howbeit, I thank you.

(I. ix. 68-70)

The battle over, his energy drains from him and with aristocratic negligence he fails to recall the name of the poor man who sheltered him, the man for whom a little earlier he had pleaded with equally typical aristocratic magnanimity. Nietzsche, who is the father of all modern cultural historians of antiquity, would recognize at once both the largeness and the shallowness of Coriolanus's aristocratic spirit.

Coriolanus is never the theoretic, conscious Stoic that Brutus is in *Julius Caesar*. Yet there remains one pivotal moment in the play when he momentarily attains true Stoic grandeur. It comes at the end of III. iii, when the people turn on him and the tribune Brutus cries out that he should be banished as an enemy of the people. Coriolanus looks down at them and says, 'I banish you' (III. iii. 125) and turns his broad back on them. The Senecan *dicta* are all there. The mind is its own place. The Stoic man is citizen of the world, and cannot be exiled. But at the same time we see something else, a red-faced child, stamping and crying through his tears 'I'll send *you* away!' Here intuitive cultural history intersects with intuitive psychology. The moment is powerfully mimetic, with a comprehensiveness and, at the same time, a particularity which will not easily be matched. It is also pure genius.

'The Merchant of Venice' and 'Othello'

Shakespeare saw that Rome was not England. He also saw that Venice was not London.

Venice, to the Elizabethans, was in some ways what Hollywood was to the rest of the world in the 1930s, or perhaps it would be better to say a mixture of Hollywood and Paris: *the* glamorous, daring, brilliant, wicked city. Even today as the senile, jewel-encrusted Bride of the Adriatic sinks malodorously beneath the waters of the Lagoon, one can glimpse, in the real city, what the effect must once have been. The rest of the world is black, white and grey and here alone, among gilded lions, rosy brick and white marble stained with green, is the Coloured City. The most neutral description of Venice begins to sound like overwriting. Many things, to be sure, have changed. The city of sexual licence has become oddly puritanical; notices in the *vaporetto* stops alert the visitor to the possible indecorousness of his or her costume. Meanwhile the frescoed walls still blaze with the great Venetian scenes of social splendour, ruffs, brocade, fruit, wine and amazing people. Here is the only adequate equivalent in visual art to the Shakespearean mode of, say, *Antony and Cleopatra*. The painters of his own land, Isaac Oliver or Nicholas Hilliard, lacked the necessary physical amplitude and much more besides. In Shakespeare's time travellers' reports of the city abounded and moralists debated whether it was better, in the name of Experience, to send one's son to Venice (with all its attendant perils)[22] or to provide him with suitable books about the place instead.

But the strangest thing of all, to the Elizabethan Englishman, is still unsaid. In 1597 (the probable date of *The Merchant of Venice*) the cycle by which we are sustained was plainly visible to any inhabitant of this country. The food he ate he saw first in his own or his neighbour's fields. Even in the nineteenth century Thomas Hardy tells in the fourteenth chapter of *The Mayor of Casterbridge* how from the streets of an ordinary English country town you could actually nod to the men cutting corn in the fields. Corn, bread, beans, pigs, cows, sheep, wool, cloth, all made a natural sense, authorized and watched over by the seasonally changing English sky. But Venice is actually built in the sea. Salt, undrinkable seawater flows in its great streets. Again and again the traveller to Venice must have thought, first, 'How can anyone live in this barren place?' and, next, 'How can these people be so rich?' No trees, no grass, but everywhere brick, marble, porphyry, bronze and gold. Here was a people living in a way that in Shakespeare's time must still have seemed partly unnatural, for they appeared to live on money alone. Money, traditionally defined as the medium of exchange, itself barren, had here proved strangely fruitful and multiplied itself hourly in the market place.

To put the case in this simple way involves both exaggeration and some distortion. The English practised usury and Venice had her subject territories. Yet the fundamental contrast retains a certain force. Venice was the single, most spectacular example of the power of wealth to beget wealth, and its miraculous setting in the sea is emblematic of that power. Venice is the landless landlord over all.

The crucial part of this finds expression in Shakespeare's *The Merchant of Venice*. It is in a way futile to search for the sources of Shakespeare's knowledge of Venice. By the time he came to write *Othello* he was able to consult Contarini's *The Commonwealth and Government of Venice*, perhaps in Lewis Lewkenor's translation of 1599. But meanwhile London was full of vigorous talk and Venice was an excellent subject of conversation. For all we know Shakespeare may have visited Venice himself in 'the missing years'. The word 'merchant' alerts us first. In his plays set in England merchants hardly figure. We may revive the original impact of the title if we substitute 'the Capitalist' for 'the Merchant', but such 'equivalents' are never truly equivalent. Then, the imagery of money, the chink of coins pervades this play as it does no other. Moreover, this golden imagery is in places pointed very sardonically; it is applied with an almost brutal directness to the central romantic love story of the play. There was of course a convention of applying the language of finance to love, but the point of the convention lay in a paradox, the paradox of applying the lowest and most contemptible terms to the highest and at the same time most human situation, love. Thus the usual thing is to set the metaphor at odds with its application. The lady 'out-values value', makes wealth into poverty as long as she is lacking, and so on. In place of this serviceable and well-worn ingenuity *The Merchant of Venice* offers a disquieting simplicity. Bassanio tells of his love in these words:

> In Belmont is a lady richly left,
> And she is fair and fairer than that word,
> Of wondrous virtues.

(I. i. 161–2)

First he tells us of the money and then, in simple, joyous juxtaposition, of her beauty and virtue. Bassanio is not an out-and-out fortune-hunter who is after Portia for her money. He really loves her and her wealth is simply a component of her general attractiveness. There is a certain repellent ingenuousness about Bassanio. He can trust his own well-constituted nature. It would never allow him to fall in love with a poor woman; for, after all, poor women are not attractive. After such a start a strange light is cast on the rest of his speech:

> her sunny locks
> Hang on her temples like a golden fleece,
> Which makes her seat of Belmont Colchos' strond,
> And many Jasons come in quest of her.

(I. i. 169–72)

The Golden Fleece in another context would have been a paradox of love language. Here it is uncomfortably close to the centre of Bassanio's interest.

Shakespeare deliberately involves Bassanio's love from the outset in a faintly humiliating financial atmosphere. But he plants no overt stylistic signals of what he is about so that the effect is faint indeed. The flow is as smooth as that of any poem by Drayton or Daniel and one almost begins to suspect Shakespeare of a cynical contempt for his audience ('I'll make them drink this and they'll never know what they swallowed') were it not for the fact that, in the trial scene, he plainly relies on the fact that some of this, at least, has stuck in the mind. Bassanio's first move in his courtship is less than heroic. It is to touch his friend Antonio for a loan so that he can improve his sartorial image.

It is curious how wit can consist in the very avoidance of an expected complexity. One may compare the conversational practice known in the slang of forty years ago as 'kidding on the level'; the speaker makes a remark which sounds ironic but the real joke lies in the fact that every word is literally intended: 'Hello darling, you know I hate your guts.' Shakespeare with his strangely bland coupling in this play of the language of love and the language of money is in a manner kidding on the level. Even Portia, who is generous in her love, speaks of her own money as one of her attractions in a strangely unconscious manner when she says to Bassanio,

> You see me, Lord Bassanio, where I stand,
> Such as I am. Though for myself alone
> I would not be ambitious in my wish
> To wish myself much better, yet for you
> I would be trebled twenty times myself,
> A thousand times more fair, ten thousand times more rich,
> That only to stand high in your account
> I might in virtues, beauties, livings, friends,
> Exceed account. But the full sum of me
> Is sum of something which, to term in gross,
> Is an unlesson'd girl.
>
> (III. ii. 149–60)

Notice how wealth is twice placed at the summit of an ascending rhetorical scale involving character and beauty. The accountant's language, 'to term in gross', is uncomfortably close to what is actually going on. An imprudent director – I could not call him perverse – might well have Bassanio surprised by these words in the very act of appraising with his eye the value of the room's hangings.

But Portia is not really unconscious. She understands Bassanio with that peculiar, pitiless clarity of love which characterizes all the great Shakespearean heroines, these women who so utterly transcend their contemptible lovers. After she has said that she will pay off Antonio's debt for Bassanio, she says to her betrothed,

> Since you are dear bought, I will love you dear.
>
> (III. ii. 315)

The play on 'dear' is not wholly comfortable and, at the same time, the love is real and unstinting.

It is perhaps not surprising that this speech should help to make one of the principal 'echoes' of the play:

> 'Tis dearly bought, 'tis mine, and I will have it.
>
> (IV. i. 100)

This time it is not one of the nice people who speaks. It is Shylock and he is talking about a pound of flesh cut from the breast of Antonio.

The Merchant of Venice is about the Old Law and the New; about the low Jewish justice of an eye for an eye and a tooth for a tooth and the way this justice is transcended by Christian charity and mercy. The climactic trial scene is archetypal. The black-clad Jew haggling for the flesh of the fair-skinned Christian, the supervening figure of Justice who is also Love, all this is the stuff of legend. It recalls the medieval *Processus Belial*, as has often been observed,[23] in which the Virgin Mary defends Man against the Devil who lays legal claim to his soul. Behind this analogue lies the doctrine of the atonement itself, in which God paid the legal price for man with his son who was also himself. In the fact of such powerful patterning all ethical ambiguities, we shall be told, must surely fall silent. The Jew is wicked, unhappy, usurious, greedy, vengeful. The Christians are happy, generous, forgiving. This, it might be said, is the plain meaning of the play, and it takes a determined 'Transparent' critic to darken it. In fact it is not difficult to do so. For as soon as we enter the fiction and treat the figures of the drama as possible human beings in a possible, great mercantile city, everything feels slightly different.

It is true, of course, that certain archetypes operate powerfully in the play. But it is not true that they are the only thing there, that the mind should be arrested at their level of generality, that there is nothing behind them. It is Shakespeare's way to take an archetype or a stereotype and then work, so to speak, against it, without ever overthrowing it. Shakespeare himself darkens the pristine clarity of these ethical oppositions and he does so, in the first instance, with allusions to money. To this he adds the figure of Antonio, about whom shadows gather from the beginning. If Bassanio's love for Portia sounds uneasily shallow and mercenary, Antonio's love for Bassanio is disquietingly intense. The stereotypical impression of Christian society in *The Merchant of Venice* is of a world of felicity, conviviality, parties, easy commerce of like spirits, harmony. In all this Antonio is from the first incongruous. He is melancholic. Later, when he is in great peril, he sees himself as in some way polluted and wishes to die:

> I am a tainted wether of the flock,
> Meetest for death; the weakest kind of fruit
> Drops earliest to the ground, and so let me.
>
> (IV. i. 114–16)

In the first scene of the play Antonio is left alone with Bassanio and says, with an air of one coming to the point,

> Well; tell me now what lady is the same
> To whom you swore a secret pilgrimage,
> That you to-day promis'd to tell me of?
>
> (I. i. 119–21)

Bassanio does not answer, but dwells at length on his lack of cash. Antonio with extreme generosity places at his friend's disposal,

My purse, my person, my extremest means.

(I. i. 138)

The reference to 'person' and 'extremest means' evidently looks forward to the horror so narrowly averted in Act IV. The 'Opaque' critic will feel an impulse at this point to arrest the structure of allusion at the level of thematic motifs: Antonio's words 'pre-echo' the situation in Act IV as an early musical phrase may 'pre-echo' a major development in the last movement of a symphony. The 'Transparent' critic will not be patient of such impediments to humane inference; he will at once begin to wonder if Antonio, aware of the dangerous extremity of his own love for Bassanio, senses the obscure likelihood of a violent outcome. Some may go further, and surmise a kind of deathwish in Antonio. None of this is verifiable or has the force of necessary truth. A moderate alliance of Opaque and Transparent criticism might tell us that Antonio speaks with sudden violence because of the strength of his love, but neither foresees nor deliberately invokes the later horror; that is 'inadvertently' alluded to, by a species of dramatic irony. But what happens to the ordinary spectator, sitting in the audience? It is possible that the majority of spectators, since 1597, had no conscious reaction at all; simply did not separately 'notice' the connection between Antonio's words. But those who did, explicitly, notice the connection will have construed it in terms of character, to a greater or lesser extent. For the bias of theatrical apprehension, oddly enough, is to 'Transparency'. The figures on the stage are apprehended as people. The very tawdriness of the visible means of presentation in a theatre renders this compensatory exercise of Transparent interpretation the more necessary. Otherwise all audiences would see as Natasha saw in Tolstoy's *War and Peace* (VIII. ix) and drama would die. In the history of drama Brechtian alienation is very much the special case, but even it is not fully Opaque, entirely formalist. Brecht, admittedly, deliberately arrests the apprehension of the spectator at the level of the ostentatiously artificial means; he 'foregrounds' the mechanisms of his art. But he counts on a residuum of unused imaginative sympathy, which he is able to channel the more efficiently in the direction of 'doctrine'. In so far as this channelling occurs (and it is essential to his enterprise) his art is neither abstract nor formalist. Meanwhile it is manifestly, *creakingly* unlike other forms of dramatic experience. It may resemble the drama of 'primitive' societies as that drama appears to a cultural outsider, but the *Towneley Play of Noah*, say, never felt to its first observers as Brechtian drama feels to us.

The most natural inference from any or all of the Transparent interpretations of Antonio's words, from the most modest to the most speculative, is that Antonio loves Bassanio with a love so intense as to throw Bassanio's more decorous love for Portia into unhappy relief. Some may feel that this secondary inference is merely monstrous and inherently improbable. But in a manner the thought of Antonio in love occurred to Solanio within the play before it occurred to any spectator or reader outside it, for at I. i. 46 he suddenly says to Antonio,

> Why, then, you are in love.

Antonio answers, 'Fie, fie!' Solanio treats this as a negative but, strictly speaking, it is not. The New Arden editor J. Russell Brown notes with admirable precision that it is 'an exclamation of reproach rather than a clear negative'.[24] Of course Solanio does not suggest that Antonio is in love with Bassanio. He merely plants the idea that Antonio's melancholy is connected with love and then the play itself, with overwhelming singleness of purpose, directs us to a single love object. Antonio's love is exercised against the bias of financial interest. Setting aside the more obvious impediments, one could not imagine Antonio speaking of Bassanio in the unconsciously self-interested way Bassanio spoke of Portia. Bassanio sees Portia as the centre of his future happiness and wealth. Antonio looks very differently at Bassanio; he sees the beloved extinction of both wealth and happiness.

A seed is thus planted at the back of our minds and the progress of the drama brings it to an obscure flowering. In II. viii Solanio describes the parting of Bassanio and Antonio, in which Antonio was unable to hold back his tears, and comments, 'I think he only loves the world for him' (II. viii. 50). While the dapper Bassanio seeks joy and a fortune in Belmont, Antonio, for mere love, faces mutilation and death in the city. When all seems to be over Antonio says to Bassanio,

> Commend me to your honourable wife;
> Tell her the process of Antonio's end;
> Say how I lov'd you; speak me fair in death;
> And, when the tale is told, bid her be judge
> Whether Bassanio had not once a love.
>
> (IV. i. 268–72)

What gives the business of the ring-begging in V. i its extraordinary tension if it is not the half-buried conflict between male love and heterosexual love? Here formally – and not so formally – a brief dramatic 'minuet' enacts the rivalry of Antonio and Portia. At its end, although we are in a comedy and the figures are pairing off in the soft Italian night, Antonio does not get a partner. We may remember that great, drab line from the Sonnets:

I may not evermore acknowledge thee.

(xxxvi. 9)

Given this 'transparent' psychological intuition the story of the cas-
kets ceases to be an inert, decorative centrepiece and becomes charged
with latent irony. Bassanio, dressed up to the nines with someone else's
money, is mockingly rewarded with the gift proper to plain virtue. The
leaden casket bore as its legend,

Who chooseth me must give and hazard all he hath

(II. vii. 16)

W.H. Auden in one of the most brilliant critical remarks of the century
observed that this requirement is met by two people in the play, neither
of whom is Bassanio.[25] It is met by Antonio and Shylock. That is where
the real *agon* lies.

I have granted that the stereotype gives us a mercenary Shylock and
merciful Christians (the Christians being 'above' vengeance) and that
this stereotype is observed in the play. But we have already seen how Shylock's savage ' 'Tis dearly bought' was pre-echoed, in a more elevated
setting, by Portia. 'My daughter! O my ducats!' cries the grief-stricken,
confused, mercenary Shylock (II. viii. 15). 'Like a golden fleece', says
Bassanio (I. i. 170).

I will make fast the doors, and gild myself
With some moe ducats, and be with you straight.

(II. vi. 49–50)

says Jessica to her Christian lover, as they make off in the night with the
turquoise Leah gave to Shylock when he was a bachelor (III. i. 105). All of
which gives added force to Shylock's plea at the trial, where he says, in
effect, 'Remember me? I'm the usurer, the man who makes deals. So
where is the pound of flesh which is owed me?'

In the course of the play we are told certain things about the state of
Venice. The Christians have among them 'many a purchased slave'
(IV. i. 90). Jews are employed when ready capital is needed. They are
considered as aliens (as emerges when Shylock forfeits his goods and
places his life at the Doge's mercy, on the ground that he sought the life of
a *Venetian* citizen). All this Auden brings out in his admirable essay.
Shakespeare is clearly aware of the covert manner in which Christian
merchants make money breed, which is by the ancient doctrine a kind of
usury ('usury' originally referred to any form of interest and was
later – very revealingly – restricted to *excessive* interest). Shakespeare
is likewise aware of the lower, 'coarser' kinds of interest for which Shy-

lock and his kind are needed. He shows with great clarity the almost exclusively mercantile character of the Venetian economy:

> the trade and profit of the city
> Consisteth of all nations.

(III. iii. 30–1)

Here it is Antonio who speaks. The tenor of his argument is that justice must be maintained because if it is not foreign investors may withdraw their money. It is hard to imagine a similar subordination of justice to the profit motive in one of the English histories. In this way Shakespeare shows both the separateness and the economic symbiosis of Christian and Jew.

In I. iii Antonio tells Shylock that he makes no use of usury (line 65) and Shylock in reply tells the curious story of Laban, who agreed with Jacob that he (Laban) should have any particoloured lambs that were born while Jacob could have the others. At conception time Laban set peeled wands before the ewes, who subsequently gave birth to particoloured lambs. Antonio in reply eagerly distinguishes 'venturing' from 'usury'; Laban, he insists, merely trusted in God, he had no power of his own to affect the outcome of the bargain. Or are the ewes to be understood as themselves signifying gold and silver. . .? Shylock, sardonic, uncooperative, turns the question aside (91):

> I cannot tell; I make it breed as fast

Antonio, one senses, is not confident that he has won the argument (it is hard to be sure that Laban did not intervene, with his peeled wands, for had he simply wanted to accept God's dispensation he could surely have waited till it became evident at lambing time). Antonio's words 'The devil can cite scripture for his purpose' are the words of a man who is holding fast to a conviction that his opponent must be wrong, but cannot quite see how. Meanwhile we sense that Antonio's money (whether by 'venturing' or indirect usury) may breed as fast as Shylock's. He is the merchant, after all.

We thus have a curious situation in this play. Shakespeare employs throughout a latent system of allusions to the economic character of Venetian society and this system of allusions, instead of corroborating the stark opposition of good and evil proposed in the play's main action, subtly undermines it. The economic allusions tell us – against the simple plot – that the Jews and the Christians are deeply similar, for all are mercenary. The general vice which Christians ascribe to the Jews is one of which they are themselves – in a less obvious manner – guilty. The Jews therefore perform a peculiar ethical function in that they bear the brunt of the more obvious dirty work necessary to the glittering city. This counter-system of allusions is organically joined to the drama as a whole and therefore exhibits artistic form. But at the same time it is mimetic of reality, in a pretty specific manner. For it can hardly be pure coincidence that Venice really was thus. A recent historian of Venice in the sixteenth century, Brian Pullan, notes, 'Jews were deemed to be there for the purpose of saving Christians from committing the sin of usurious lending', and again, 'The Venetians had consistently combined the attitude of ritual contempt for the Jews with a shrewd and balanced appreciation of their economic utility.' He quotes the diarist, Marino Sanuto, 'Jews are even more necessary than bakers to a city, and especially to this one, for the sake of the general welfare.'[26] It is quite obvious that Shakespeare, Sanuto, Pullan are all discussing a single, real object.

As commonly with Transparent criticism there is a penumbra of unverifiable, remoter possibilities. Since these also compose a relevant system they are worth noting. Shakespeare's sense of background may be very detailed indeed. Anyone who knew anything about Jewish religion would be aware that Shylock, no less than Antonio, was out on a limb. First, the practice of usury is, in the Jewish religion also, tainted with moral dubiety. *Leviticus* 25: 35–7 simply forbids usury, but *Deuteronomy* 23:19–20 permits the exaction of interest from a stranger, though not from a brother (hence the title of Auden's essay). Thus as the Christians need the Jews, so the Jews need the Christians to practise usury on. The symbiosis is more perfectly symmetrical than we may have thought. Shylock, however, breaks with his religion, in particular with *Deuteronomy* 24:6, when he agrees to take Antonio's *life* as a pledge. The passage in *Deuteronomy* uses the metaphor of a millstone: 'No man shall take the nether or the upper millstone to pledge: for he taketh a man's life to pledge'; the metaphor suggests that 'life' is here equivalent to 'means of living'. We may compare *Ecclesiasticus* 34:22, 'He that taketh away his neighbour's living, slayeth him.' Shylock makes precisely this equation at IV. i. 371–2:

> you take my life
> When you do take the means whereby I live

This pattern of scriptural reference would tend to reinforce an impression, already subliminally present in the play, that the Christians, in taking away Shylock's capital, are doing to him what he wished to do to Antonio. The act of mercy has an inner likeness to the act of revenge. Shakespeare completes the ironic pattern by making Antonio say to Portia, 'Sweet lady, you have given me life and living' (V. i. 286). It is typical of Shakespeare's genius that in his great comedy of economic reality he finds the single point where language most powerfully asserts the interdependence of economics and humanity, in the etymological affinity between a person's *life* and a person's *living*. This is in its turn analogous to the economic and ethical meanings of *worth* and *value*.

One effect of Shakespeare's economic subtheme is to make one suspect that the high-minded talk of the Christians is a luxury available only to the dominant class. Old money can afford to talk in this way. We notice that Portia speaks of mercy when Shylock is sharpening his knife for Antonio, but as soon as the tables are turned and Shylock is on the run, Gratiano cries out again and again that Shylock must hang. Shylock is in fact forgiven and the central ethical plot is clearly dominant at this point. Yet even here one senses something less than ethical, a faint smell of patronizing contempt in the very exercise of mercy. Again, though Shylock's money is new and the Christian's old, the misfortune of Antonio the merchant shows us that we are now in a world in which even old money can be horribly at risk. Portia alone has so much old money that she rises above the rest, as Belmont rises above Venice in the sweet summer night. In this way a cruel reductive pun is worked, dramatically rather than verbally, on the notion of transcendence.

That Shakespeare's picture of Venice is not one of minute, documentary accuracy is obvious. The law shown in this play, for example, is fairy-tale law, not real law. But Shakespeare's art in this play remains – not only in the obvious triumphs of probable human motivation at the level of individual character, but also at the less accessible level of influences and conditions – cognitive, with a breath-taking intelligence. He saw the economic peculiarity of Venice and then made the second, greater leap of perceiving how an economic fabric may condition the very nature of moral action: mercy and charity lose their primal simplicity; in the new order personal loyalty, bereft of traditional feudal support, is both sharpened and made more dubious. The ancient stratagem of the Atonement, whereby God sends his substitute to take on himself our sins and save the world, fascinated Shakespeare both in this play and in *Measure for Measure*. There a figure of Christian mercy discovers that his city needs not mercy but rigorous justice, finds a substitute to do his dirty work for him and, when the substitute is drawn into evil of the worst sort, forgives him with a charity at once generous and insulting. In both plays Shakespeare admits what others might have wished to exclude, the ugly anthropological ancestor of the Atonement, the scapegoat, the unhappy creature on which a society vents its bad conscience.

But the most difficult point remains. These half-buried echoes and subauditions in the play really do compose a structure, and an exciting subversive thesis. But they are not the play. After years of pious criticism the views of A.D. Moody and H.C. Goddard are very seductive. Moody says, 'Shylock avows the moral sense by which they actually live. We can see that in condemning Shylock they are condemning their own sins. It would seem then that they are making him literally their scape-goat. . .or, as H.C. Goddard puts it, "They project onto him what they have dismissed from their own consciousness as too disturbing." '[27] But in agreeing with this we are in danger of forgetting the real generosity, however produced, of the Christians, the real ferocity, however explained, of Shylock. They did forgive Shylock. Shylock would have torn open the breast of Antonio. These are things which no theatrical experience of the play will ever let you forget. As William Empson says, we must view the Bassanio–Portia relationship with 'a generous scepticism which can believe at once that people are and are not guilty.'[28] So Shakespeare will not let us rest even here. The subversive counter-thesis is itself too easy. We may now begin to see that he is perhaps the least sentimental dramatist who ever lived. We begin to understand what is meant by holding the mirror up to nature.

Shakespeare's other play about Venice, *Othello*, has been the occasion of a classic dispute in Transparent criticism. There is disagreement about the hero: is he, in fact, heroic? Othello's speech at the end of the play causes most of the trouble:

> Soft you; a word or two before you go.
> I have done the state some service, and they know't –
> No more of that. I pray you, in your letters,
> When you shall these unlucky deeds relate,
> Speak of me as I am; nothing extenuate,
> Nor set down aught in malice. Then must you speak
> Of one that loved not wisely, but too well;
> Of one not easily jealous, but, being wrought,
> Perplexed in the extreme; of one whose hand,
> Like the base Indian, threw a pearl away
> Richer than all his tribe; of one whose subdu'd eyes,
> Albeit unused to the melting mood,
> Drops tears as fast as the Arabian trees
> Their med'cinable gum. Set you down this;
> And say besides that in Aleppo once,
> Where a malignant and a turban'd Turk
> Beat a Venetian and traduc'd the state,
> I took by th'throat the circumcised dog,
> And smote him – thus.
>   (He stabs himself)

(V. ii. 341–59)

T.S. Eliot in 'Shakespeare and the Stoicism of Seneca'[29] observed that in this speech Othello seems to be 'cheering himself up': 'He is endeavouring to escape reality, he has ceased to think about Desdemona, and is thinking about himself' (p. 130). F.R. Leavis in his 'Diabolic intellect and the noble hero'[30] picked up a word applied by Eliot to the Stoic hero, 'self-dramatization', and said that this speech by Othello, though it begins in quiet authority, ends precisely in self-dramatization (pp. 151–2): no tragic hero this, but one who has learned nothing from his misfortune and would rather rant than think. On the other side stands Dame Helen Gardner. In her article, 'The noble Moor',[31] she reaffirmed the essential nobility of Othello, his generosity, the greatness of his heart, his absoluteness and disinterestedness; and many felt that the cynics had been silenced.

My general argument, so far, has been that Shakespeare's mimesis is unusually comprehensive. He moves forward on a total front. He imitates individuals but he also imitates contexts. My response to this disagreement of Transparent critics is to stand further back for a while. There are more things in this play than the figure of Othello, and it may be that in understanding some of them we shall understand him. to begin with we may be utterly formalist and ask what kind of play *Othello* is.

Shakespeare's plays have come down to us in the triple division into comedies, histories and tragedies laid down by the editors of the First Folio. There is in this division a large measure of editorial accident, for the three categories are not co-ordinate. *Richard II* is, clearly, a history, but, equally clearly, it is also a tragedy. Indeed it is formally a better tragedy than *Othello* in that it deals with the fall of a prince. *Othello*, on the other hand, is about an almost bourgeois Italian household, a misunderstanding and a murder at a level which involves no repercussions among nations. Its social milieu is that normally inhabited by comedy. This social difference is enough to stamp *Richard II* as central tragedy and *Othello* as peripheral tragedy.

Othello, to be sure, is not the only Shakespearean tragedy to deal with upper-middle-class goings-on. *Romeo and Juliet* refers to a similar section of society, but then it has long been commonplace to observe that *Romeo and Juliet* opens like a comedy. The long dynastic rivalry of Montagues and Capulets brings us nearer to the proper political stature of central tragedy than anything that can happen behind Othello's closed front door.

But there is the phrase 'domestic tragedy'. Is this appropriate to *Othello*? The phrase 'domestic tragedy' is commonly used to connote a distinct genre: all those Elizabethan and Jacobean plays which dealt with real-life murders and scandals, such as Jonson's and Dekker's *The Lamentable Tragedy of the Page of Plymouth*, Yarrington's *Two Lamentable Tragedies, A Yorkshire Tragedy* (about a man who murdered his two children) and *Arden of Faversham* (about the murder in 1551 of Thomas Arden by his wife), Wilkins's *The Miseries of Enforced Marriage*, Heywood's *A Woman Killed with Kindness*. It is fairly obvious that these plays catered for appetites which are served today by the more sensational Sunday newspapers. The title pages of these domestic tragedies repeatedly strike a note of prurient censoriousness which is immediately recognizable. *Othello* is not in any straightforward manner a member of this class, although we may note in passing that both *The Miseries of Enforced Marriage* and *A Woman Killed with Kindness* deal, like *Othello*, with the then uncommon theme of marriage. Moreover, Michel Grivelet has pointed to the popularity among writers of domestic tragedy of the *novellas* of Bandello, Boccaccio and Cinthio.[32] The principal source of *Othello* is a novella by Cinthio. Again, the stories of domestic tragedies tend to crop up later in ballads. This is true of *Arden of Faversham* and it is also true, as it happens, of *Othello*.

The authors of these plays seem not be have used the term 'domestic tragedy' themselves. The word 'domestic' was used of 'what goes on in a house' (in accordance with its etymological derivation from *domus*, 'house') and also of national as opposed to foreign affairs. Thomas Heywood does occasionally play on this ambiguity,[33] but in the only place where he uses 'domestic' to designate genre ('domestic histories'[34]) he is referring to chronicles of England. The earliest example in the *Oxford English Dictionary* of *domestic* as opposed to *regal* (where the *Dictionary* offers the slightly misleading gloss 'devoted to home life') is from Davenant's *Playhouse to be Let*:[35]

> Kings who move
> Within a lowly sphere of private love,
> Are too domestic for a throne.

Nevertheless, it is plain that the idea of a contrast between the tragedy of courts and the tragedy of private, household events was current in Shakespeare's time. The unknown author of *A Warning for Fair Women* (1599) refers to his play as 'a true and *home-born* tragedy'. Yves Bescou has remarked that in *A Woman Killed with Kindness* the house is itself a principal character.[36] But in the common run of Elizabethan domestic tragedy there is admittedly little sense of tension between the idea of tragedy and the idea of domesticity.

Here Shakespeare is unlike the rest. For if we say that *Othello* is his domestic tragedy we must note that in this case the term connotes a paradox, domestic and yet a tragedy, tragic and yet domestic. If this is acknowledged the phrase has a certain utility as a description of the play. Thomas Rymer's celebrated attack on *Othello*, published in 1693, turns primarily on the fact that the play is bathetically domestic. Speaking of its moral, he says,

> First, This may be a caution to all Maidens of Quality how, without their Parents consent, they run away with Blackamoors. . . . Secondly, This may be a warning to all good Wives, that they look well to their Linnen.[37]

Othello's tragedy indeed is strangely – and formally – introverted; it consists in the fact that he left the arena proper to tragedy, the battlefield, and entered a subtragic world for which he was not fitted. *Othello* is the story of a hero who went into a house.

Long ago A.C. Bradley observed that, if the heroes of *Hamlet* and *Othello* change places, each play ends very quickly.[38] Hamlet would see through Iago in the first five minutes and be parodying him in the next. Othello, receiving clear instructions like 'Kill that usurper' from a ghost, would simply have gone to work. Thus, as the classic problem of *Hamlet* is the hero's delay, so the classic problem of *Othello* is the hero's gullibility. The stronger our sense of Othello's incongruity in the domestic world, the less puzzling this becomes. Certainly, *Othello* is about a man who, having come from a strange and remote place, found his feet in the world of Venetian professional soldiership – and then exchanged that spacious world for a little, dim world of unimaginable horror. 'War is no strife/To the dark house and the detested wife' comes not from Othello but from a comedy,[39] but it will serve here. Its note of peculiarly masculine pain and hatred can still score the nerves. It is therefore not surprising that Shakespeare avails himself of the metaphor of the caged hawk. Desdemona says, 'I'll watch him tame', at III. iii. 23. The real process of taming a hawk by keeping it awake and so breaking its spirit is described at length in T.H. White's *The Goshawk* (1953). Othello turns the image round when he says of Desdemona,

> If I do prove her haggard,
> Though that her jesses were my dear heart-strings,
> I'd whistle her off and let her down the wind
> To prey at fortune.

> (III. iii. 264–7)

He speaks formally of Desdemona, but it is hard not to feel that in the last words it is his own dream of liberty which speaks.

Othello is also about insiders and outsiders. The exotic Moor finds when he leaves the public, martial sphere that he is not accepted, is not understood and cannot understand. The Venetian colour bar is sexual, not professional. Iago plays on this with his 'old black ram. . .tupping your white ewe' (I. i. 89–90) and the same note is struck by Roderigo with his 'gross clasps of a lascivious Moor' (I. i. 127). Othello's gullibility is not really so very strange. Coal-black among the glittering Venetians, he is visibly the outsider, and in his bewilderment he naturally looks for the man who is visibly the insider, the man who knows the ropes, the sort of man who is always around in the bar, the 'good chap' or (as they said then) the 'honest' man. And he finds him.

There are two schools of thought on the sort of actor who should play Iago. School A chooses a dark, waspish fellow. School B chooses a bluff, straw-haired, pink-faced sort of man, solid-looking with no nonsense about him. In production School B triumphs, for the role, cast in this way, becomes both credible and terrifying. Although Iago is everywhere spoken of as a 'good chap', he has no friends, no loves, no positive desires. He, and not Othello, proves to be the true outsider of the play, for he is foreign to humanity itself. Othello comes from a remote clime, but Iago, in his simpler darkness, comes from the far side of chaos – hence the pathos of Shakespeare's best departure from his source. In Cinthio's *novella* the Ensign (that is, the Iago-figure) with a cunning affectation of reluctance, suggests that Desdemona is false and then seeing his chance, adds, 'Your blackness already displeases her.'[40] In Shakespeare's play we have instead a note of bar-room masculine intimacy, in assumed complicity of sentiment. Iago says, in effect 'Well, she went with black man, so what is one to think?' (III. iii. 232–7). Othello's need to be accepted and guided makes him an easy victim of this style. The hero is set for his sexual humiliation.

From the beginning of the play Othello is associated with outdoor weather, with openness: 'The Moor is of a free and open nature' (I. iii. 393); 'But that I loved the gentle Desdemona,/I would not my unhoused free condition/Put into circumscription and confine/For the sea's worth' (I. ii. 25–8). Note the important word 'unhoused' and the powerful emphasis on the last four monosyllables. In II. i, set on the quayside in Cyprus, the language bursts into a profusion of images of wind and weather, before it brings Othello down from the high seas into the encircling arms of his wife. The effect is best represented by sporadic quotation: 'What from the cape can you discern at sea?/Nothing at all, it is a high-wrought flood./I cannot twixt the heaven and the

main/Descry a sail./Methinks the wind hath spoke aloud at land;/A
fuller blast ne'er shook our battlements./. . . The chidden billow seems
to pelt the clouds;/The wind-shaked surge, with high and monstrous
mane,/Seems to cast water on the burning Bear,/And quench the
guards of th'ever fixed Pole. . . . The town is empty; on the brow
o'th'sea/Stand ranks of people, and they cry "A sail!". . . . Great Jove
Othello guard,/And swell his sail with thine own powerful
breath,/That he may bless this bay with his tall ship,/Make love's
quick pants in Desdemona's arms. . . . O my soul's joy!/If after every
tempest came such calms' (II. i. 1–6, 12–5, 53–4, 77–80, 182–3). The
diminuendo is marvellously managed: the bay becomes the arms of
Desdemona, the tall ship Othello himself. When, in III. iii, Othello
thinks his married happiness is irretrievably lost, he makes a formal
speech of valediction. This speech turns insensibly from a farewell to
married contentment into the real farewell, the real loss, which is the
loss of that military action and freedom in which alone Othello's true
personality could move:

> I had been happy if the general camp,
> Pioneers and all, had tasted her sweet body,
> So I had nothing known. O, now for ever
> Farewell the tranquil mind! farewell content!
> Farewell the plumed troops, and the big wars
> That makes ambition virtue! O, farewell!
> Farewell the neighing steed and the shrill trump,
> The spirit-stirring drum, th'ear-piercing fife,
> The royal banner, and all quality,
> Pride, pomp and circumstance, of glorious war!
> And O ye mortal engines whose rude throats
> Th'immortal Jove's dread clamours counterfeit,
> Farewell! Othello's occupation's gone.
>
> (III. iii. 349–61)

The word 'big' in line 353 is exactly right. He is surrounded by things
which are too small to fight with, things like handkerchiefs. When,
later in the same scene, he envisages a dark release from the dreadful
circumscription of the house, once more a great flood surges in the
language of the play:

> Like to the Pontic sea,
> Whose icy current and compulsive force
> Ne'er feels retiring ebb, but keeps due on
> To the Propontic and the Hellespont;
> Even so my bloody thoughts, ...
>
> (III. iii. 457–61)

Othello's gradual disintegration is mirrored in his style of speech, at first swiftly authoritative, then broken and at last full of a barbaric extremism. The thing is done slowly through the play, but there are certain speeches in which the entire triple development is gone through in little. When near the beginning of the play the truculent gang comes crowding in with weapons and torches, Othello easily controls them:

> Keep up your bright swords, for the dew will rust them.
>
> (I. ii. 59)

When he is brought before the Duke and the Senators in I. iii he is at first similar. Asked to account for his conduct he gives the reverend 'signiors' a very gentlemanly account (smooth, unflustered, almost majestic) of the way he won Brabantio's daughter (I. iii. 128-70). There is no sign of any break in this style until we reach line 260. Here Othello's language suddenly becomes problematic, so much so that most editors assume that the text is corrupt. The speech appears in Alexander's edition of the *Works* in the following form (Desdemona has just asked to be allowed to go with him to the wars):

> *Othello*   Let her have your voice.
> Vouch with me, heaven, I therefore beg it not
> To please the palate of my appetite;
> Nor to comply with heat – the young affects
> In me defunct – and proper satisfaction;
> But to be free and bounteous to her mind
> And heaven defend your good souls that you think
> I will your serious and great business scant
> For she is with me.
>
> (I. iii. 260-8)

The crux occurs in the baffling third and fourth lines, which remain puzzling even after they have been amended and repunctuated, as here, by a modern editor. In the case of this play, it is not easy to determine whether the first Quarto of 1622 or the Folio of 1623 has the higher authority. In the crux before us, however, this thorny problem fortunately does not arise, for the two are virtually identical. The first Quarto gives: 'Nor to comply with heat, the young affects in my defunct, and proper satisfaction'. The difficulties are evident. Is 'affects' a noun, in apposition to 'heat', or a verb (the relative pronoun 'which' having been elided) which would turn 'young' into a noun, the object of 'affects'? Should we change 'my' to 'me' (as Alexander did) so that we can read 'the young affects in me defunct' as an absolute construction, equivalent to 'the youthful passions being dead in me'? Does 'proper' mean 'legitimate' or 'my own'? Quite obviously, the sentence is a mess. But a Transparent reading may suggest that nevertheless we can accept it as it stands; that is, if we look *through* the fractured form to the possible person we may understand the forms as we never could if we looked at form alone.

A certain meaning comes through, and indeed it is strange. Othello seems to be saying, 'Do not think that I am asking for this out of lust, for I am past all that, rather I am interested in Desdemona's mind.' This does not have to be a full profession of impotence (though the powerful word *defunct* might be held to imply even that), but only of diminished desires, but this in a newly married hero is sufficiently arresting. Attempts[41] to make *defunct* bear some such meaning as 'discharged' or 'freed' by analogy with the Latin *defunctus periculis* ('freed from perils') will not do. This sense is not found elsewhere in English and, even in Latin, only emerges when there is an accompanying ablative (*periculis*). If Othello had said, 'defunct *from x*', this gloss might have been defensible, but he did not. No audience hearing these words would understand 'discharged'. Othello, beginning to explain that his request does not arise from lust, for the first time loses control of his sentence and so, we may infer, of his thoughts. Why?

Desdemona has just intervened in the men's world of senatorial debate with a sexual candour almost as startling as Othello's sexual retreat:

> My heart's subdu'd
> Even to the very quality of my lord:
> I saw Othello's visage in his mind;
> And to his honours and his valiant parts
> Did I my soul and fortunes consecrate.
> So that, dear lords, if I be left behind,
> A moth of peace, and he go to the war,
> The rites for why I love him are bereft me,
> And I a heavy interim shall support
> By his dear absence. Let me go with him.

(I. iii. 250–9)

There is no serious doubt that 'rites' in line 257 is a reference to the consummation of the marriage. This is what throws Othello off balance. She began by speaking of his mind – that part was excellent, carried no danger in terms of the stereotype of the lascivious Moor – but then she asked to be allowed to consummate the marriage. Othello's status in Venetian society is strong as long as it is kept separate from questions of sexuality. His speech is a stumbling, eager attempt to quash the implication of lasciviousness and to recover balance by catching at Desdemona's initial emphasis on mental affinity. The two speeches, Desdemona's and Othello's, are chiastically arranged: ABBA, mind, desire, desire, mind, but Othello's answering version is strangled and broken. To emend is to make it smooth. But the very roughness can be seen as correct, if one intuits a person in the part.

The editorial questions may still need answers (I think 'affects' is probably a noun and that 'proper' means here 'my own') but an actor can deliver the speech as given in the first Quarto, if he is allowed to stammer or hesitate. It remains true that the speech, thus unamended, would count as the most extreme piece of naturalistic confusion in the canon (though Leontes' speech, 'Affection! thy intention stabs the centre' in *The Winter's Tale*, I. ii. 138–46, comes very close). The collapse of Othello's language is microcosmic of the collapse of his personality in the entire tragedy.

Othello was perplexed in the extreme before Iago went to work on him. Marriage itself disoriented him. Naturally, his valediction of marital happiness became a valediction of the military life. It was there that he last knew himself. We are now in a position to return to his final speech before he stabs himself (V. ii. 341–59). Othello quietly stops the captors who would lead him away; he speaks briefly of his service to the state and then asks that, when the story of his actions and his fate is told, it should be fairly told; if it is fair, it will tell not of a pathologically jealous man but rather of a confused man, one who threw away a treasure and weeps for it; moreover the story should also include the slaying of the Turk long ago in Aleppo. As he tells of the slaying of the Turk, he kills himself on the clinching word 'thus'.

In this speech the pathos of the outsider reaches a climax. It is true that Othello has not attained full understanding, but there is a kind of dignity, for that very reason, in 'perplexed in the extreme' (V. ii. 349). In the course of the speech his mind flinches away from the mangled, unintelligible scene around him, back to his heroic past, when he had an honoured part to play. It is no accident that Othello's memory, in its search for a feat proper to be remembered, should light on the slaying of the turbanned Turk. To assert his Venetian status to the full he needs as enemy a spectacularly foreign figure. Yet, as we watch him, we *see*, not a Venetian but – precisely – a spectacularly foreign figure. That this is art of the highest order rather than accident is brought home by the conclusion of the speech. For at the moment when Othello comes, in his remote narrative, to the slaying of the foreigner, before our eyes he stabs himself, in a horrific parallelism. It is as if as his last act of devoted service, his last propitiatory offering to the state, he kills the outsider, Othello.

Let us now turn to the questions we posed at the outset. Is the rhetoric of his speech self-dramatizing, histrionic, or is it noble? I answer, it is noble, but its nobility is tragically deracinated. I said before that Othello's tragedy lay in the fact that he left the arena proper to tragedy. The logical 'shimmer' of this suggestion affects our perceptions of his final speech. Nobility thus isolated and astray is infected with absurdity, but the very absurdity is tragic. Othello's rhetoric is the rhetoric of a shame-culture (as we defined that term in our discussion of the Roman plays). Othello's shame-culture is more primitive, more thoroughly pre-Stoic than Coriolanus's, and his difference from the society around him is also greater.

Othello is actually *simpler* than those around him. A shame-culture identifies glory and virtue. The manner in which this survived in Shakespeare's time (and, to some extent in ours) was in the notions of honour and reputation. Thus Cassio harps desperately on his 'reputation' as 'the immortal part' of himself (II. iii. 253–7). But it is in Othello that we find the notion of reputation, not as something extrinsic but as the centre of his moral identity, operating with enough force (as Iago knows) to kill him. At I. iii. 274 Othello says, in the first Quarto, 'Let. . .all indign and base adversities/Make head against my reputation.' There he is insisting still on a confidence which is seriously threatened. But then, in a marvellous scene, Iago gets to work within Othello's mind, thinking his thoughts aloud for him and he knows well on which nerve he should press:

> But he that filches from me my good name
> Robs me of that which not enriches him
> And makes me poor indeed.
>
> (III. iii. 163–5)

In the world of professional military action Othello was a human being. When he passed through the door of the house he became a kind of nothing. The word 'occupation' is in our day and was in Shakespeare's a relatively colourless word (it had a few extra meanings then, but that is by the way). Shakespeare is therefore doing something very deliberate when he places it at the climax of Othello's speech of valediction at III. iii. 349–61: 'Othello's occupation's gone.' He is making sure that we notice that the idea of profession or métier has an ethical status in Othello's mind which it does not naturally have in ours.

Venice in *Othello* is the same city we saw in *The Merchant of Venice*. Othello is thus no feudal baron or chieftain, but a professional mercenary, paid by the state. Thus a certain continuity of economic reference links the two plays. But in *Othello* Shakespeare plays down the references to money. Instead he develops at greater length something which is also present in *The Merchant of Venice*. At III. iii. 31 Antonio said, 'the trade and profit of the city/Consisteth of all nations'. Venice is the landless city where different kinds and races meet in a strangely abstract effort of aggrandizement. The sea is the medium of their wars as money is the medium of their wealth. This, in *The Merchant of Venice*, yielded the endlessly fruitful contrast between a Jewish and a Christian consciousness. In *Othello* it permits the study of a primitive consciousness yoked to the service of a complex, civic society. Venice is for Shakespeare an anthropological laboratory. Itself nowhere, suspended between sea and sky, it receives and utilizes all kinds of people.

Othello in his last speech is reverting to the earlier phase. Utterly beaten by his domestic environment, he goes back into his heroic past and delivers his formal vaunt (characteristic of the shame-culture hero from the boasts of the Homeric warrior to the *beot-word* of the Anglo-Saxons, and thence to the 'I killed me a b'ar when I was three' of the American folk hero) though, at the beginning of his speech at least, Othello is restrained by his civilized environment. The speech, properly delivered, should not sound more and more shrilly histrionic as it goes on. On the contrary, it should gather strength and confidence. The actor must draw himself up to his full physical height. Of course there is immense pathos. For – though we dispute their judgement – we are now in a position to account for the reaction of Eliot and Leavis. Othello's behaviour, if judged by the *mores* of the city, *would* be merely theatrical. It may really have a therapeutic function, if not of 'cheering him up', of galvanizing muscles trained to kill. But ultimately all talk of self-dramatization is a product of the discrepancy between Othello's own nature and the place in which he finds himself. Shame-culture is more concerned than later cultures with outward behaviour; indeed, it locates identity in outward features. Thus for a shame-culture what in us would be artificial posturing may be a means of recovering one's true self. For all the pathos of incomprehension Othello is at last more authentically himself than at any time since the beginning of the play. This recovery of self, however achieved, corresponds to the 'moment of insight' customary in tragedies and successfully prevents *Othello* from turning into a 'sick' paraphrase or serious parody of tragic form. The core of Othello's nobility is real. He has reached a clearing in the forest, a small but sufficient open space in the labyrinth. He has come to a place where, once more, he has a job to do – a job like the jobs he did before – and he knows how to do it well. It is to kill himself. His words recall his feats against the foreign dog and his conclusion is another feat, both like and horribly unlike those.

Thus *Othello* joins the basically economic insight into cultural variation which we find in *The Merchant of Venice* to the contrast of heroic and civic cultures which is so finely treated in the Roman plays. Although Othello postdates Coriolanus and is more primitive than he, there is nevertheless implicit in what I have been saying a shadowy version of the 'evolving human nature' we saw in the Roman plays. The civic state naturally succeeds the heroic. Othello does not merely belong to another culture but to an earlier one. In the first of the three great dramatists of ancient Greece, Aeschylus, there is virtually no distinction between motive and public situation (this is a continuation of a shame-culture refusal to separate inner and outer). The dilemma of Orestes is essentially public: one god says 'Do this,' another god says, 'Do that.' There is no question of attributing hesitation or procrastination to Orestes as a feature of his character (indeed, he can hardly be said to have character). This holds to some extent for Othello, or for Othello's conception of Othello. Remember here Bradley's remark, cited earlier,[42] about Hamlet and Othello changing places. One thing Othello does not suffer from is hesitation or infirmity of purpose. Between the thing which is to be done and the doing of it no mental shadow falls.

At a later stage of cultural evolution people become aware that their actions are not only provoked by the outside world but are also inwardly motivated. The notion of self, as we saw, begins to contract. The shame-culture hero *is* his strength, his gleaming arms, even, at times, his cloud of assisting goddesses. Later we begin to assume that the self is separate from such external factors; we say 'Oh, yes, she did well in the four-hour examination, but that's just because she happens to have a strong constitution – it's not *merit.*' I suppose this is the present phase for most of us. Can one *imagine* a further phase? By continuing the trend, we would get an even more narrowly contracted ego, perhaps one which might even view its own motives as separate from itself. Certainly a person like that would seem civilized – rather horribly so – and would be a proper product of a world grown very old..

One cannot ascribe to *Othello* as developed a conspectus of evolving human nature as we find in *Julius Caesar* and *Coriolanus* but it may be, nevertheless, that in *Othello*, some four or five years later than *Julius Caesar*, Shakespeare began to push harder at the idea I have just let fall. If Othello is the underevolved man, who is overevolved? The answer is Iago. For if the workings of Othello's mind recall the oldest literature we have, Iago's evoke a literature as yet unwritten, the literature of existentialism, according to which any assumption of motive by the ego is an act of unconditional, artificial choice. Mark Antony is strange but Iago is far stranger. Mark Antony exploits the emotion he really feels; Iago chooses which emotions he will experience. He is not just motivated, like other people. Instead he *decides* to be motivated. He concedes that he has no idea whether Othello has had sexual relations with his wife. He simply opts, in a vacuum, for that as a possible motive.

I think I know how this astonishing idea occurred to Shakespeare. In the seventh story of the third decade of the *Hecatommithi* of Giraldi Cinthio, the following passage occurs (I quote from the careful translation by Raymond Shaw, given in an appendix to M.R. Ridley's New Arden edition of *Othello*[43]):

> The wicked ensign, caring nothing for the loyalty due to his wife or the friendship, loyalty and duty he owed the Moor, fell passionately in love with Disdemona and turned all his thoughts to seeing whether he might enjoy her. . . . Everything that the ensign did to kindle in her a love for him was useless. So he imagined that the reason was that Disdemona had become enamoured of the captain and so decided to put him out of the way. Furthermore he changed the love that he bore the lady into the bitterest hatred.

The important phrase is 'So he imagined' and the crucial word is 'so'. The Italian, which Shakespeare may have read, reproduces this feature. I assume that in fact it is merely verbal slackness on Cinthio's part. But, taken literally, it implies that the ensign *deliberately* imagined that something was the case, and this impression is reinforced by the active voice of 'changed' a few lines below where we might have expected 'his love changed'. Most readers would hardly notice these two tiny anomalies. But Shakespeare, I suspect, did notice them, and paused in his reading. For here is the germ of the existentialist Iago.

'Henry IV': Prince Hal and Falstaff

I have said that Shakespeare likes to take a stereotype and then work against it. The stereotype of Prince Hal in relation to his father, Henry IV, is that of the uncontrolled young man, sowing his wild oats, in rebellion against an authoritarian father. Shakespeare has no sooner set this up for us than he begins to undermine it.

First, he contrives a dramatic echo-chamber, by giving Hal a secondary father. His name is Falstaff. W.H. Auden observes that, if you look at Hal's associates, they are really rather odd.[44] What sort of people would one expect to find in company with a prince out on the tiles? Every generation has its own word for the answer to this question: Corinthians, rakes, bucks, blades, *jeunesse dorée*, mashers, Bright Young Things, the Beautiful People. These are not what we find about Hal. Admittedly there is one who is certainly smooth and may be young, Poins, but thereafter the stage is engrossed by an extraordinary collection of aged and seedy persons: an obese alcoholic of advanced years, various strutting scarecrows from that strange Elizabethan underworld of discharged officers and decayed soldiers, and some superannuated prostitutes. Why?

The best answer (the reader may be surprised to find me granting this) is not one resting on psychological probability. It is thematic. It is Falstaff that Shakespeare needs and all the rest is a sort of moving cloud of circumambient Falstaffiana. Shakespeare needs him first of all, as I have suggested, as a parody-father. We saw how in *Othello* Shakespeare made use of an immediate, visual contrast to enforce the theme of the outsider – the black Othello among the shining Venetians. So here (though it is somewhat less obvious) he needs a visual tableau: a grey-haired, physically disgraced old man and a superb youngster. They should *look*, for a moment, like father and son. The point is underlined in the famous scene in which Falstaff plays the part of King Henry admonishing his errant son (*1 Henry IV*, II. iv. 418–64). Here we are formally presented with the required tableau.

It does not reinforce but definitely and immediately reverses the stereotype. Instead of the stern father and the 'dropout' son, we have the exact opposite. The jaded slang of the 1960s may bring out the paradox. Falstaff is an aged hippy (fundamentally uncontrolled, given over to the pleasure principle, certainly a dropout from practical society, with his own drug – alcohol – and his own lyrical mode of speech, contemptuous of legal and other convention); meanwhile Hal, we gradually learn, is a rigidly controlled personality, dedicated to effective government and the subordination of personal pleasure to legal and political ends.

At the end of I. ii, in Part 1, Prince Hal is left alone on the stage, and pronounces his famous, explanatory soliloquy.

> I know you all, and will a while uphold
> The unyok'd humour of your idleness;
> Yet herein will I imitate the sun,
> Who doth permit the base contagious clouds
> To smother up his beauty from the world,
> That, when he please again to be himself,
> Being wanted, he may be more wond'red at
> By breaking through the foul and ugly mists
> Of vapours that did seem to strangle him.

If all the year were playing holidays,
To sport would be as tedious as to work;
But when they seldom come, they wish'd for come,
And nothing pleaseth but rare accidents.
So, when this loose behaviour I throw off
And pay the debt I never promised,
By how much better than my word I am,
By so much shall I falsify men's hopes;
And, like bright metal on a sullen ground,
My reformation, glitt'ring o'er my fault,
Shall show more goodly and attract more eyes
Than that which hath no foil to set it off.
I'll so offend to make offence a skill,
Redeeming time when men think least I will.   (I. ii. 188–210)

Is the Prince making cold-blooded political use of the people who suppose him to be their friend? This is the kind of speech which Levin Schücking held up to show the primitive dramatic technique of Shakespeare;[45] it is not naturalistic, for in naturalistic drama we are encouraged to notice not only the content of the speech but also its manner, so that when, say, Leontes tells us in _The Winter's Tale_ that he knows his wife is unchaste we infer from his distracted manner that his judgement is awry. But with speeches of 'direct self-explanation', such as Hal's, Schücking suggests that any such inference is out of place. They are a spoken equivalent of the programme note. The actor, though he continues to say 'I' rather than 'he', in effect doffs his role and comes forward to explain things to the audience. Thus the object of the prince's speech is reassurance: 'Do not be anxious about this young man; he is going to be a great king in due course.'

With regard to the present speech this view seems to me substantially correct. It is not of course the direct address to the audience as mankind which we find in medieval drama; nor is it the 'logical joke' type of audience reference common in the Renaissance theatre. Shakespeare has the Prince stand watching the retreating backs of those he has just been joking with and, once they are securely out of earshot, address them in terms which (within the drama) are intended rather to articulate his own thoughts than have any effect on them. Formally (if that is the kind of criticism we are to engage in) the speech is not a direct address to the audience but an apostrophic soliloquy (that is, a soliloquy which is formally, but only formally, addressed to another person). But, at the same time, such soliloquies are formally distinct from the dramatic texture of the rest, and the extra-mimetic function of reassurance is quite inescapable.

Even if the actor may begin in a fairly naturalistic manner – musingly – the speech rapidly gathers formal momentum, and the element of *virtual* address to the audience grows stronger.

But it by no means follows from any of this that the speech has ceased to be mimetic. It is a rule of explanatory soliloquy that we should attend strictly to content. Very well, let us do that.

Implicit in the formal account has been a suggestion that any feeling of shock we may have felt at the Prince's cold manipulation of people is removed if we refuse to infer character and restrict ourselves to information. But this speech does not say, 'Though I am now keeping vile company, all will be well, since a sudden change will come over me, and the surprise which this will create will be wholly salutary for the realm and the crown.' What it makes utterly clear is that Hal himself proposes to bring about this transformation deliberately. The disquieting element of cool manipulation is not something we infer from a naturalistic interpretation of Hal's manner, it is something we are told. If the speech is self-explanation and provides the audience with information, this is part of the information it provides. Everything, to be sure, depends on the meaning of the word 'that' in the following lines:

> Yet herein will I imitate the sun,
> Who doth permit the base contagious clouds
> To smother up his beauty from the world
> That, when he please again to be himself,
> Being wanted, he may be more wond'red at
> By breaking through the foul and ugly mists . . . .

selfish & manipulating

(I. ii. 190–5)

The word 'that', in this context, undoubtedly means 'in order that'.

This insistence on an uncomfortably intrusive purposive particle where we might have expected a more neutral grammar of mere consequence is precisely what led, in the final speculation of our last section, to the 'existentialist' Iago. The distance between Prince Hal and Iago is great but not, perhaps, unbridgeable. W.H. Auden (the presiding genius of this part of the book) noted[46] a curious similarity between this speech by the Prince and one of Iago's soliloquies, similarly placed, early in the play:

> For when my outward action doth demonstrate
> The native act and figure of my heart
> In compliment extern, 'tis not long after
> But I will wear my heart upon my sleeve
> For daws to peck at: I am not what I am.

(*Othello*, I. i. 62–6)

Both passages are Machiavellian in style; that is, they evoke an ethos of devious cunning. This also works against the critic who believes that a formalist reading can dispel all distaste. It is an inference from the manner, but not a naturalistic inference; it is a formal one.

Let us confess that this is a strange speech, marked by a very considerable tension. Shakespeare adopts a 'naive' technique, but he does so with a complex sense of context and for a particular effect. The actor who allows the text to speak in him will find that he gradually freezes as the speech proceeds. The director who understands this process may ensure that a strong light falls on the actor's almost unmoving face, on the line, 'Herein will I imitate the sun.' The sun is the emblem of royalty. The office of the king may thus momentarily shine through the actor figurally, and become a felt presence on the stage.

But, when every concession has been made, the speech is not naturalistic; forms are at work which are not the transparent forms of realism; the speech purveys information rather than betraying an attitude: the result is that we find ourselves presented with an essentially mimetic statement about the *character* of Prince Hal. The presumption of twentieth-century criticism – that choric exegesis precludes characterization – is shattered when the choric information turns out itself to be, baldly and explicitly, information about character. It is never good practice with Shakespeare to ignore or repress worrying, initially unwanted complexities. Far better to assimilate them, to imagine and to think. When one is watching or reading Shakespeare, this thinking can be done almost subliminally, with a wise passiveness. When criticizing or interpreting Shakespeare, one must think explicitly.

The speech certainly contained great comfort for the Tudor audience, but it is a comfort shot through with unease. There is nothing unhistorical in the supposition that an Elizabethan could have been repelled by manipulation of people's affections. The Machiavellian 'twinge' in the style is not there by chance. But (and here a Tudor would have been more perceptive than a modern audience) it is all directed to the good end of stable government. And so Prince Hal is a White Machiavel. This powerful moment of confession which is also a self-dedication and a kind of promise precedes and sets the dominant tone for what follows. It is not wiped out by Warwick's observing in Part 2 at IV. iv. 68–72 (long after our conception has formed) that the Prince kept low company to educate himself in the moral variety of his people.

Falstaff, who is all intelligence, knows everything about the Prince except this, his chilling, profoundly moral, private plan. Nevertheless, Shakespeare illogically permits two episodes in which Falstaff learns the truth. One of them is the celebrated rejection of Falstaff by the new-made

King Henry V, but that poses no problem of consistency in Falstaff because it comes at the end. The more problematic one occurs in the tab leau scene with which we began, where Falstaff plays the part of the Prince's father (*1 Henry IV*, II. iv). When Falstaff has had his turn, the game is reversed, Hal plays his father and Falstaff plays the Prince. The fun is uproarious but through it we begin to sense a profound collision and awakening. Falstaff finds that he is pleading for the Prince's love and, at the second when he discovers he can never have it, is interrupted by a loud banging on the door; breathless figures with urgent news come blundering *across* the duel between Hal and Falstaff – now at last explicit. So the moment is seen, once, in total clarity, and then muffled in extraneous noise.

Prince	. . . wherein worthy, but in nothing?
Fal.	I would your Grace would take me with you; whom means your Grace?
Prince	That villainous, abominable misleader of youth, Falstaff, that old, white-bearded Satan.
Fal.	My lord, the man I know.
Prince	I know thou dost.
Fal.	But to say I know more harm in him than in myself were to say more than I know. That he is old – the more the pity – his white hairs do witness it; but that he is, saving your reverence – a whoremaster, that I utterly deny. If sack and sugar be a fault, God help the wicked! If to be old and merry be a sin, then many an old host that I know is damn'd; if to be fat be to be hated, then Pharaoh's lean kine are to be loved. No, my good lord: banish Peto, banish Bardolph, banish Poins; but, for sweet Jack Falstaff, kind Jack Falstaff, true Jack Falstaff, valiant Jack Falstaff – and therefore more valiant, being, as he is, old Jack Falstaff – banish not him thy Harry's company, banish not him thy Harry's company. Banish plump Jack, and banish all the world.
Prince	I do, I will. [*A knocking heard.*

[*Re-enter* BARDOLPH, *running*]

Bardolph	O, my lord, my lord! the sheriff with a most monstrous watch is at the door.
Fal.	Out, ye rogue! Play out the play: I have much to say in the behalf of that Falstaff.

[*Re-enter the Hostess*]

Hostess	O Jesu, my lord, my lord!
Prince	Heigh, heigh! the devil rides upon a fiddlestick; what's the matter?

Hostess	The sheriff and all the watch are at the door; they are come to search the house. Shall I let them in?
Fal.	Dost thou hear, Hal? Never call a true piece of gold a counterfeit. Thou art essentially mad, without seeming so.

(*1 Henry IV*, II. iv. 443–76)

Notice in this exchange how at one point a laugh is killed, or at least checked. 'Valiant Jack Falstaff' raises the laugh but 'old Jack Falstaff' silences it with truth. When the Prince answers, from a masklike face, 'I do, I will', the secret is out.

When I quoted Falstaff's words flung desperately across the violent interruption, I made use of an emendation. The First and Second Folios and the string of Quarto editions (the fifth of which was probably the copy-text for the First Folio) all give 'made' where I have given 'mad' at II. iv. 476. The word 'mad' is an emendation, but it is pretty well the smallest emendation possible. This becomes clear if we imagine the passage written in an Elizabethan hand. Shakespeare almost certainly wrote a secretary hand, in which case the words might have looked something like this:

In this hand *d* is written ᔑ and *e* is written backwards as ᔑ . The *d* is a little taller, may have a closed loop at the bottom and a large loop at the top, but it is undoubtedly very like an *e* and in actual specimens of secretary hand the two letters are sometimes quite indistinguishable: you can tell which is which only by context.

Let us suppose that Shakespeare wanted to write the word 'mad', spelling it, as he may well have done, with two *d*'s. It might then look like this.

And of course this can be read as 'made'. Indeed it says 'made', taken letter by letter, just as much as it says 'madd'.

All of this would become a good deal weaker if we knew that Shakespeare strongly distinguished his *d*'s and his *e*'s and avoided spellings like 'madd'. We have no conclusive evidence on this point, but such evidence as we possess points the other way. The only specimen of handwriting, apart from some signatures, which has a good chance of being Shakespeare's is to be found on three pages of the manuscript

'Book of Sir Thomas More', the passage written in what is usually called 'Hand D'. This passage is one of several 'additions' to the text by revisers. The word *mad* does not occur on any of these three pages, but a great deal of doubling of letters does occur. The writing of Hand D spells 'got' with two *t*'s, 'sit' with two *t*'s, 'sin' with two *n*'s, 'cut' with two *t*'s and 'dogs' with two *g*'s. Such a man, one feels, would scarcely flinch from 'mad' with two *d*'s. Moreover, several of the *d*'s in the manuscript are identical in form with the *e*'s; for example, in the upper half of folio 9, the *d* of 'God' in the first line is like the *e* of 'power' in the fourth line; the *d* of 'hands' (thirteenth line) is like the *e* of 'kneels' (sixteenth line). The graph is very close all the time.

It might be thought that, given the fact that 'made' and 'mad' are common words, Shakespeare's supposed manner of writing and spelling should have led to frequent textual confusion. In fact, however, although both words are common they are very different in force and meaning; as a result context usually precludes confusion. But, for all that, there are several cases in the text of Shakespeare of possible confusion of these forms; for example, in *The Winter's Tale*, at III. iii. 115, the Clown says, in the Folio, 'You are a mad old man' but most modern editors accept Theobald's substitution of 'made'. The 1609 Quarto of Sonnet 79, 'Expense of spirit in a waste of shame', gave 'made in pursuit' for line 9.

Given all this it is very nearly a question of printing the reading one prefers. The Folio editors in the seventeenth century made no bones about it. It would seem that as soon as they spotted 'made' they changed it to 'mad'. The New Arden editor in our own century was obviously tempted to do the same thing but drew back because he felt 'mad' gave a difficult or impossible sense. Does it? 'Essentially made' – now that is really difficult. The phrase is explained as a continuation of the previous talk about true gold and counterfeiting, and 'essentially made' is supposed to mean 'made of true gold'. The suggestion is highly implausible. It is not Shakespearean English (or any other). No parallel usage, as far as I know, has ever been shown for *essentially* in this sense. But 'essentially mad' on the other hand is obviously good Shakespearean English. Does not Hamlet say, 'I essentially am not in madness,/But mad in craft' (*Hamlet*, III. iv. 187–8)? The sense 'mad' in this passage is both clear and powerful. Falstaff has seen that the Prince does not have any friends at all and he, the semiprofessional fool, suddenly cries out, 'Why, you're the crazy one; You don't look it, but you are!' Hal is inside out. Instead of concealing his human features beneath a stiff, impersonal mask, he wears the golden mask of kingship beneath an ordinary, smiling human face.

Thus the stereotype of wild son and authoritarian father is reversed. Falstaff is that other kind of archetypal old man who derives by a kind of creative misreading from Paul's *vetus homo*,[47] the old man we must put off in order to put on the new; the old Adam, the unregenerate, the happy inhabitant of a fallen world which remains, if not Eden-like, then Arcadian, excluded from the New Jerusalem. Falstaff says, 'Dost thou hear, Hal? Thou knowest in the state of innocency Adam fell; and what should poor Jack Falstaff do in the days of villainy? Thou seest I have more flesh than another man, and therefore more frailty' (*1 Henry IV*, III. iii. 164–7). Paul calls the old Adam 'the body of Sin',[48] an expression which immediately and naturally invites joyous elaboration from Falstaff. But what now of Hal's father? Surely there the stereotype is straightforwardly maintained?

In fact, it is not. We learn this largely from the parodic structure of the play. Falstaff cannot be a figure of authority because he is a criminal. But what if the King is himself a criminal? This is a subversive idea, and there is no doubt that it is present in the plays. The dubiety of the King's right to rule is fundamental. The Prince knows that it is dubious and all his dedication hinges on the decision that it is better to maintain a usurpation than to let the realm slip into anarchy.

There is a certain sort of learned critic who loves to point out that Falstaff must be classified as an evil force, since he stands for drink, conviviality and pleasure and has no sense of his responsibility to the great cause, the putting down of rebellion. All this depends, perhaps, on the authenticity and rightness of the order which is being maintained. But these same learned critics come at length in their dogged progress upon the fact that the King's rule is inauthentic. The rebels are not more rebellious than the King himself. The effect of this is to reopen the ethical debate about Falstaff. Dr Johnson was right when he reminded the reader – who, be it noted, he assumed all those years ago, would be distressed at the departure of Falstaff – that Falstaff utters no single 'sentiment of generosity' in the course of the plays.[49] Yet Auden can see Falstaff as a parabolic figure of charity.[50] How is this?

It is partly an effect of style. Falstaff speaks a golden Shakespearean English which makes him the centre of a small world of joy wherever he goes. Above all, in the very jaws of senility and death, he is life, and whenever he comes near there is a real danger that the great warlords will be seen for what they perhaps are – mere bloody men, agents of death.

Yet (with Falstaff one has to go on and on saying 'yet' since he is 'poem unlimited'), even while Falstaff impugns the practical mystique of the ruler, he is made the great expression in the plays of what we

may call the impractical mystique. Falstaff, who cannot get on with live
King Henry, is on the best of terms with dead King Arthur. If a sense of
England as a ruined Arcadia or Eden survives at all in *Henry IV* it is
because of Falstaff. This comes partly from the language of the Falstaff
scenes with its preference for immemorial, rustic ways of measuring
time – 'I have known thee these twenty-nine years, come peascod-
time' (*2 Henry IV*, II. iv. 368–70). There is a speech in *As You Like It*
which brings Falstaff to mind, and it is possible to piece together why
this is so. Charles says to Oliver,

> They say he is already in the Forest of Arden, and a many merry men
> with him; and there they live like the old Robin Hood of England.
> They say many young gentlemen flock to him every day, and fleet the
> time carelessly, as they did in the golden world.
>
> (*As You Like It*, I. i. 105–9)

Falstaff says in his first scene, 'Let us be Diana's foresters, gentlemen of
the shade, minions of the moon' (*1 Henry IV*, I. ii. 25–6). Falstaff might
almost be describing that band of Kentish poachers who stole deer from
Penshurst park after blacking their faces and calling themselves the
servants of the Queen of the Fairies.[51] But notice that in Falstaff's
speech we have, as in Charles's speech, the forest and the gentlemen – surely merry ones, too. Then in Part 3 Pistol speaks of 'golden
times' (V. iii. 95) and Silence sings in a quavering voice of Robin Hood
(V. iii. 102). And so the elements of the *As You like It* speech are reassembled.

Then there is the trail of references to King Arthur (King over the lost
England). These are of increasing power. In Part 2 at II. iv, Falstaff
enters singing, 'When Arthur first in court' (II. iv. 33) and then breaks
off with a request to Francis to empty the jordan. Then in the great
pastoral-comical-elegiacal scene, III. ii, Shallow says that long ago he
was Sir Dagonet in Arthur's show (III. ii. 273). Since, according to
Malory, Dagonet was Arthur's fool and Shallow here plays fool to
Falstaff the effect of the allusion is to turn Falstaff for a second into a
grey echo of Arthur himself. But the best comes in *Henry V*. There
Pistol, the Hostess, Nym, Bardolph and the Boy are talking about the
way Falstaff died and wondering whether his soul is in hell or heaven.
Bardolph cries out, 'Would I were with him, wheresome'er he is, either
in heaven or in hell!' But the Hostess answers,

> Nay, sure, he's not in hell: he's in Arthur's bosom, if ever man went
> to Arthur's bosom. 'A made a finer end, and went away an it had

been any christom child; 'a parted even just between twelve and one,
ev'n at the turning o' th' tide.

(Henry V, II. iii. 7–14)

Comic malapropism can be strangely powerful. The Hostess has confused the story in Luke about Dives and Lazarus with the story of Arthur.
To that most potent story she has joined the story Luke tells of the poor
leper who was shut out from the rich man's gate, as Falstaff was shut out
from the presence of Hal, and how the poor man was after death raised up
to Abraham's bosom while the rich man was left in hell (is there anyone
left who can believe that Shakespeare was unequivocally against Falstaff
when the imagery can do things like that?). To that scriptural story the
Hostess has joined the legend of the old king who lies sleeping under
Snowdon or perhaps Glastonbury Tor till we need him again.

Thus the anti-father. But, as I have suggested, the Prince's relation
with his real father is likewise, though less obviously, subversive of the
stereotype. Once again it is the old man who is the outlaw and the son is
the possible agent of control. The old man looks hungrily to his son for an
authority he could never attain himself. One could imagine various possible reactions in a son faced with such a father, such a kingdom: a des-
pairing withdrawal from political life, an equally desperate ferocity. Hal
falls into neither of these. Instead, he commits himself, body and soul to
confirming, both morally and by force of arms, the power of the crown.
He knows that he is more completely alone than anyone else, more,
even, than his father. His situation requires of him more perhaps than
should be asked of anyone. It requires him to extinguish his humanity in
the interests of the realm. E.M. Forster once wrote that if ever he was in a
position where he was forced to choose between his country and his
friend he hoped he would have the guts to choose his friend.[52] People
respond warmly to the passage but I suspect that they do so because
betraying one's country is a remote abstraction to most of us. Whether or
not the cause is just, whether the realm is holy or corrupt, treachery on
the part of the king must mean suffering, on a horrible scale. As Angelo,
the fallen archangel of *Measure for Measure*, said, the good man in office
must learn to pity people he does not know, has never seen (II. ii. 101).

Hal's White Machiavellian speech in which he explains his strange
purpose produces, in the author of this book, a distinct physical symptom, a tightening at the back of the throat. The same symptom is produced in the same subject by Sonnet 94:

> They that have power to hurt and will do none,
> That do not do the thing they most do show,

> Who, moving others, are themselves as stone,
> Unmoved, cold, and to temptation slow –
> They rightly do inherit Heaven's graces,
> And husband nature's riches from expense;
> They are the lords and owners of their faces,
> Others but stewards of their excellence.

This seems to be one of the sonnets addressed to the Friend, the young, beautiful man whom Shakespeare loves and whose unresponsiveness is seen by Shakespeare at one moment as a kind of blasphemy and at others – by an immense effort of will – as admirable.

If this were the nineteenth century I should now be permitted to speculate – to wonder whether Prince Hal was not founded on the beloved Friend, whether our difficulties with the Prince may not arise from the fact that we, unlike Shakespeare, are not in love with him, so that for us he gives light but not warmth, to wonder whether the rejected Falstaff, the myriad-minded, the genius with words, the messy, disordered man, might not be an ectype of Shakespeare himself, who in this sonnet made an intense effort to give praise to the other sort, to the beautiful, reserved man. Such speculations, though untestable, are not fundamentally irrational.

It may be said that the public mimesis of possible realities is one thing, and the dark genesis of a work in the private affections of the poet another, but reality is a turbulent ocean which endlessly overflows dykes and breakwaters of this kind; the terms for interpreting even an ostentatiously fictitious profession of love are modified by our sense of its source; we may strive to restrict 'source' to fictional 'persona' but the restriction is artificial, requires an unsleeping vigilance to enforce it; left to themselves the most literate, the most literary readers of *The Waste Land* will sense, behind the epicene Teiresias, the learned and quizzical American poet. But, for all that, the inferences have become unmanageable. It is better to stick to what we can see; and we can see a little (I am still trying to understand the tightening at the back of the throat).

The phrase 'lords and owners of their faces' objectively recalls the Prince, for the *face* is associated with royalty from Richard II smashing the looking glass to the almost surrealist speech in *Henry V* where Hal, now the King, imagines his features turning to unfeeling stone (III. i. 11–14). Moreover the preservative coldness of the Friend strongly resembles Hal's – he too husbands England's riches from expense. But the sonnet ends in a barely controlled revulsion of feeling which is not, as far as I can see anywhere reflected in the dramatic sequence from Part 1 of *Henry IV* to *Henry V*.

In Prince Hal Shakespeare gives us a mode of goodness which is embarrassing. The man is attractive but behind his easy manner lies something very unattractive and it is that unattractive something which is most deeply, most uncomfortably involved with real virtue. But the Prince is not quite a saint and the conflict of humanity and dedication can make a fool of him (where people like Hotspur and Falstaff, oddly enough, are secure). In Part 2, at IV. v, the old King lies dying in the Palace of Westminster. There has been talk of Prince Hal, his way of life, of the fact that at this of all times no one knows where he is. Then Westmoreland comes with good news: the rebellion is over. The King cries out, 'O Westmoreland, thou art a summer bird,/Which ever in the haunch of Winter sings/The lifting up of day' (IV. iv. 91–3). But the shock of the good news is too great and now he is conveyed to the inner room. The crown is placed beside him. Then, out of step and out of time, the Prince suddenly enters, talking in too loud a voice, for which he is politely rebuked by Warwick. The Prince moderates his voice and says that he will sit beside the now sleeping King. The rest withdraw and the Prince's eyes fall on the crown: 'O polish'd perturbation! golden care!' (IV. v. 23). Then his eye strays to a downy feather which has settled by the mouth and nostrils of the King; it lies there, unmoving, and the Prince is suddenly sure that his father is dead:

> My gracious lord! my father!
> This sleep is sound indeed; this is a sleep
> That from this golden rigol hath divorc'd
> So many English Kings. Thy due from me
> Is tears and heavy sorrows of the blood
> Which nature, love and filial tenderness,
> Shall, O dear father, pay thee plenteously.
> My due from thee is this imperial crown,
> Which, as immediate from thy place and blood,
> Derives itself to me. [*Putting on the crown*]
>   Lo where it sits –
> Which God shall guard; and put the world's whole strength
> Into one giant arm, it shall not force
> This lineal honour from me. This from thee
> Will I to mine leave as tis left to me.
>
>   (IV. v. 34–47)

But the King is not dead. Again he revives, to find himself alone. He calls for Warwick and the rest. Where is the Prince? And then, a moment later, '*Where is the crown?*' – 'Is he so hasty that he doth suppose/My sleep my death?' (IV. v. 61–2). Then Warwick returns to say that he found the

Prince weeping in the next room and that he is coming at once. The Prince enters and the King orders all the rest to leave. Hal speaks first:

> I never thought to hear you speak again

(IV. v. 92)

The King's answer is savage:

> Thy wish was father, Harry, to that thought.
> I stay too long by thee, I weary thee.

At last the Prince is allowed to make his excuses, to explain what he has done. This he performs brilliantly and touches his father's heart:

> There is your crown,
> And He that wears the crown immortally
> Long guard it yours! [*Kneeling*] If I affect it more
> Than as your honour and as your renown,
> Let me no more from this obedience rise. . . .
> Coming to look on you, thinking you dead –
> And dead almost, my liege, to think you were –
> I spake unto this crown, as having sense,
> And thus upbraided it: 'The care on thee depending
> Hath fed upon the body of my father;
> Therefore thou best of gold art worst of gold. . . .'
> Thus, my most royal liege,
> Accusing it, I put it on my head,
> To try with it – as with an enemy
> That had before my face murd'red my father –

The King is won by the speech and calls his son to sit by him on the bed. This is the part which, above all, produces the constriction in the throat. For the most terrible thing about this scene is that the Prince, in the most venial way, lies. He did not address the crown as an enemy, nor was it in that spirit that he took up the crown in his hands. Shakespeare, I think, does not want us to make any mistake about this, for he shows us the two things in succession, first the taking up of the crown and then the Prince's account, given under pressure. We know that when the Prince thought his father dead he experienced two great emotions one after the other; first real (and immense) grief for his father, and then a quite different feeling: 'Now it has come; now I am the King.' In the story which he tells his father he changes things, so that his thoughts are of Henry throughout.

Yet we can hardly say that we have 'seen through' Hal, discovered the cold ambition that lies beneath. Shakespeare refuses to make it so easy for us. What we have seen and what the Prince has dissembled is, precisely, not ambition, but dedication. This is merely the worst of his ordeals. There is indeed a fierce irony in the fact that this was the Prince with the common touch, the easy manner with all sorts and conditions, for no character in Shakespeare, except perhaps Iago, is so utterly alone.

The scene between the Prince and his father is very like that other great and complex scene, written about a year afterwards: the quarrel scene in *Julius Caesar* with its double version of the death of Portia. Henry dies, lives and dies again and so, in a manner, does Portia (though outside the scene). The sense of anguished back-tracking over what was said only moments before ('I said an elder soldier, not a better./Did I say better?' *Julius Caesar*, IV. iii. 56–7) is common to both. Strongest of all is the sense in both scenes of a good man, in a state of near disintegration, exerting all his skills, all his *art*, to prevent horror and chaos from taking over, and the audience being made, in a way which is almost unseemly, privy both to the mendacity (almost invisible with Hal, palpable with Brutus) and to the heroic effort of moral will. Both Brutus and the Prince are in a manner made fools of, yet in either case the phrase 'made fools of' is too coarse for the work it needs to do. Cassius's comment, extraordinary in its combination of affectionate admiration, charity and analytic intelligence,

> I have as much of this in art as you,
> But yet my nature could not bear it so.
>
> *(Julius Caesar,* IV. iii. 192–3)

corresponds to the King's answer to the Prince, loving yet somehow finding space within that love to register the *rhetorical* skill of what the Prince has just done:

> O my son,
> God put it in thy mind to take it hence
> That thou might'st win the more thy father's love,
> Pleading so wisely in excuse of it!
>
> *(2 Henry IV,* IV. v. 178–81)

Both scenes shows us more than we are accustomed to receive. Both force on us the radical opposition of nature and art in a manner which will not permit the resolution of the 'nature' half of the opposition into further covert rules of art (which is what formalist critics allege). Instead the dramatist turns the tables by reminding us that art is actually employed *in* life, by Stoic commanders or anointed princes, when life is most itself, most amorphous, most crushing. The fact that a playwright has contrived the whole impression by means of fictions in no way abolishes this point. For his fiction is unintelligible unless we permit ourselves the (wholly natural) recourse to real human behaviour. The element of recalcitrant 'mere probability' is so strong in these scenes that it is not only conventions of Elizabethan drama which are subtly contested. Our own comforting conventions, in which we codify our admiration of the good and our contempt for the bad, are themselves contested, so that people do not care to say, even to themselves, that Brutus, or Prince Hal lied. More often than not the thought has actually been repressed before the spectator has left the theatre. It is not that the mirror of nature shows us spectacular blemishes (these can be accommodated, neutralized and then enjoyed by way of an appropriate rhetoric). Shakespeare shows us the painful enmeshing of falsity with good feeling as it actually happens. The scenes, from every formal point of view, are chaotic. But they have a glaringly obvious, single, clarifying source in reality itself.

Prince Hal is a late-born man, delivered over to a world which has lost its freshness. His father obtained his crown by deposing Richard II. Richard, though in many ways a fairly repellent person, was the true, anointed king, God's regent upon earth. This fact alone has power to irradiate the England of the play, *Richard II*. The dying Gaunt rebukes the King for his betrayal of the realm, yet throughout his famous speech (II. i. 31–66), except for a single phrase, the praise of England remains in the present tense. The England of the usurper, Henry, lacking its point of intersection with the divine order, is greyer, less definite, less heraldic. War is seen less in terms of its high intelligible crises and more in terms of sheer mess – 'bloody noses and crack'd crowns.' 'I never did see such pitiful rascals. . . . Tut, tut; good enough to toss; food for powder, food for powder; they'll fill a pit as well as better: tush, man, mortal men, mortal men.' 'There's not three of my hundred and fifty left alive, and they are for the town's end, to beg during life' (Part 1, II. iii. 90; IV. ii. 62f; V. iii. 36f).

Part 1 of *Henry IV* opens with an overwhelming impression of weariness, of more to do than can be done – 'So shaken as we are, so wan with care. . . .' *Richard II* was about the fall of a king, but it was a true king that fell, and this gives the drama a unified and spectacular tragic structure. With the two loosely joined parts of *Henry IV* we get a cooler dramatic technique, inclining more to piecemeal exploration and an agnostic pluralism. In both *Richard II* and *Henry IV* we find scenes of meditation on the idea of England as a ruined garden but they are very different. In *Richard II* we have a tiny, jewelled allegory, in which two unnamed gardeners, in measured verse, liken the conduct of a kingdom to their own simple art. All is structured, everywhere there is correspondence and analogy, all thoughts begun are concluded. But in *Henry IV* we have instead the Gloucestershire scenes, in which Falstaff, Shallow and – name of names – Master Silence ramble on together in the orchard of Shallow's decaying farm. These scenes are extremely naturalistic – almost Chekhovian – full of inconsequential remarks, voices trailing away into nothingness, of memories, mundane queries about such things as the present price of bullocks, of a sense of imminent death. In the absence of conclusive structures we are given an atmosphere, compounded of last year's apples, the grey heads of old men, of sweetness and barrenness, and of futility.

This is the non-kingdom which Hal is to inherit from his father. Somehow he must unify the kingdom, make the crown real again. This is the proper context of the strange speech of 'direct self-explanation' with which we began. He has a mission (and there can be no doubt that it is a fully moral mission – unless the country is unified the blood and suffering will be endless). He dedicates himself utterly to the mission and, in its service, to a strange plan. He needs, on his inheritance, to seize the initiative, and for this he must be master of an element of spectacular surprise. In fact the people must be surprised (in the etymological sense of the word – 'taken unawares') by majesty. But if majesty is to surprise it must be preceded by its opposite – ignominy, irresponsibility. And so the bizarre logic of the situation tells Hal that he must humiliate himself in preparation for his sudden blaze. He must appear to neglect his royal responsibilities, must fritter his time away in vicious idleness, with criminals and drunks, until the moment comes. Like Kim Philby in our own time, he has proposed to himself a life of systematic duplicity; a life of endless conviviality in which he is to have no friend, no possibility of ordinary candour.

The two parts of *Henry IV* probably belong to the years 1596–8, overlapping *The Merchant of Venice*, some two years earlier than *Julius Caesar* and about six years earlier than *Othello*. *Coriolanus* may be dated anywhere between 1605 and 1608. In each of these plays we have found some notion of cultural evolution. We have already noticed a transformation of the context, a change in England itself at the beginning of *Henry IV*. The England of *Henry IV* is not the England of *Richard II*. While the anointed king was still on the throne, the country itself seemed still partly taken up into the supernatural. Parables, allegories, Eden, Paradise naturally express the character of this island in the older play. But the England of the usurper has been abandoned to the bleak natural order.

But in order to see whether the notion of cultural evolution is present in the two parts of *Henry IV* we must bring Hotspur into the discussion. Hotspur is culturally more primitive than Hal. Auden observes[53] that under the old kings the country had functioned fairly loosely as a set of small baronies, earldoms and the like, in which the dominant loyalties were local, personal, feudal. This is offered as a statement of a fact available to Shakespeare. A change of mental set, a change in instinctual morality was needed before people learned that their duty to a king they never saw undercut their duty to the man who fed and protected them. It is clear that in Hotspur this change has not occurred.

His energy is half-divine, and his language breathes a freshness which no one else in the play can match. Hal looks at him with a kind of envy – the moral world in which he moves is so simple. At II. iii. 1 he enters reading a letter; 'He could be contented – why is he not, then?' Hotspur cannot comprehend the hypothetical. Bacon wrote, *antiquitas saeculi, iuventus mundi*,[54] 'the age of the ancients was the youth of the world.' He was arguing, in a highly guarded fashion, for the moderns against the ancients and brilliantly turned the tables by saying, 'If it's age you like you should read the moderns; we are far older than they, who lived in the world's infancy.' So Hotspur, who belongs to the old order, is above all young. When he receives his death-wound from the Prince he cries,

> O Harry, thou hast robb'd me of my youth
>
> *(1 Henry IV*, V. iv. 77)

Responsibility, prudence, caution, strategy mean nothing to him. Honour is his watchword and honour means fighting, with a complete disregard of personal safety or the probability of victory. Only at the end, when his last battle is impending, does Hotspur begin to think (the measured, bitter reply to Blunt in IV. iii brings the change of style which marks the change of heart). Shakespeare brilliantly makes him wish (at V. ii. 48) that only he and Hal might fight that day. Here Hotspur's impetuosity is fused for a moment with pity for the other victims of war. But impetuous he remains. At the end of V. ii he will not stay to read the letters brought by the messenger. The King wishes his son were like Hotspur, but it would have been disastrous if he had been. Prince Hal is like Virgil's Aeneas in that he is burdened with a sense of history and the crushing obligations implied by the likely succession of events. Aeneas has his Hotspur in Turnus, the young, impetuous leader of the Latins. For both Aeneas and Prince Hal the most important relationships are lineal. Each is dominated by the idea of his father, by Anchises and by the King. Thus for Aeneas the lateral relation with Dido is a distraction which must be crushed.

Here, it may be thought, the analogy breaks down. Hal has no Dido, no mirror love to bear him from his purpose; in the sequence from Part 1 of *Henry IV* to *Henry V* we have no tragic queen who dies of a broken heart.

Yet someone (if we can believe Pistol, and I think we can) lay dying of a heart 'fracted and corroborate' (*Henry V*, II. i. 121). The analogy with the *Aeneid* is indeed broken by an explosion of genius, yet at the same time in a manner sustained. We have come back to Falstaff. For Shakespeare has chosen to give us something hilarious: a Dido in the form of an Anchises. The great distracting love of *Henry IV* is an old man, and he drinks.

Falstaff is not like Hotspur a specimen of an earlier culture. Rather, he spans and sums in his person all change, all shocks. He is as Arthurian as he is Henrician, as Arcadian as he is English, paradisal and fallen. Introduced in Part 1 as irrelevant to clocks ('What a devil hast thou to do with the time of the day?' says the Prince at I. ii. 7), he is, as we learn in Part 2, soon to die. He is an old man but he is also a sort of timeless baby. The Hostess's account of the death of Falstaff is a wonderful description of a baby: 'I saw him fumble with the sheets, and play with flowers, and smile upon his finger's end' (*Henry V*, II. iii. 15). There is a point when the two images are held in separation, and then glimmer and join. Falstaff says, 'I was born about three of the clock in the afternoon, with a white head and something a round belly' (*2 Henry IV*, I. ii. 176-7). We hear the words and, as we listen, what do we see? A white head and a round belly.

4
The new mimesis

The example of Shakespeare

In recent literary theory the concepts of anthropology have loomed large. We have learned that our thinking does not operate in a vacuum of pellucid neutrality, but is conditioned by the prevalent forms of our culture. Culture, no longer the transparent medium of thought and art, has been made visible by anthropology, shown to have a palpable substance which is subject to historical change.

The application of this insight to literature occurred first, as might have been predicted, in the study of ancient Greek literature. The achievement is largely a German one and is conveniently summed up in the earlier history of the concept of alienation. Today it is popularly supposed that 'modern man' is alienated and that ancient religious cultures, conversely, were 'integrated'. Since the term 'alienation' was appropriated by Marx and given an economic application, its history has been complex. In its non-Marxian form, as used by Feuerbach, it was in fact especially applicable to the religious culture of ancient Greece. This culture was 'alienated' in that man was deprived of characteristics properly his, such as freedom, spontaneity, mind and emotion, and these were ascribed to gods.[1] It was as if man saw his own nature written on the heavens before he saw it in his own breast. Nietzsche in his turn wrote *The Genealogy of Morals* (1887) in which he suggested that morality was itself subject to cultural evolution: 'good' in archaic Greece was harshly external in its reference to the 'noble' characteristics, beauty, felicity, strength (here the notion of a shame-culture is clearly anticipated).

Bruno Snell in his *Discovery of Mind*[2] stressed the absence both of inward depth and of spontaneous mental activity in Homeric heroes. They do not decide; their actions are rather determined by gods. This happens because what we construe as a mental event is by Homer construed as divine intervention. Where we might say, 'He had an erotic impulse', Homer will say, 'Aphrodite breathed in him.' In the Homeric formulation, the impulse is not his.

Snell's book was followed in England by E.R. Dodds's *The Greeks and the Irrational*.[3] Dodds carefully analysed the apology given by Agamemnon in the nineteenth book of the *Iliad*: Agamemnon says, 'Not I [*ego*] was the cause of this act, but Zeus and my lot and the Erinys that walks in darkness, they it was who in the assembly put wild folly in my understanding, on that day when of myself (*autos*) I took Achilles' prize from him' (86f.). The passage seems to imply that *ego* and self (represented by *autos*) are not coextensive, so that you can say easily in Greek what you cannot say in English, 'Myself did it, but I did not.' Passions are conceived as external to the ego and indeed as external to the man, in that they are not symbolized by gods but consist in divine action (sometimes this is causal, as in the Homeric passage quoted, sometimes direct, as in 'Aphrodite breathed in him'). Nevertheless this agency falls within the province of the self. Agamemnon is not here exculpating himself; he accepts responsibility and agrees to pay retribution.[4] Then John Jones, in his *Aristotle and Greek Tragedy*[5] drew attention to the way Aeschylus, the earliest of the three great Greek tragedians, cannot show *psychological* hesitation; we are always confronted with a *public* dilemma; one god says this, another says that. The difference between the Aeschylean and the Euripidean Orestes lies precisely in this. Euripides has become master of a distinctively psychological language and is thereby enabled to show us a fully human hesitation. Brooks Otis, in his masterly, quasi-structuralist *Virgil: A Study in Civilized Poetry*,[6] sees the Latin epic as a psychologizing introversion of the Greek; the funeral games of *Aeneid*, v, are a 'subjectivized' rewriting of Homer, Homer's starkly external values are likewise internalized as *pietas*.

The body of thought here sketched gives us the history of ancient culture in a developing, narrative form. As the distinctively psychological language grew, we are told, it took over functions previously discharged by god-language. Thus Fragment 119 of Heraclitus, 'Character is a man's destiny-god', assumes a pivotal importance in the story, for this is one of the places where the two languages are weighed, one against the other.

The picture bristles with difficulties. Hugh Lloyd-Jones in *The Justice of Zeus*[7] showed us a Homeric world less destitute of morality than Snell and Dodds had pretended. Homer meanwhile certainly has a psychological vocabulary coexisting with the religious. At *Odyssey*, iv. 712 we read, 'I know not whether some god sent him on or whether his own spirit stirred him to go.' In *Iliad*, V. 180f. Lycaon plainly considers it in a manner unfair that Diomede is helped to fight by a god; he does *not* draw the circle of Diomede's heroism outside the divine assistance and say, 'He is a truly great warrior, a god-helped warrior.' Perhaps most fundamental of all, the presumption that the theological vocabulary preceded the psychological appears to create an infinite regress. If it is impossible to describe, say, a human decision without expressing the process in terms of divine action, how is one to describe a decision *on the part of a god*? The application of the same logic implies that this in its turn must be translated, through the usual hypostatized allegory, into action by some prior god, and so on *ad infinitum*. In fact this is not what happens in Homer, our earliest text. Rather, the gods and goddesses freely decide, think and emote. Obviously then, Homer has these concepts and it is difficult to see where he could have got them from if it was not from human beings. The old epigram about man seeing himself in the heavens before he saw himself directly gets more puzzling the more one thinks about it. The thesis which ascribes an absolute priority to the theological language over the psychological seems very doubtful. But that such a priority is intermittently operative in archaic literature is clear. The German criticism of Homer remains one of the most challenging and important efforts to explore and understand a profound difference of culture.

I have outlined this body of writing because it is the tradition which lies behind my own interpretation of Shakespeare in this book. Yet Snell, with his investigation of the prior categories which modify poetry 'from below', clearly belongs, in several important ways, to the formalist camp. Indeed his work triumphantly vindicates the real critical usefulness of such an approach. But although my account of Shakespeare has been largely conducted in terms given to me by Dodds and Snell, there is one immense difference. For Snell, cultural differences are *betrayed, not scrutinized* by literary texts.

When he analyses the manner in which Homer's references to intelligence are restricted to the idea of multiplicity ('many-minded') while

the later lyric poets have access to the idea of depth ('deep-minded')
Snell, from the Olympian advantage of vast historical distance and
extensive knowledge, perceives conceptual constraints of which the
poets themselves were presumably unconscious. This is part of the
excitement of his approach. Even while it disquietingly suggests that
our own culture may be similarly subject to unnoticed conditioning, it
shows how the truly historical critic can perceive and so master these
conditions. When, however, I came to apply the conception of a changing culture to Shakespeare, I treated the poet, not as mere matter or
evidence, but as a fellow intelligence. The Shakespearean criticism
which is *logically* analogous to the Greek criticism of Snell and Dodds is
that of E.E. Stoll. The comparison feels wrong, partly because Stoll's
work is so much lower in quality than theirs and partly because Stoll did
not attempt to pass below literary categories to more fundamental conceptual categories. To do the full job one would have to map the use in
Shakespeare of such quasi-ethical terms as 'honour'. But as soon as one
begins to do this, one discovers the fundamental indocility of all
Shakespeare's writing. He refuses passively to submit to one's analysis,
but is for ever popping up at one's elbow with suggestions and insights
quite as subtle as anything one can produce from the vantage point of
modern anthropology and cultural history. One attempts 'the Olympian conspectus' and finds oneself still looking *up*.

Of course Shakespeare's writing 'betrays' the Elizabethan view of
Rome as it 'betrays' the Elizabethan view of royalty. But he also thinks
about these things and these categories with a freedom which is evidently cognitive. Therefore he has appeared in this book as an ally in the
enterprise of cultural history. He is not only a specimen but also an
analyst, not only a late 'text' but also an early 'criticism'. His dramatic
analysis of the difference between Brutus and Mark Antony, between
Othello and Iago, between Hotspur and Prince Hal is logically co-ordinate with Brooks Otis's analysis of the difference between Homer's
Achilles and Virgil's Aeneas.

In the cultural analysis of ancient texts there is a running presumption that the hope of truth is increasingly confined to the analysis itself
and is removed from the material analysed: *their* perceptions are unconsciously conditioned but *we* can identify the conditions. The example
of Shakespeare is endlessly rebellious against this arrogant relegation.
Even when one works with seemingly modern tools of thought, such as
the concepts of cultural history, one finds that Shakespeare is there
before one. The inference is obvious: the text refuses to relinquish what
I have called 'the hope of truth'. Its level of *cognitive* activity is so high
that later attempts to compass even the latent character of thought-

categories find that its most radical moves have been anticipated by the poet. The easiest way – no, the *only* way – to account for this is to say that Shakespeare was looking very hard at the same world (400 years younger, but still the same world) that we are looking at now.

It may be objected that the presence of similar patterns of 'cultural evolution' in plays with widely different chronological settings shows that these patterns cannot be objective. If culture really 'evolved' a Mark Antony after it had 'evolved' a Brutus, why should it, so many hundreds of years later, have to repeat what looks like a more primitive version of the same operation with Hotspur and Hal? Is it not obvious that these tensions, on which I have sought to impose a high-toned fashionable gloss of historical jargon, are really the *eterne mutabilitie* of human nature, perennial, unhistorical variations of temperament?

That the various 'historical' relations in a manner echo one another I would not wish to deny. One of the effects of my analysis is to throw upon the screen certain recurrent moments: the quarrel of Brutus and Cassius is like the misunderstanding between Prince Hal and his dying father; the admiring 'art plus nature' comment of Cassius after the near-humiliation of Brutus is like the 'art plus nature' comment of King Henry, after his son, likewise, has come very close to humiliation. My scrutiny of the 'histrionic status' of Othello's last speech runs parallel to my scrutiny of Prince Hal's notorious soliloquy. The 'panning down' to the visual presentation of the exotic Othello is, in method though not in matter, like the 'panning down' to the white head and round belly of Falstaff. To notice these things is perhaps to learn a little more about the formal art of Shakespeare. But it is equally clear that Shakespeare notices unique historical factors. Brutus is a distinctively Roman Stoic. The fact that Othello is more primitive than Coriolanus is immediately accounted for by his uncivil origin. Nor is it surprising that a gentlemanly backwoodsman like Hotspur should be less 'culturally evolved' than, say, the Epicurean Cassius. The final brutal test of cognitive mimesis must be the real world itself. In the world we do *not* find a linear progression in reality, to contrast with the echoing systems of Shakespeare. Rather we find a like (if not identical) system of echoes. It is consistent to claim both that a heroic culture is earlier than a civic, 'co-operative' culture, and that the heroic culture survives (say, in boarding schools). It is consistent, because in the earlier period the heroic culture was dominant and in the later it is vestigial. This is the kind of correspondence we should expect in a poet dealing with fictional probabilities.

The 'overevolved' characters are a little more puzzling. In my historical analysis I almost went so far as to say that these were people *who had not yet arrived*, are imagined, not recognized by Shakespeare. Yet, if Mark Antony is one, Shakespeare has placed him, historically, in ancient Rome and, if Iago is another, he has placed him in Renaissance Venice. Both, it would seem, are credible in the settings given. Yet even in such settings (both urban and unstable) we may suppose that certain individuals may anticipate a trend which later becomes more prominent. There is no need to suppose that Shakespeare arrived at his conception by pure imaginative extrapolation with no foundation in direct experience. The empirical foundation need be no more than an evanescent mood, a fugitive exchange of words. For Shakespeare this would be enough.

Similar considerations apply to the critical case I made concerning *Othello* against Eliot and Leavis. An opponent might object that my very theory of cultural evolution does not merely 'account for' the reaction of Eliot and Leavis, it makes it wholly inescapable. For we are all equally members of the later culture, and so have no choice but to describe Othello's behaviour as histrionic. This argument assumes that cultural episodes are closed and homogeneous. It should be clear by now that I on the contrary regard them both as subject to exceptions and as capable of perceiving and responding to other cultures as such. Indeed, it is peculiarly the formalist who will tend to assume that such cultural episodes will be 'closed' or 'windowless'. It seems obvious in fact that they are ventilated by cognitive access to the unfamiliar, and indeed without such cognitive access cultural history itself would be impossible. If we were truly 'locked into' the concepts of the twentieth century we should simply see the varying concepts of other centuries as gibberish. Indeed, we would not even know that we *were* locked in. This is the old paradox whereby even the most severe cultural formalist is obliged to claim cognitive truth for his own historical analysis and by doing so undermines the credibility of his absolute thesis.

Thus, while there are indeed conditioning forms of thought, they can be used cognitively; they can encounter recalcitrance and are in any case 'ventilated' with more open forms of cognition, which permit a degree of understanding even of other cultures. Shakespeare, naturally, exhibits the preliminary conditioning of the Elizabethan period; every other Elizabethan likewise exhibits it. But then Shakespeare likes to apply his own thought forms to recalcitrant material; he is luminously capable of fundamental understanding of other forms, other cultures. In this he differs from most, perhaps all of his contemporaries.

In my 'anthropological' interpretation of Shakespeare I deliberately adopted the Transparent language of criticism; that is, I considered the characters in the plays as possible human beings and not just as functions in a formal system. When I gave examples (pp. 80–1 above) of Transparent criticism, the shining example was Auden's lines about Brueghel's *Fall of Icarus*. Accordingly, when I came to write at length in the Transparent mode about Shakespeare I took Auden's *The Dyer's Hand* as a guiding thread. That book, above all, shamelessly and most fruitfully, assumes that Shakespeare treats realities. Poets often think thus.

I have throughout conceded that the most cognitive, the most pellucidly mimetic passages in literature are conventionally ordered, but have insisted that the presence of convention does not preclude truth or probability. The tendency of my argument has often been to rehabilitate older critical postures, which twentieth-century formalism has thrown into contempt.

But, it must be said, the phrase 'merely conventional' has often been used disparagingly, implying want of substance, by those very critics I seek to rehabilitate. Notice, however, the adverb 'merely', which implies that convention may be differently and more usefully employed. Nevertheless, we must be careful here. The phrase 'merely conventional' is not restricted to passages which, though highly polished, are untrue or improbable. Indeed it is often applied to truisms. It seems rather that the phrase is used when the formal arrangement of a line obtrusively recalls that of other passages and usurps our attention at the expense of the line's reference. All lovers of literature are familiar with this experience and justly resent its being blandly forced upon them. But I suspect that among professional teachers it can easily get out of hand. As with art history, so with literature, the teacher is artificially directed, by the terms of his or her job, to elicit such repetitions, and then to differentiate author from author, period from period, by modifications in the formal character of their work. Thus we come to a line like Sidney's 'Foole, said my Muse to me, looke in thy heart and write' with a predisposition to locate its precedents, and to place it in the web of analogical structures. I question whether even the most literary Elizabethan readers had their attention channelled (for all their love of phrase and echo) in quite this harshly exclusive manner. In fact it seems to me entirely possible that many of them read the line as I read it in my teens, as another exciting foray out of mere Petrarchan bead-stringing into the dense reality of love. And with Shakespeare's anti-Petrarchan sonnets the intuition is stronger still. Shakespeare's Sonnet 21, beginning 'So is it not with me as with that Muse,' makes two things quite clear: first that the disparaging concept, if not the actual phrase, 'merely conventional', did figure in his consciousness, and second that his own poem is not offered as merely an alternative convention. Of course it is possible for experts to point out that anti-Petrarchanism is itself a repeated formal posture and it is conceivable that Shakespeare may have intended some such intuition to arise in his reader. But to admit the thought 'and this also is mere convention' is to turn the poem into a wry joke.

I have little doubt that this is just what is done in *As You Like It*, II. i. Duke Senior opens the scene with a set speech in praise of their new home in the forest, far from the pomp of Court. Virgil in his *Eclogues* praised the uncourtly world as a place of lyric ease: 'Tityre, tu patulae recubans sub tegmine fagi', and in his *Georgics* he praised it on the opposite ground that it formed character through labour. The Duke's praise rests on grounds more fundamental still. The uncivil world is alone real. When the wind blows till it bites, Duke Senior tells us he can smile and say, 'This is no flattery; these are counsellors/That feelingly persuade me what I am' (II. i. 10–11). But he says all this in an obtrusively formal manner, and at the end of his speech, Amiens, the courtier, pronounces obsequious judgement:

> Happy is your Grace,
> That can translate the stubbornness of fortune
> Into so quiet and so sweet a style

(II. i. 18–20)

The Duke preaches realism and is then praised for his power to transmute reality into *style*. Note that Amiens says 'into' where ordinary usage might have led us to expect 'in'. This all but imperceptible conceptual oddity is of course anticipated in the Duke's own imagery, which presents an almost surrealist transformation of nature into various forms of language – stones into sermons, running brooks into books. At the beginning of his speech the Duke reminded us of Adam. Adam may have named the beasts, but he never thought to translate them into their own names. The Duke praises grim reality but is in truth the father of all formalists. He is in no way offended by Amiens's compliment. It does not occur to him that he might be annoyed. We have here a clue to the Duke's dislike (strangely intense for so happy a comedy) of Jaques. As I have said elsewhere,[8] the Duke is a fantasist ineffectively disguised as a realist, while Jaques is a realist very effectively disguised as a fantasist.

My point is that, although oppositions of nature and artifice can be reduced to their own formulations either through artistic inadvertency or as a deliberate effect of sophisticated irony, this is not true of every such opposition. Consider *2 Henry IV*, II. iv. 224–84, the episode in which Prince Hal and Poins eavesdrop on Falstaff's dalliance with Doll

Tearsheet. I offer this as a typically Shakespearean example of *writing against the grain of convention*. I take it that the given convention against which Shakespeare works is roughly as follows: the splendid young bloods must first eavesdrop on and then expose the folly of the ageing boaster. Shakespeare first makes sure that we are given enough clues to establish this convention in our minds. But then he turns at once to the marvellous and subtle labour of its subversion. To begin with, he gives to Falstaff that golden language of which we have already spoken, but to the Prince and Poins he gives a thin, sour diction. Listen first to Falstaff:

> What stuff wilt have a kirtle of? I shall receive money a Thursday. Shalt have a cap to-morrow. A merry song, come. It grows late; we'll to bed. Thou't forget me when I am gone.
>
> (*2 Henry IV*, II. iv. 263–7)

Now listen to the Prince and Poins:

> Prince   Would not this nave of a wheel have his ears cut off?
> Poins   Let's beat him before his whore.
>
> (II. iv. 245–7)

Next, he has a lute play softly throughout the conversation of Falstaff and Doll. Then, while the absurdity of the love-making is in no way blurred, it seems that Doll, who weeps to think of Falstaff's passing, may really love the old fraud. Auden in his essay 'The Prince's dog' gives too little weight to this. He thinks of Falstaff as an *opera buffa* character, a vainglorious boaster who imagines that he has great power over women when really he has none.[9] What Shakespeare shows us is – typically – much more interesting than that: an old man who has very great power over some admittedly pretty seedy women. Lastly and most crucially of all to the subversion of the stereotype, Shakespeare gives to Falstaff, not to Hal or Poins, a truly comprehensive consciousness of what is happening. 'Saturn and Venus this year in conjunction/What says th'almanac to that?' (II. iv. 253–4) says the Prince, and we laugh, not very *happily*, at the wit. Not happily, because the purging force of the exposure of vice and folly is all lost as soon as we realize that Falstaff himself is fully aware of the ridiculousness of love between those who will soon die:

> Thou dost give me flattering busses. . . .
> I am old, I am old
>
> (II. iv. 258, 261)

This time there can be no question that the dramatist hopes for expert appreciation of the way something which appears to be a resistance

offered by nature to convention is really an ironically pleasurable con-
test of conventions. The ways in which the understanding of Falstaff
and the affection of Doll are conveyed do not present an obtrusively
repetitious formal aspect, perhaps because there is no obvious formal
trope involved. The conventions of the English language and of drama
are observed, but the detailed content of the scene has no obvious literary or ideological source, but at the same time a blindingly obvious
source in nature. Which is exactly what Shakespearean criticism
urgently affirmed, when first it found its voice. Indeed, such things as
the pathos of old age, the terror of death, the value of love are not so
much too *novel* to be counted as tropes, as *too general, too familiar.*
Although I have said that, more than anything else, it is repetition which
produces that usurpation of attention which in turn invites the description 'merely conventional', I must allow that in some areas of life a sort
of endless repetition is easily tolerated, becomes once more unnotice-
able, so that the mind is freed again to engage with meaning. The word
'and' is not a cliché. The sadness of old age is not a literary trope.

I have noted the tendency in teachers of literature, confronted with a
literary opposition of convention and nature, to react in a reflexive
manner, to cry out, in joyous consciousness of their own erudition, that
the so-called 'nature' half of the antithesis is itself a conventional trope.
And in some highly conscious artists this balletic movement of the
sensibility is anticipated, producing a work of ironic self-reference.
This, indeed, seems to mark the point of maximum strenuousness in
much modern criticism. In Shakespeare it represents an early and (for
him) undeveloped phase of his art which he effortlessly outgrew.

The young man who wrote *Love's Labour's Lost* could turn anything
into dapper verse. Where others begin with a problem of poverty,
Shakespeare began with a problem of wealth. *Love's Labour's Lost* is in
part about the vice of premature articulateness, of the too-swiftly-
available formula. The lovers must repent their falsely conventional
professions of love, and then subject their very professions of repent-
ance to a fresh purgation.

> | Berowne | Henceforth my wooing mind shall be express'd |
> | | In russet yeas, and honest kersey noes. |
> | | And, to begin, wench – so God help me, law! – |
> | | My love to thee is sound, sans crack or flaw. |
> | Rosaline | Sans 'sans', I pray you. |

(V. ii. 412–16)

Love's Labour's Lost is a 'happy comedy' and yet it is laced with something like hysteria. The infinite regress of reflexive consciousness

whereby each new profession of sincerity can be reduced to its too-expert formula becomes a kind of abstract avenging spirit, creating below the surface an accelerating panic in the natural festive process of the comedy, until at last Shakespeare must mortify his own comic conclusion with news of a death and the separation of the lovers, before escaping, through a kind of literary miracle, into the final, immemorial songs of spring and winter. This avenging spirit pursues him in other early plays, notably in those which we may call, following Schlegel and Bradley, 'the tragedies of thought.'[10] Richard II is plagued not so much by Bolingbroke as by his own capacity for conceptual anticipation: Bolingbroke does not force Richard from the throne, he moves into spaces successively vacated, with elaborately conscious art, by Richard. Hamlet is oppressed by a consciousness which cannot any longer connect with natural events or even natural emotion. Thus Shakespeare's first response was to build his problem of premature articulateness into the objective emotional economy of the drama; to set the dog which had been hunting *him* upon his hero. Later he learned to convey action and passion without this convulsive intervention of formal consciousness. Often he will avail himself of ancient tropes and deep-laid conventions but without that early, restless impulse to register his own consciousness of what is formally involved. When Shakespeare exchanged the gardeners' allegory of *Richard II* for the Gloucestershire scenes of *2 Henry IV*, he moved from a mode in which form is emphatically patterned and asserted to a mode in which form is broken. It seems to me entirely appropriate to say that with this fracturing of the more obtrusive symmetries comes an intuition of reality. For – to descend to the utterly simple – people do in fact talk in discontinuous sentences. The fact that an *obtrusive* discontinuity can became an obvious formal device should not blind us to the way it is used by Shakespeare, which is to convey the taste of reality.

Ockham's beard: a note on latency

Maurice Morgann's essay on the dramatic character of Falstaff is one of the most resolutely Transparent pieces of criticism ever written:

> There is a certain roundness and integrity in the forms of *Shakespeare*, which give them an independence as well as a relation, insomuch that we often meet with passages which, tho' perfectly felt, cannot be sufficiently explained in words, without unfolding the whole character of the speaker. . . . The reader will not now be surprised if I affirm that those characters in *Shakespeare*, which are seen only in part, are yet capable of being unfolded and understood in the

whole; every part being in fact relative, and inferring all the rest. It is
true that the point of action or sentiment, which we are most concerned in, is always held out for our especial notice. But who does not
perceive that there is a peculiarity about it, which conveys a relish of
the whole? And very frequently, when no particular point presses, he
boldly makes a character act and speak from those parts of the composition which are *inferred* only, and not distinctly shown. This produces a wonderful effect; it seems to carry us beyond the poet to
nature itself, and gives an integrity and truth to facts and characters
which they could not otherwise obtain: and this is in reality that art
in *Shakespeare* which, being withdrawn from our notice, we more
emphatically call *nature*. A felt propriety and truth from cases
unseen, I take to be the highest point of Poetic composition. If the
characters of *Shakespeare* are thus *whole*, and as it were original,
whilst those of almost all other writers are mere imitation, it may be
fit to consider them rather as Historic than Dramatic beings; and
when occasion requires, to account for their conduct from the *whole*
of character, from general principles, from latent motives, and from
policies not avowed.[11]

Here Morgann suggests that we may properly assume an area of latent
meaning in Shakespeare, not explicitly presented by him but accessible
to inference. Evidently, there is a connection between Morgann's plea
for latent meanings and his extreme-realist reading of the plays. It is
clear that he would not have been at all surprised by the observation
that he, Morgann, on occasion said things about Falstaff which had not
been said first by Shakespeare. This point, so far from being a brilliant
undercutting of his enterprise, is in fact anticipated by him. He suggests – and indeed, properly considered, the suggestion is hard to resist
– that the meaning of Shakespeare's plays cannot be confined to that
which is explicitly and formally stated in them. If this is granted, one
cannot censure Morgann *merely* for indulging in inference. I myself
believe that certain of Morgann's inferences are extravagant, but my
ground for saying this is not 'Shakespeare does not mention this', but
(because I accept the method of inference) 'Shakespeare does not imply
or hint this.'

Morgann knew that if he could induce his reader to acknowledge a
latent area, the business of exploring that area (by surmise and inference) would naturally involve some reliance on the known character of
the real world. If a play is viewed as formally closed, as giving the kind of
meaning which is coextensive with the forms employed, it is easy to
shelve genuine mimesis, to restrict oneself to the analysis of a wholly
autonomous system of conventions. At the opposite extreme, we all

interpret the words we hear in the course of our practical lives from fellow human beings, by playing our knowledge of the linguistic convention against our knowledge of the real situation in which the words are uttered. Morgann is in fact proposing that where literature proposes probable human beings it is wholly natural and proper to apply one's sense of what is likely in real life, in making sense of an evidently incomplete (*deliberately* incomplete) presentation.

Morgann's critical conception of latency, or 'undermeaning' is historically highly significant. His conception is thoroughly radical. The previous history of the concept of undermeaning stretches back to the Greek term ὑπόνοια which meant 'guess' or 'inference' before it meant 'covert meaning'. The development of the stiff, formal apparatus of allegorical interpretation from this concept is very curious. The Greeks continued to recite and revere the poems of Homer long after their society had assumed a profoundly different shape from that which Homer had known, generating a different set of moral priorities. It seems clear that many of the bizarre early attributions of allegorical significance to Homer arose from the fact that the obvious meaning had become embarrassing or unacceptable.[12] In particular, where the behaviour of Homer's gods seemed barbarous or merely immoral, it must have been a relief to be encouraged to see them as, for example, allegories of physical processes. Allegorical readings produced in this way are obviously subcritical, non-cognitive. They exist, not to explicate a latent area genuinely implied by Homer, but only to allay later, extraneous anxieties.

When Virgil came to write the *Aeneid* in about 30 BC he knew that he must match the achievement of Homer but in such a way as to please his contemporaries. The authority of the archaic Greek poet was still such as to determine the formal surface of Virgil's poem. But the inner significance, especially the morality, was another matter. Of course, by the time Virgil wrote, both the *Iliad* and the *Odyssey* were themselves, as I have suggested, a curiously double affair. Homer as he was taught in the Roman schools was variously allegorized and moralized. But while this may well have given Virgil the hint he needed for writing the great poem of introverted significance, we cannot say that Homer, for the Romans, simply *was* a moral poet, in exactly the same way as Virgil. Virgil laboured in order that all those moral significances imposed by the learned on the ancient epic should be genuinely and authentically latent in the new. Thus Virgil perfected the art of *idem in alio*, of the new world implicit in the old.

He was able to bring off this achievement in good faith because of an objective, cognitive presumption about history. History is itself *objec-*

tively structured in an analogical manner; Augustus in Virgil's own time really was a second Aeneas; Cleopatra really was a second Dido. Virgil could not have reappropriated for art the extraneous under-meaning of the scholars without this corroborative fidelity to the realities of history. Of course we may now dispute the fact that Augustus was a second Aeneas, as we may dispute any other under-standing of history. In thus inviting his reader to bring to his under-standing of Aeneas some sense of the later leader Augustus, Virgil is in one respect doing what Morgann did (for Morgann interpreted Falstaff by bearing in mind what others such as he might be expected to do or have done). But there is an important difference. The mimetic referent, or check, is specified by Virgil; for Aeneas it is not just any leader such as he, but, uniquely, Augustus.

This narrowly patterned determination of meaning smacks of formal constraints; it may indeed be conditioned by the formal, tick-tock allegorizing of the Roman classroom. Instead of a penumbra of inference constrained by genuine probability, we have a specifically controlled correspondence, very like the autonomous systems of metaphor. Virgil may actually have thought that reality itself was so structured, but, for all that, the presence of such patterning with most readers will inevitably create a presumption of *formal* determinants, that is, a presumption of art rather than nature. And indeed there is one aspect of Virgil's art where covert or secondary meaning really is wholly of this kind. When Dido and Aeneas first make love the heavens darken and a great storm breaks. This is the famous sympathizing Nature of Virgil, so different from the golden, indifferent Nature of Homer. The passion of the sky seems to provide an answering undermeaning for the passion of Dido and Aeneas. But now 'undermeaning' no longer denotes an area of probable inference. Rather it is merely a given answering pattern and one, moveover, which is, in an unusually pure sense of the term, ficti-tious.

One may argue desperately that Virgil believed great events were attended by portents, and so on, but one knows in one's bones that the storm in *Aeneid*, iv, is pure literary art, invention. The sky darkens, not because it would have happened, but because it is an 'acted metaphor' of passion. The habit of implication and correspondence has broken free of its roots in a corroborative reality and, so freed, can function as a secondary language. The sympathetic cosmos in Virgil is not probable in itself but should be construed as essentially metaphorical. So con-strued, it can then perform the richly cognitive work which metaphors perform. The correct way to apply the probability test to Virgil's sympa-thetic cosmos is not to ask 'Would the sky really weep?' but to ask, 'Is passion really like that weeping sky?'

When secondary meaning develops thus far it is no longer appropriate to speak of undermeaning or latency. The correspondence must be fully available, formally, for now the significance and any mimetic force will lie in the use and reference of that very correspondence. This is the pattern which came to dominate the history of polysemy and undermeaning. The model of the symbol and its significance replaced (except in a very few cases, of which Morgann is one) the model of the incomplete formal utterance, the meaning of which must be supplemented from an awareness of the real world.

In this process the late example of Freud is instructive. Freud supposed that human behaviour and discourse were systematically incomplete, and postulated a latent area (the unconscious) accessible to expert inference. But Freud has been suspected with some reason of 'rigging' this scheme. His area of latency, the unconscious, is so effectively hidden that most of us cannot pronounce on it at all. It is offered as real, indeed, as more fundamentally real than anything else – but the reader is not encouraged to explore it by consulting the world he knows. Meanwhile Freud himself peopled this realm with figures which are oddly reminiscent of the old literary allegory: the hirsute, bestial Id, the austere Super-Ego, even the togaed Censor. It is as if Freud, in his anxiety to outstrip fellow workers in the field, cast his net further into the darkness than they, but found that in doing so he had gone too far for any sort of empirical corroboration, and therefore fell back, for want of real material, on the old *metaphors*. The correspondence of the Freudian censor to the behaviour it is invoked to explain is in fact not causal but manifestly semantic; the image of the Censor, itself luminously clear, perfectly *expresses* the idea of restraint.

The latent area which Morgann found in Shakespeare is frequently psychological. It is a matter of 'motives not acknowledged'. We might have thought, therefore, that in Freud, rather than in the history of literary allegory, we should find a true analogue of Shakespeare. But it is not so. Freud's latent area proves more purely fictive (more 'literary'!) and less mimetic than Shakespeare's. Some may say that Freud's 'images', viewed as such, are richly informative. I would not agree. They seem seldom to function in a genuinely heuristic manner. In truth, Freud is the allegorist, Shakespeare the psychologist.

Lest this doctrine of inferential criticism be thought to smack too much of mere licence to write whatever comes into one's head, I would add that a sound literary criticism must be ready to point to the actual motifs, in the text of Shakespeare, which set inference and speculation in train, and provide a loose criterion of relevance. In part the sense of a penumbra of more or less convincing possibilities is created, or started, by Shakespeare's habit of variation (*variatio*). Where Racine successfully encapsulates each thought in a single magisterial phrase, Shakespeare seems instead to throw out varying expressions at a venture. The implication is that there is a reality other than the expressions, to which they more or less successfully approximate. King Lear says to Regan,

> I prithee, daughter, do not make me mad.
> I will not trouble thee, my child: farewell.
> We'll no more meet, no more see one another.
> But yet thou art my flesh, my blood, my daughter;
> Or rather a disease that's in my flesh,
> Which I must needs call mine: thou art a boil,
> A plague-sore, or embossed carbuncle
> In my corrupted blood.

> > (*King Lear*, II. iv. 217–24)

In this speech one is aware of a scattering effect in the language, but at the same time of a driving central impulse to compass a single end, which can be named (it is Regan) but not exhausted by description. In highly formal art the description and the 'object' are indistinguishable and formalist criticism seeks to extend this character to all literature. In real life, of course, we find incessantly that our descriptions fall short. A formalist confronted with a speech like this may try to hold the mind at the mere series of epithets, but their evident incompleteness, together with the familiarity of the experience of such incompleteness in daily life, renders this critical tabu utterly artificial. The dramatic form of the play provides (in Regan) a referent extrinsic to the forms of this individual speech, and the speech itself in its turn by its very incompleteness (which we begin to fill up from non-literary experience) endows Regan with inferential substance. The rising scale of 'my flesh, my blood' is successfully summed and explained with 'my daughter' but then that description is not enough for Regan, and the King veers sharply away into the language of diseased flesh. Even the comparatively trivial variation,

> We'll no more meet, no more see one another,

which would surely have Racine reaching for his blue pencil, begets in the mind a sense that *this* imagined encounter is something unique. Language can only map its position and rough dimensions. The thing itself is other.

But variation merely sets the mind working. Shakespeare then authorizes certain lines of inference by incorporating traits of character which are odd, yet not absolutely incompatible with the dominant explicit picture. If there is a danger that such a moment will look like mere authorial inadvertence he will often follow it up, a little later, with a second similar hint. Brutus in *Julius Caesar* is noble and scrupulous. But when he imagines the assassination of Caesar his language becomes heightened and exalted in a way which is not wholly comfortable:

> Let's be sacrificers, but not butchers, Caius . . .
> Let's kill him boldly but not wrathfully;
> Let's carve him as a dish fit for the gods.
>
> (II. i. 166–73)

The 'dominant' note of moral scrupulousness is struck: Brutus is recommending moderation. But after the manly simplicity of 'Let's kill him boldly', 'Let's carve him as a dish' is altogether less sympathetic; it is mildly troubling, slightly weird. One begins to wonder if there is after all a dark impulse to cruelty which is now pressing so hard upon his personality that this singular, oddly 'aesthetic' vision of carving another human being momentarily usurps his mind. The line is there and if it were the only such moment we would be justified in ignoring the fugitive and off-key impression it creates. But when the murder is done, Brutus's language is once more strange:

> Stoop, Romans, stoop,
> And let us bathe our hands in Caesar's blood
> Up to the elbows, and besmear our swords.
> Then walk we forth, even to the market-place,
> Let's all cry 'Peace, freedom and liberty!'
>
> (III. i. 106–11)

Brutus seems unconscious of the incongruity (and the power) of the picture he presents: men covered with blood shouting 'Peace!' Because of the earlier hint the mind now races: the image is stately, as if some ancient ritual were being described. Indeed a ritual is alluded to but it is here inverted in a nightmare manner. The ritual thing to do after a murder is to cleanse oneself of pollution, to wash away the blood with water. Brutus instead invites his fellow assassins to cover their arms in blood. It is as if his hypertrophied conscience, which tried to hold off from the horrific central fact of murder, has found its proper therapy in a wild ceremonial assertion that, in this most just of murders, the murder itself is an act of cleansing, the blood is not to be purged because it is itself a purgative; Pilate washed his hands (see *Richard II*, IV.i.239) but not thus. At the same time the ordinary horror of the blood makes

Brutus sound almost schizophrenic: logical, imaginative, yet unaware of reality and driven by it in ways he does not comprehend.

None of this psychologically coherent train of explanation could have been achieved if we had not allowed ourselves to think of Brutus as a human being, and supplemented the artfully broken text with extra-literary conjecture. The speeches in question, if they are assessed within the conventional 'field' of Elizabethan literature, must appear merely anomalous. The suggestion is tenable. But if the opposite approach repeatedly yields coherent results (and it does) the formalist is then obliged to account for that very phenomenon and can in effect do so only by conceding that the readers are being improperly rewarded for licentious extra-literary reference.

If, on the other hand, it is said that such criticism is very dubious, I would agree. I deliberately chose a point at which the indications shade off into uncertainty. One cannot dwell on these moments analytically without giving a spurious impression of definiteness and confidence. My present purpose is only to point out that Shakespeare himself provokes such speculations, but – in the theatre, at least – normally controls them through the 'dominant' motifs. Brutus, I have no doubt, remains a noble Roman. But I wonder about his repressed motives and I believe Shakespeare ensured that I should do just that. It is a common vice of would-be subversive criticism to expatiate on these evanescent yet obscurely exciting implications as if they were the whole picture and as if mere 'stock effects' were unimportant. Conservative scholars usually say that such critics 'over-read' their author, impose readings which are not present in the text. It would be nearer the truth to say that they 'under-read' him. The dark meanings are present, but they do not overthrow the rest. A full reading of Brutus must acknowledge his nobility.

Shakespeare, more perhaps than any other writer, creates a cloud of alternative or overdetermining explanations round his figures. One begins to sense that there are two ways of using the intelligence: to solve difficulties and to start them. Those who assume that intelligence is essentially concerned with solutions find themselves at a stand when they are asked to explain the intelligence of Shakespeare: no problems were solved by him. Kierkegaard was once sitting at a café table in the Frederiksberg Gardens when it forcibly occurred to him that the world was full of highly competent persons clearing up difficulties; obviously, there was a need for someone who could find fresh difficulties; this, he resolved, would be his role: to shed a little darkness on the world.[13] With Shakespeare 'darkness' must be a relative term; rather we are dazzled with excess of light. Our practical choices, our explanatory assumptions are indeed impeded by the superabundance of causes and motives. For Shakespeare chose a form of intellectual activity in which he was not obliged to observe the principle of parsimony in explanation. Ockham's razor, 'Entities are not to be multiplied beyond necessity', is vital in science and useful in everyday life, if one is hoping to avoid having to repeat one's actions, is looking for the most economic practical course. But in life we sometimes wish, in a more disinterested manner, to enlarge our sense of the possible variety of our fellow human beings, and this variety is in fact very great. It is proper – indeed, it is *intellectually* proper – that we should see other human beings as over-determined by an indefinite number of different kinds of cause, material, physical, economic, purposive, pathological, and should be further aware that each of these can be indefinitely subdivided. Shakespeare teaches us this truth. His works may thus be likened to Ockham's beard, golden, luxuriant, not yet subdued (happily) by the famous razor.

Conclusion

What is the new mimesis? It is not a programme for writers. Some readers may have come to this book expecting to hear the rallying cry, 'Show in your fiction the impossibility of ever showing things!' I have driven round this track a hundred times and I know its meagre extent. My word to the writers is, 'Try the world' (where 'try' covers 'attempt', 'test', 'provoke' and 'woo'). But I have no illusions about the power of criticism over art and would not wish things otherwise. Thus, with regard to artistic practice it might be claimed that 'the new mimesis' is neither more nor less than the old mimesis, were it not for the fact that artists always find new ways of imitating through form the indefinite richness of reality. The new mimesis is a new *theory*, and its essence is the reconciliation of form with veridical or probable representation. The artists indeed have seldom felt any difficulty in this alliance; rather it has been the ordinary medium of their activity. But theorists and readers most certainly have. It is part of my point that the theory presented here should be a mere unregarded truism with centuries of practising writers and mildly shocking to present theorists. Auerbach's magnificent conspectus in his *Mimesis* was governed by two organizing ideas, first that the presence of a marked style ('high style' or 'low style') was implicitly incompatible with 'serious realism', and second that the conception of reality itself underwent a fundamental change (transcendent in the middle ages, naturalistic in more recent times). Both these ideas, as Auerbach employs them, are reasonable. But they easily slide into a metaphysical form which is no longer innocent: the first can become the doctrine that the presence of style or form actually precludes reference to reality and the second can lead to the presumption that reality is itself a fluid social fiction.

Both of these propositions are rejected in this book. All representation of reality is conventionally ordered; it is never possible in a finite work to exhaust reality; always we receive a selection only; even a pronounced 'high style' may select and defer to realities; the sense that reality has been displaced by 'mere form' occurs when our *attention* is usurped by obtrusive (often repetitious) formal characters. Meanwhile, shifts in the conception of reality may be understood as involving actual error; the medievals for example may have been wrong in thinking – if they did – that reality is confined to the transcendent realm. That this suggestion now sounds coarsely philistine is an indication of the present state of our assumptions, yet serious philosophers continue to strive to get these things right, where 'right' is conceived as different from 'wrong'. When philosophers claim that absolute, universal Truth is unattainable they mean that it is *wrong* to claim such knowledge and *right* to disclaim it – so that 'wrongness' and 'rightness' remain at the centre of their discourse. But the very idea of rightness has now taken on the quality of 'scandal' (in Kierkegaard's quasi-scriptural use of the term). Otherwise and elsewhere the shifts in our conception of the real may be construed cognitively as variations in the area illuminated by a moving beam, as different answers naturally and properly elicited by different questions. Certainly the mere fact of change in the conception does not automatically show that the conception is autonomously fictive, free-floating. That would be a simpler world than the one in which we live.

Mimesis has long been considered merely in terms of its own changing modes. But mimesis is mimesis *of* something, or it is not mimesis. It exists in tense relation with that which is other than itself. I plead that a sense of that 'other' be reincorporated in our critical and theoretical activity.

What follows practically from this conception of mimesis? Four things: first a different way of reading topoi (major formulae repeated in the history of literature); second the licence to ask 'Is this true?' or 'Is this likely?' when reading fiction; third a renewed sense of the variety of reality; fourth a renewed sense of evidence. Let us take these one by one.

Great repeated formulae (if presented in a certain way by teachers) can easily come to be felt as formulae only. They are obviously liable to that usurpation of our attention by formal characters to which I referred a little earlier. In Homer's *Iliad* Glaucus says that the generations of men are as numerous as the leaves that strew the earth in autumn and grow again in spring (V. 146–8). In the *Odyssey*, when the hero comes to the misty, sunless limit of the world, the ghosts of the dead crowd round him, brides and unmarried youths, wretched old men and wounded warriors in their bloody armour (xi. 36–41). In Virgil's *Aeneid* the great host of the dead, mothers, men, heroes, boys and unmarried girls, in numbers like the leaves which fall at the first frost of autumn or the birds which gather at the onset of winter, stand on the banks of the river praying to be carried over (vi. 305–13). In Dante's *Inferno* the dead come on in such numbers that the poet can scarcely believe that so many people have died. They fling themselves into the river of death like leaves falling (iii. 55–6, 112–14). In Milton's *Paradise Lost* the legions of the fallen angels lie thick as the leaves which clog the brooks in Vallombrosa (i. 301–3). In Eliot's *The Waste Land* the crowd flowing over London Bridge is identified with the great multitude of the dead: 'So many,/I had not thought death had undone so many' (62–3).

This is one of the greatest topoi. We may notice that it is not inertly repetitious. Sometimes birds come in, sometimes not. In Milton the reference is not even to the human dead but to the fallen angels. This, like Shakespearean 'variation' projected upon a huge historical sequence, may suggest different attempts to get at something other than the expressions; the idea that the number of those who have left the light is both unimaginably vast and profoundly natural. But an exclusive concentration on either the formal continuities or the formal variations, though encouraged in academic teaching, anaesthetizes our reading. There is a kind of reader who, in encountering any instance of the topos, will think not only of all the other poets who have said this, but also of the thing they are saying: how many people must have died since the world began. Such readers allow their minds to be dazed for a moment by this multitude, as the eye is dazzled by the numbers of the leaves in a forest. But such readers, I suspect, are not as common as they used to be.

In citing the examples I deliberately avoided quotation, consciously committed the 'heresy of paraphrase' to enforce the idea of extrinsic reference. The pressure to quote became much stronger as I moved to examples in my own language and was finally irresistible in the case of Eliot. This is not simply because one's own language is more familiar and quotable. Eliot's lines are themselves formalist to a greater degree than any of the earlier examples. Indeed Eliot himself *quotes* (Dante) where the others *echo* the earlier versions (I do not know what Homer is echoing but I would wager that he is doing so). Yet even with Eliot the thought of the Terrible Dark Multitude persists, and it, together with Homer, Virgil, Dante and Milton, energizes the lines.

I have paid most attention in this book to especially assertive realism, to moments which, so to speak, surprise the mind with truth: the still, preoccupied figures of Vermeer, the richly overdetermined characters of Shakespeare. But these, though they are necessarily formulated by art, do not seem formal to most people. Topoi on the other hand are obviously formal and yet move us mimetically (or do so if the teachers will let them). In *Henry IV*, Part 1, the First Carrier says, 'Heigh-ho! an it be not four by the day, I'll be hanged; Charles' wain is over the new chimney' (II. i. 1–3). Here is a real shiver of Truth. One senses, across the intervening centuries the darkness, the inn yard without artificial illumination, the eyes straining upward, for a moment to pick out the known shape of the new chimney and the stars above it. This is what they must have done, in the cold time before the sun came up. And the passage is only minimally formal. Yet when I read these lines I remember another occasion which is not, at first, literary at all, a sweet-smelling summer night after the sun had set and some light remained, when I found myself thinking spontaneously, 'The shapes of the buildings and the covering of the paths have changed, but just *this* light, just *this* quality in the air may have been noticed, and breathed, a thousand years ago' – in other words, 'On such a night as this. . . .' *This* of course, is, a topos. But it came to me with all the sharpness of the intuition which Shakespeare's lines about the star over the chimney produce, and it came to me, at first, without a single attendant literary quotation. If someone had told me at that moment that in fact, because of twentieth-century pollutants, the air could not have been the same a thousand years ago, the observation, though unwelcome, would not seem a philistine irrelevance; on the contrary I would have been keenly interested.

To introduce this sort of anecdote into a literary discussion is now slightly offensive; it breaks a tabu; it is a vulgar intrusion of the personal. But having gone so far I will go a little further. When, a few years ago, a person I knew died, I was meditating how best to describe him in a written piece and found myself thinking that whenever he had talked I had never wished him to stop. This also, as it happens, is an ancient formula. I never wrote the piece but if I had it would have included this phrase. Even a mild formalist would then have concluded that the phrase was there only because its previous literary life had generated it afresh. But they would be wrong. It would have been there because it was true. The fact that such things are not usually concretely verifiable by the reader is not disabling. One may read on the assumption that truth is possible or on the assumption that truth is wholly irrelevant. The two ways of reading feel quite different.

My second consequence was the licence to ask of works of fiction, 'Is this true?' or 'Is this likely?' It may be thought that this is a licence no one needs, since we do it all the time anyway. In fact the practice has been reduced and, in a way, quite properly reduced, as a result of progress in our awareness of cultural history. The person who heavily observes that Chaucer's reliance on astrology is erroneous is rightly condemned for his ignorance of history. But it is perfectly proper, after one has recognized the area of cultural or conventional determination, to ask again, 'Is this true?' The current etiquette of literary discussion has made it harder than it used to be to dissent from, say, a coherent religious view presented by a figure from the past. Liberal humanists betray no trace of indignation as they explain the tenets of Calvinism; the history of ideas is flattened into a mere series of cultural phenomena. The great nineteenth-century edition of Pope by Elwin and Courthope[14] is rancorously unsympathetic to Pope's brand of deistic religion. Its commentary on *An Essay on Man* is full of abrupt, orthodox contempt, breaking out at times in indignant rebuke. Maynard Mack's Twickenham edition[15] on the other hand, is generously receptive to the cultural richness offered in the poem. Yet in the Victorian edition the poem seems live and in Mack's it seems like the contents of a museum, dead. 'The traditional view,' says Mack, and forthwith supplies corroborative references. The idea of agreeing or disagreeing, despite the fact that the *Essay on Man* is a didactic poem and 'much affirmeth', seems not to occur to him.

In a similar manner the criticism of Samuel Johnson, even where we dissent from it, is live and treats works as live. When he inveighed against the pastoral unreality of *Lycidas*,[16] Johnson had not failed to notice that the poem was written in the pastoral convention. He noticed it and disliked it. I suspect that if one attempted to tell him that his criticism was absurd since art has nothing to do with nature, one would be swiftly dismissed from his presence. If, on the other hand, one were to argue (mimetically) that pastoral is the genre which honestly imitates our dream values, acknowledging their unfoundedness even while it accurately catches their inner poignancy, he might listen. C.S. Lewis is rare among modern critics in being prepared to acknowledge the further step, always implied by mimesis. He quotes a sentence from Sidney about a lover kissing a footprint and notes that this may have happened in real life – and then adds, 'Many readers may ask whether the reality is not as foolish and tasteless as the fiction?'[17] F.R. Leavis, sometimes with a curiously naive disregard of conventional determinants, was similarly willing to ask, 'Is this true?' or (more frequently) 'Is this right?'

Of course poets play with meanings. But a *total* contempt for all the constraints imposed by truth is rare. Critics who ask, 'Is this true?' will occasionally notice and resent contradiction. They will be rebuked for this by ordinary formalists (*experto crede*) who will point out in their turn that *coincidentia oppositorum* has always been one of the chief pleasures of poetry. But as soon as one scrutinizes such *coincidentiae* with an eye to truth one discovers that they are almost invariably carefully guarded from lapsing into mere contradiction; a *formal* contradiction masks a material coherency. When Romeo says,

O heavy lightness! serious vanity!

$$(Romeo\ and\ Juliet,\ I.\ i.\ 176)$$

we do not suspend our objection to contradiction on the ground that this is poetry, and one sense is being played against the other. Rather, we intuit that he is talking about love, which is in one respect as light as air and in another is a source of sadness; this enables us to interpret and resolve the formal contradiction. The Aristotelian questions 'In what respect?' and 'In what sense?' will normally resolve a *coincidentia oppositorum*, and this resolution actually presupposes the third dimension of mimetic reference. It would be a foolish criticism which objected on grounds of substantive contradiction to such figures of rhetoric. But meanwhile genuine contradiction occasionally occurs. Pope says in one place that all are equally happy and in another that the good are happier than the rest (*Essay on Man*, ii. 238–74; iv. 310). This is not a *coincidentia oppositorum*.

My third 'consequence' was a renewed sense of the variety of reality. I would be unhappy if this book were to give the impression that literary realism was confined to precise visual description and psychological insight. In fact literature is remarkable for its responsiveness to the more fugitive aspects of the real; in particular to shifting *appearances* as distinct from more stable entities. A shifting appearance is part of the fabric of reality in so far as it actually occurs. We apply the word 'unreal' or 'illusory' to such moments in so far as they beget expectations which are subsequently disappointed. A wall seen by moonlight may look thick. The look is illusory in that the wall when inspected on other occasions proves to be thin. But the look was real in that the wall really did look thus. If we are willing to consider the unstable presentations of the world equally with the stable ones, we shall find that literature may be more frequently mimetic than we had supposed.

We are tolerably accustomed to acknowledging the mimetic force of lines like Tennyson's

> Wavers on her thin stem the snowdrop cold.[18]

But what of a line like

> Now lies the Earth all Danae to the stars.[19]

This is poetry at its fictive height, mythological, figurative, visionary. Danae in ancient legend was impregnated by Zeus who came to her in the form of a shower of gold. Tennyson applies the myth, in a context of sexual exaltation, to the earth, as if the earth were waiting to be ravished by the stars as Danae was ravished by the gold. In fact Danae was never so visited by Zeus, the earth is not ravished by the stars. No poetry could be further removed, it might be thought, from truth. But if we acknowledge the working of myth and metaphor and *then* ask, 'Do they communicate a truth?' the answer is less easy.

A traditional way to deal mimetically with this line would be to say that it described Tennyson's mind. I would suggest that it is a degree more public in its mimesis than that description suggests. It describes the way the earth can seem to a person in a heightened state of erotic awareness. That 'seeming' will be differently construed by different people: some will suggest that the atmosphere is merely imposed by the subject, others will be willing to see whether the earth may itself be such as to satisfy in certain ways expectations and perceptions so conditioned. The bias of poetry, with its continuous attention to phenomenal characters, is commonly to the second view. But we need not settle this question now. Tennyson's line is both richly metaphorical and profoundly if intractably empirical. It is drenched with feeling which it does not merely betray but also powerfully represents.

Today it is a favourite pastime of critics to expose the conventions operating in the most pellucidly realistic writing. If only to keep a proper balance it is useful occasionally to register the mimesis which is observed in ostentatiously formal or flippant writing. The very ostentation of pattern can be made to serve a mimetic end. Let us take Johnson's 'A short song of congratulation':

> Long-expected one-and-twenty
> Ling'ring year, at last is flown,
> Pomp and Pleasure, Pride and Plenty,
> Great Sir John, are all your own.
>
> Loosen'd from the Minor's tether,
> Free to mortgage or to sell,
> Wild as wind, and light as feather

Bid the slaves of thrift farewel.

Call the Bettys, Kates and Jennys
Ev'ry name that laughs at Care,
Lavish of your Grandsire's guineas,
Show the Spirit of an heir.

All that prey on vice and folly
Joy to see their quarry fly,
Here the Gamester light and jolly,
There the Lender grave and sly.

Wealth, Sir John, was made to wander,
Let it wander as it will;
See the Jocky, see the Pander,
Bid them come, and take their fill.

When the bonny Blade carouses,
Pockets full, and Spirits high,
What are acres? What are houses?
Only dirt, or wet or dry.

If the Guardian or the Mother
Tell the woes of wilful waste,
Scorn their counsel and their pother,
You can hang or drown at last.[20]

At one level the jingling verses (like the movement of one of the songs from *The Beggar's Opera*) reflect the rattling life of the man described; at another they create a formal smokescreen so that the strain of Tory moralism can assume the advantage of surprise. Here it might be said that the first level is mimetic but the second wholly formal. Yet even that is dubious, since there is a sense in which Johnson's poem mimics a stratagem of parodic scorn often employed in real life. Meanwhile the implication of the poem, that inheritance imposes responsibility, is not merely played with but is, as near as may be, objectively proposed by Johnson. His poem is formally flippant, but the flippancy and the formalism are part of a complex mimetic point.

The twentieth century has found many new ways of being formally playful. As an analogue-with-a-difference to Johnson's poem we may consider E.E. Cummings's 'Anyone lived in a pretty how town':

anyone lived in a pretty how town
(with up so floating many bells down)
spring summer autumn winter

he sang his didn't he danced his did.

Women and men (both little and small)
cared for anyone not at all
they sowed their isn't they reaped their same
sun moon stars rain

children guessed (but only a few
and down they forgot as up they grew
autumn winter spring summer)
that noone loved him more by more

when by now and tree by leaf
she laughed his joy she cried his grief
bird by now and stir by still
anyone's any was all to her

someones married their everyones
laughed their cryings and did their dance
(sleep wake hope and then) they
said their nevers they slept their dream

stars rain sun moon
(and only the snow can begin to explain
how children are apt to forget to remember
with up so floating many bells down)

one day anyone died i guess
(and noone stooped to kiss his face)
busy folk buried them side by side
little by little and was by was

all by all and deep by deep
and more by more they dream their sleep
noone and anyone earth by april
wish by spirit and if by yes.

Women and men (both dong and ding)
summer autumn winter spring
reaped their sowing and went their came
sun moon stars rain[21]

Here the nursery jingle is strongly felt as pattern and musical sequence
but at the same time elicits certain characteristics of the world. At the
simplest level the poem echoes the sound of bells. In the line, 'with up
so floating many bells down', the word 'floating', with its unvoiced
initial consonant, its long first syllable and its sense, suggesting suspen-

sion, momentarily impedes the line, just as the sound of bells is momentarily impeded between buildings as one passes within earshot. Bells themselves, we realize when we have read the poem, with their submusical courses loosely echo the ramshackle cycle of birth, life, marriage and death. At the same time various childlike simplicities are evoked: 'pretty' in the second line is a deliberately undeveloped word; at the same time the clattering impetus of the metre is allowed to subvert normal word order, producing a pleasing inconsequence. As a result the town is for a moment like a town of dolls' houses. Real American towns (here I lean a little harder on the mimetic hypothesis) can often look thus.

As the poem goes on we may watch the backward drive to childhood modes and objects of perception producing undifferentiated primitive conceptions: 'was by was'. Yet a simple stand of echoic realism enforces the meaning:

> when by now and tree by leaf

is partly made of possible human utterances, ' "When?" by "now!" ', but the harsh differentiation of punctuation is banished by the poet, in obedience to an intuition of primal simplicity. When near the end he slows down the motion of the line,

> all by all and deep by deep,

he imitates the repose of death.

It may be said that 'evocation' and 'echoing' are not true mimesis and should not be confused with realistic representation. I have no quarrel with anyone who wishes to define these terms thus narrowly. In this book 'mimesis' is used very generally to connote any deliberate relation to the real, as opposed to epiphenomenal or 'betrayed' relation. It is enough for my purpose if it be granted that neither Johnson nor Cummings merely suspends reference and plays with empty categories.

If we fully admit the mimetic dimension, literary criticism becomes harder. We are transformed from cartographers to explorers, exposed to dangers, difficulties and even actual pains unknown to the formalist. As an example of problematic mimesis I offer a single phrase from Wordsworth's description of skating in his childhood: 'To cut across the reflex of a star.'[22] The problem here is to determine the mode and proper reference of the mimesis. Wordsworth in *The Prelude* establishes a practice of vivid recollection, where specific accuracy is implicitly claimed. But is it possible, on however clear a night, to see in ice the reflection of something as faint as a star? Furthermore, one could not skate *across* such a reflection because it would retreat before one as one moved. I became aware, as I entertained these doubts, that in the time of Francis Galton, and still more in the time of Gilbert White, it would have seemed wholly natural to investigate the phenomenon. Accordingly, not without a certain self-consciousness at the picturesque nature of what I was doing, I wrote to a friend in Canada, to ask his views. He told me that one can see a star reflected in ice, but was less clear on the possibility of skating across the reflection. Another friend (a physicist) suggested that it could be done only by flinging out a leg while at the same time holding the head steady in something approximating to its initial position. The tentative conclusion I draw from this is that Wordsworth was referring to a real reflection of a star but never performed the gymnastic feat described by my scientific friend; that his poetry is not minutely descriptive of stable facts (like Crabbe's for example) but is infiltrated by an impulse to catch the moment as it was felt by the skater. Wordsworth saw the reflection and instantly sped across the spot on the ice where he had seen it. The factual inaccuracy with which he telescopes this as skating *across the reflection itself* conveys with brilliant accuracy the speed of the original experience, in which the motion is performed almost before the percept has faded from the retina. When Wordsworth revised this passage for the 1850 version, he tamed the image by inserting a line to explain how in fact the star fled before him. One suspects that the later version, though physically correct, is the product of reflection, while the earlier version was the purer product of memory.

Literature, in that it reveres appearances equally with stable presentations, preserves a notably egalitarian conception of reality. In doing so it composes an immense implicit critique of all those movements of reductionism, from seventeenth-century mechanism to twentieth-century positivism which have dogged philosophy. In like manner (*pace* Auerbach) Chaucer in the middle ages implicitly contested the transcendentalist conception of reality then in the ascendant. I do not mean by this that he undermined religion, only that he implicitly opposed any *confinement* of reality to a transcendent plane.

My fourth 'consequence' was a renewed sense of evidence. With this I return to the metaphysical concerns of my opening chapters, but at the same time there is an immediate and practical implication for schools and universities. The resolution of substance into form, fact into convention, is absorbed by students in a fundamentally uncritical manner. At one time there was much talk of 'naive realism'. We are in danger of producing from our universities a generation of naive relativists. 'Everything is subjective' is a frequent catchphrase and passes for wisdom. The retort, 'Was *that* a merely subjective observation?' is either brushed aside as mere logic-chopping or else has the unintended effect of plunging the first speaker into a yet deeper abyss of gloomy (yet still pleasurable) scepticism. The attempt to differentiate true and false, probable and improbable, used sometimes to seem pompous because it was in any case so obvious, so fundamental. Now, it is often construed, weirdly, as an extension of fascist authoritarianism, as if to prefer true statements to false ones were like preferring white people to black people or Gentiles to Jews. To the ordinary reader some of the more extreme anxieties of this book must appear almost paranoid, and it will be thought that I attack positions which no one could possibly hold. There is real force in this view. There is a sense in which no one can *really* be a consistent radical formalist and survive as a human being. But even half-beliefs can have consequences. In the case of formalism, the consequence is a sense that, since all human 'demonstration' is really a sort of cultural rationalization, one's own incentive to *demonstrate* truths is diminished or destroyed. It is a primary contention of this book that any such inference is unfounded. This book is logically conservative, but I have tried to explain that without such conservatism socialism itself is baseless. I reject the passive epistemology of Locke. I delight in *particular* demonstrations of cultural determination. I am sure that a projective faculty operates in all learning. But I adhere, in a way which is now unfashionable, to the corrective status of the object.

Our literary culture is at present much more alive, much more active than it was twenty years ago. But there is in this activity something febrile. The very energy, as it accelerates, exhibits more and more the character of a malaise. The ordinary appetite for truth is replaced by a competitive cynicism, which stimulates but does not feed the mind. If we wish to produce by education people who are intellectually just, truth-loving, responsive to evidence and curious, now is the time to pause and take stock.

Literature can represent reality, but it can also invent, cheat, play, enchant. These, however, are not mere unconnected parallels. Text is texture. Representing, inventing, cheating, playing, enchanting are variously and unpredictably interwoven. They all, always, involve meaning, and meaning is never wholly private to the individual, never radically independent of the public world. It is true that, if we could not form images in advance of experience, we could not interrogate reality and so establish true and probable utterance. But such pre-empirical imagining is also preliterary. Language grows when certain schemes prove operable in relation to the real. Literature, even that most thoroughly liberated from the constraints of realism, differs from visual art in that it lives in language, and the meanings with which it *plays* must first have *worked*, or they would not be meanings. Sometimes, indeed, literature composes new, radically interrogative schemata which elicit new elements from reality, extend our perceptions, and this is mimesis working with its greatest (heuristic) power. But such moments are rare. What we usually find is either 'dominant mimesis', where representation is the aesthetic end or purpose of the work, or else, still more commonly, 'instrumental mimesis', where meanings are organized in the service of ends which may be indefinitely (and gloriously) extravagant. This book is not a plea for the superiority of realistic fiction; it is rather a plea that no form of literature be regarded as wholly insulated from this varying world. Hesiod said that the Muses were the daughters of Memory. But the better genealogy is that attributed to Alcman by Diodorus, the Sicilian: the Muses, in his account, were the daughters of Earth.[23]

Notes

Chapter 1 Shaking the concepts

1 This and all subsequent quotations from Shakespeare are taken from *William Shakespeare: The Complete Works*, ed. Peter Alexander, London, 1951.

2 *Leviathan*, i. 5, in *The English Works of Thomas Hobbes*, ed. Sir William Molesworth, London, 1839–45, vol. 3, p. 37.

3 See the facsimile edn of J.I. Cope and H.W. Jones, St Louis, 1959, pp. 40, 62, 112–13.

4 *Some Thoughts concerning Education*, pp. 7, 124, in *The Educational Writings of John Locke*, ed. J.L. Axtell, Cambridge, 1968, pp. 117–18, 283–4.

5 *Dell antichissima sapienza italica*, i. 2, in *Opere*, ed. Fausto Nicolini, Milan, 1953, p. 248.

6 *Gulliver's Travels*, Pt 3, 'A voyage to Laputa', ch. 5, in the edn by Angus Ross, London, 1972, p. 169.

7 Published in 1960 (London, 2nd edn 1962) but delivered four years before in Washington, DC, as the A.W. Mellon lectures.

8 *Prolegomena to a Theory of Language*, trans. F.J. Whitfield, Madison, 1969, p. 9.

9 *The Times Literary Supplement*, 28 Sept. 1967, pp. 897–8.

10 In *Critique et Vérité*, Paris, 1966.

11 See Jonathan Culler, *Structuralist Poetics: Structuralism, Linguistics and*

the *Study of Literature*, London, 1975, p. 29.

12 First published 1942; in the edn of 1960 (London), p. 1.

13 'Tradition and the individual talent', *Selected Essays*, London, 1951, p. 15.

14 *Knowledge and Experience in the Philosophy of F.H. Bradley*, London, 1964, p. 82.

15 ibid., p. 202.

16 Ed. J. Dover Wilson, Cambridge, 1960, p. 154.

17 See e.g. Terence Hawkes, *Structuralism and Semiotics*, Berkeley, California, 1977, p. 17.

18 Vico, *Dell antichissima sapienza italica*, i. 2, in *Opere*, p. 248.

19 Claude Lévi-Strauss, *La Pensée sauvage*, Paris, 1962, p. 326; in the English translation, *The Savage Mind*, London, 1972, p. 247.

20 See e.g. Harold Bloom and others, *Deconstruction and Criticism*, London, 1979, p. vii.

21 Tzvetan Todorov, *Communications*, 11 (Paris, 1968), p. 3.

22 *La nuova scienza*, 376, in *Opere*, p. 503; in the English translation by T.G. Bergin and M.H. Fisch, *The New Science*, New York, 1948, p. 105.

23 See Isaiah Berlin, 'A note on Vico's concept of knowledge', in *Giambattista Vico: An International Symposium*, ed. G. Tagliacozzo and H.V. White, Baltimore, 1969, pp. 371–8.

24 *La nuova scienza*, 331, in *Opere*, p. 479, in Bergin and Fisch, p. 85.

25 ibid., 367, in *Opere*, p. 497, in Bergin and Fisch, p. 100.

26 'Vico and pragmatism', in *Giambattista Vico: An International Symposium*, pp. 401–24, esp. p. 414.

27 New York, 1957, pp. 425–9.

28 In *Language*, 35 (1959), pp. 26–58; see esp. p. 35.

29 *Structuralist Poetics*, p.140.

30 *Structuralism and Semiotics*, p. 17.

31 Op. cit., 1962, p. 227.

32 See his 'Phenomenal regression to the real object, I', 'Phenomenal regression to the real object, II' and 'Individual differences in phenomenal regression', in *British Journal of Psychology*, 21 (1931), pp. 339–59, 22 (1931), pp. 1–30, and 22 (1932), pp. 216–41, respectively.

33 Thouless seems not to have noticed that, strictly speaking, the perspectival shape is not a regular ellipse, but an ellipse slightly flattened on the side which is further away. The modification is so slight that it can hardly affect his findings.

34 'Phenomenal regression to the real object, II', p. 28.

35 See his *Perception: A Representative Theory*, Cambridge, 1977.

36 *Art and Illusion*, p. 255.

37 London, 1978.

38 *Soliloquies*, II. x, in *Patrologia latina*, ed. J.-P. Migne, Paris, 1845, vol. 32, column 893.

39 Op. cit., p. 247.

40 ibid., p. 246, and J.-P. Sartre, *Critique de la raison dialectique*, Paris, 1960,

p. 183. (My translation.)

41 *The Savage Mind*, p. 247.

42 ibid., p. 137, n.

43 *Cours de linguistique générale*, reconstructed from students' notes by Charles Bally and Albert Sechehaye, ed. Tullio de Mauro, Paris, 1972, p. 166. (My translation.)

44 *Was ist Metaphysik?*, Bonn, 1929, p. 19. (My translation.)

45 Letter to Edward Garnett, 5 June 1914, in *The Collected Letters of D.H. Lawrence*, ed. Harry T. Moore, London, 1962, p. 282.

46 *Civilisation and its Discontents*, trans. Joan Rivière, revised by James Strachey, London, 1963, p. 27, n.

47 Edited with a preface by Geoffrey Hartman, London—Baltimore, 1978.

48 ibid., p. 58.

49 ibid., p. 10.

50 ibid., p. 2.

51 ibid., pp. 11–12.

52 A.E. Housman, 'The name and nature of Poetry', in *Selected Prose*, ed. John Carter, Cambridge, 1961, p. 187.

53 Archibald MacLeish, 'Ars poetica', in *New and Collected Poems, 1917–76*, Boston, 1976, p. 107.

54 New Haven—London, 1980, p. 207.

55 *Psychoanalysis and the Question of the Text*, p. 55.

56 In *Parodies: An Anthology from Chaucer to Beerbohm - and After*, ed. Dwight Macdonald, New York, 1966, pp. 394–404.

57 See R. Coward and J. Ellis, *Language and Materialism*, London, 1977, p. 101.

58 *A Treatise of Human Nature*, Oxford, 1888, I. iv. 6, pp. 252–3.

59 See esp. his *Speech and Phenomenon*, trans. D.B. Allison and N. Garver, Evanston, Baltimore, 1973, pp. 4–5.

60 *L'Écriture et la différence*, Paris, 1967, p. 22; in the translation by Alan Bass, 1978, p. 11.

61 *La Prose du monde*, Paris, 1969, p. 20; in the translation by John O'Neill, *The Prose of the World*, London, 1974, p. 13.

62 'Il n'y a pas de hors-texte', *De la grammatologie*, Paris, 1967, p. 227; in the English translation by G.C. Spivak, *Of Grammatology*, Baltimore, 1976, p. 158.

63 Glasgow, 1976, pp. 23–4.

64 *Cours de linguistique générale*, p. 166.

65 ibid., p. 166.

66 ibid., p. 162.

67 *Novum Organum*, I. li, in *The Philosophical Works of Francis Bacon*, ed. J.M. Robertson, London, 1905, p. 267.

68 Jacques Lacan, *Ecrits*, trans. A. Sheridan, New York, 1977, p. 65.

69 *Cours de linguistique générale*, p. 169.

70 *De la grammatologie*, p. 16, in Spivak's translation, *On Grammatology*, p. 7.

71 *De la grammatologie*, p. 21, in *On Grammatology*, p. 10.
72 'Living on', trans. James Hubbert, in Harold Bloom and others, *Deconstruction and Criticism*, 1979, p. 81.
73 ibid., p. 84.
74 Diogenes Laertius, *Lives of the Eminent Philosophers*, ix. 61; in the Loeb edition, trans. R.D. Hicks, London, 1925, vol. 2, p. 474.
75 ibid., ix. 89; vol. 2, pp. 500-1.
76 ibid., ix. 88; vol. 2, p. 500.
77 *Treatise*, I. iv. 7, pp. 268-9.
78 See e.g. Viktor Shklovsky's essay on *Tristram Shandy* in L.T. Lemon and M.J. Reis (ed. and trans.), *Russian Formalist Criticism: Four Essays*, Lincoln, Nebraska, 1965, pp. 25-57.
79 *Being and Nothingness*, trans. H.E. Barnes, London, 1957, pp. 98f.
80 'An introduction to Derrida', *Radical Philosophy*, II (Spring 1979), pp. 18-28.
81 *De la grammatologie*, p. 234, in *On Grammatology*, p. 164.
82 *Deconstruction: Theory and Practice*, London, 1982, pp. 126-7.
83 ibid., p. 128.
84 Searle's criticisms appeared in his 'Reiterating the differences: a reply to Derrida', *Glyph*, 1 (1977), pp. 198-208. Derrida responded in his 'Limited Inc. abc . . .', *Glyph*, 2 (1977), pp. 162-254.
85 In *P.N. Review*, 6 (1979), pp. 38-40.
86 *Deconstruction and Criticism*, pp. vii-viii.
87 'The name and nature of poetry', pp. 192-3.
88 *Nausea*, trans. Robert Baldick, Harmondsworth, 1965, pp. 180, 182f.
89 ibid., p. 188.
90 In his essay, 'Differance', in *Speech and Phenomena, and Other Essays on Husserl's Theory of Signs*, trans. D.B. Allison, Evanston, 1973, p. 130.
91 See M.H. Abrams, 'Rationality and imagination in cultural history', *Critical Inquiry*, 2 (Spring 1976), pp. 447-64.
92 *Le Plaisir du texte*, Paris, 1973, p. 53.
93 Louis Althusser, *Lenin and Philosophy and Other Essays*, trans. B. Brewster, New York, 1971, p. 164.
94 In Barry Hindess and Paul Hirst, *Mode of Production and Social Formation*, London, 1975, esp. pp. 313-20.
95 From *Culture, Language and Personality: Selected Essays*, ed. D.G. Mandelbaum, Berkeley, 1949, p. 69.
96 *Structuralism and Semiotics*, p. 31.
97 Baltimore, 1978.
98 Catherine Belsey, *Critical Practice*, London, 1980, p. 36.
99 *Three Dialogues*, iii, in *The Works of George Berkeley, Bishop of Cloyne*, ed. A.A. Luce and T.E. Jessup, vol. 2, London, 1949, p. 244.
100 *Treatise*, I. ii. 6, pp. 67-8.
101 On linguistic idealism, see Roger Trigg, *Reality at Risk: A Defence of Realism in Philosophy and the Sciences*, Brighton, 1980, p. 56.
102 'Universals: Bamborough on Wittgenstein', *Proceedings of the*

Aristotelian Society, 79 (1978-9), p. 52.

103 *Collected Papers*, Cambridge, Mass., 1931-58, 8. 12. Peirce later modified this optimistic view; see ibid., 5. 494.

104 See his *From a Logical Point of View*, Cambridge, Mass., 1953, p. 44. On the intersubjectivism of Peirce and Quine, see Trigg, *Reality at Risk*, pp. 13-14, 71-4.

105 *Conceptual Idealism*, Oxford, 1973, p. 171.

106 *Reality at Risk*, p. 111.

107 *Treatise*, I. iii. 6, p. 86.

Chapter 2   The dissolution of mimesis

1 Roman Jackobson, 'On realism in art', trans. Karol Magassey, *Readings in Russian Poetics*, ed. Ladislev Matejka and Krystyna Pomorska, Ann Arbor, Michigan, 1978, p. 39.

2 ibid., p. 42.

3 ibid., pp. 38, 39, 41.

4 *Communications*, 11 (Paris, 1968), p. 2.

5 ibid., p. 3.

6 ibid., p. 2.

7 ibid., p. 3 (my translation).

8 ibid., pp. 84-9.

9 For Archilochus, see *The Oxford Book of Greek Verse*, ed. C.M. Bowra and others, London, 1930, no. 103, and *Lyra Graeca*, ed. E. Diehl, 1, Leipzig, 1949, p. 211, no. 2. For imitations, see e.g. Alcaeus, quoted in Herodotus, *History* v. 95, ed. C. Hude, Oxford, 1927, vol. ii; Anacreon, 381b, in *Poetae Melici Graeci*, ed. D.L. Page, Oxford, 1962; Horace, *Odes*, II. vii. 10, ed. E.C. Wickham, revised H.W. Garrod, Oxford, 1901.

10 *Astrophel and Stella*, 1, in *Selected Poems*, ed. Katherine Duncan-Jones, Oxford, 1973, p. 117.

11 *La Poëtique*, Paris, 1640, p. 137.

12 Ed. G. Watson, London, 1962, vol. 1, p. 35.

13 Op. cit.

14 London, 1683.

15 The translations from the 1683 text (which lacks page numbers) are my own. This passage may be found in the slightly misleading translation by J.V. Cunningham, *An Essay of True and Apparent Beauty* (Augustan Reprint Society), Los Angeles, California, 1950, p. 12.

16 *La Logique, ou l'art de penser*, III. xx, b. 2, ed. P. Clair and F. Girbal, Paris, 1965, p. 278. The work was first published in 1662 but Clair and Girbal base their edn on that of 1683.

17 Cunningham's (slightly different) translation is (again) on p. 12.

18 *Novum organum*, I. lxxvii, in *The Philosophical Works of Francis Bacon*, ed. J.M. Robertson, London, 1905, p. 278.

19 *De Veritate*, ed. M.H. Carré, Bristol, 1937, p. 77.

20 For example, Seneca, *Epistles*, xc. 16; xciv. 8; xcvii. 12; cxxii. 19, in *Seneca's Moral Epistles*, ed. with an English translation by

R.M. Gummere, London, 1961–2, vol. 2, p. 404, vol. 3, pp. 16, 366, 422; Seneca, *De Vita Beata*, iii, viii, in *Moral Essays*, ed. with an English translation by J.W. Basore, London, 1958, vol. 2, pp. 106, 120; Cicero, De Officiis, I. xxviii, in the edn with an English translation by Walker Miller, London, 1956, p. 102; Quintilian, *Institutio Oratoria*, VIII. iii. 71, in the edn with an English translation by H.E. Butler, London, 1963, vol. 3, p. 250.

21 *De Arte Poetica*, ii. 455–6, in Charles Batteaux, *Les Quatre Poétiques d'Aristote, d'Horace, de Vida, de Despréaux*, Paris, 1771, vol. 2, p. 122.

22 *Essais*, ii. 12, in the edn of Pierre Villey, Paris, 1965, p. 526.

23 *De la sagesse*, II. iii. 7, in the edn of M. Amaury Duval, Paris, 1820–4. vol. 2, p. 86.

24 Introduction to his collection, *Critical Essays of the Seventeenth Century*, 1908, Oxford, vol. 1, p. xxxii.

25 See Brian Vickers, ed., *Shakespeare: The Critical Heritage*, London, 6 vols (1974–81), vol. 5 (1979), p. 214.

26 'La vérité est presque toujours défectueuse, par le mélange des conditions singulières qui la compose', *Réflexions sur la poétique*, 24; ed. E.T. Dubois, Geneva, 1970, p. 41.

27 ibid., p. 39.

28 *L'Art poétique*, iii. 48, in Nicolas Boileaux-Despréaux, *Épîtres, art poétique, lutrin*, ed. C.H. Boudhors, Paris, 1939, p. 97.

29 Quoted by Gérard Genette in *Communications*, 11, p. 7.

30 See his *The Allegory of Love*, New York, 1958, p. 7.

31 In Vickers, ed., *Shakespeare: The Critical Heritage*, vol. 4 (1976), pp. 93–4.

32 I quote from the text in *Harrison's British Classics*, vol. 8, 1787, pp. 35–6. Armstrong published the first volume of *Sketches* in 1770 and then, in the same year, reprinted it with an additional volume in his *Miscellanies*.

33 In the edn of 1777, p. 80.

34 Op. cit., p. 91.

35 In the Yale Edition of *The Works of Samuel Johnson*, ed. A. Sherbo, New Haven, 1958– , vol. 7, p. 62.

36 See Sidney, *Defence of Poesie*, in *The Prose Works*, ed. Feuillerat, Cambridge, 1912–26, vol. 3, esp. p. 8, and David Daiches, *Critical Approaches to Literature*, London, 1956, p. 65.

37 *Dissertation sur la tragédie ancienne et moderne* (1748), in *Voltaire on Shakespeare*, ed. Theodore Besterman, Geneva, 1960, p. 57.

38 *Works*, vol. 7, p. 11.

39 In the facsimile reprint in the series, *Eighteenth Century Shakespeare*, ed. A. Freeman, no. 6, London, 1971, p. 12.

40 ibid., p. 11.

41 *La Dramaturgie classique en France*, Paris, 1950, p. 372.

42 'Essay on the art, rise and progress of the stage, in Greece, Rome and England', prefaced to vol. 9 of *The Works of William Shakespeare*, London, 1714, pp. vi–vii.

43 London, 1718, vol. 1, p. 94.

44 *The Poems of Alexander Pope*, ed. John Butt, London, 1963 (rev. 1968), p. 148.

45 *Art and Illusion*, London, 1962, p. 63.

46 See H.H Arnason, *A History of Modern Art*, Englewood Cliffs, New Jersey, 1977, p. 50.

47 W.H. Auden, *Collected Poems*, ed. E. Mendelson, London, 1976, pp. 470–1.

48 First published in 1933, reprinted in a modified form in his *Explorations*, London, 1946, pp. 1–39. Knights later changed his mind very considerably; see his 'The question of character in Shakespeare', first published in J. Garrett, ed., *More Talking of Shakespeare*, 1959, pp. 55–69.

49 Herbert Read, *Art Now* (first published 1933), London, 1960, pp. 62–3.

50 Walter Pater, *The Renaissance*, London, 1961, pp. 122–3.

51 J.A. Symonds, *The Life of Michelangelo Buonarotti*, London, 1893, vol. 2, p. 32.

52 Clive Bell, *Art*, 3rd edn, London, 1916, p. 8.

53 Evelyn Waugh, *Brideshead Revisited*, London, 1958, p. 28. Bell concedes the representation of volume on p. 27 of *Art*. His remark about butterflies and cathedrals is on pp. 12–13.

54 See Ernst Cassirer, *The Philosophy of Symbolic Forms*, trans. Ralph Mannheim, New Haven, 1953–7, vol. 2, p. 42.

55 *The Dialogues of Plato*, trans. B. Jowett, Oxford, 1875, vol. 3, p. 491.

56 *The Room, Manchester Street*, reproduced in the Whitechapel Art Gallery catalogue, *David Hockney: Paintings, Prints and Drawings. 1960–1970*, London, 1970, p. 68.

57 Laurence Gowing, *Vermeer*, New York, 1953, pp. 19–20, 23; Charles Seymour, 'Dark Chamber and light-filled room: Vermeer and the camera obscura', *Art Bulletin*, 46 (1964), pp. 323–31; Daniel A. Fink, 'Vermeer's use of the camera obscura', *Art Bulletin*, 53 (1971), pp. 493–505.

58 See Patrick Daniels, *Early Photography*, London, 1978, p. 74.

59 London, 1963, plates 18 and 19.

60 *War and Peace*, VIII. ix, in the translation by Louise and Aylmer Maude, Oxford, 1942, p. 615.

61 This happens in Terence Hawkes, *Structuralism and Semiotics*, Berkeley, California, 1977, p. 63.

62 *Communications*, 11, pp. 84–9; see above pp. 55–8.

Chapter 3 Shakespeare's imitation of the world

1 But not uncritically. See his review of Stoll's *Art and Artifice in Shakespeare*, in *Scrutiny*, 3 (1934–5), pp. 85–9.

2 In *How Many Children had Lady Macbeth?*, Cambridge, 1933, p. 21, n. The observation does not appear in the version printed in Knights's *Explorations*, London, 1946.

3 All references to Shakespeare are to *William Shakespeare: The Complete Works*, ed. Peter Alexander, London, 1951.

4 *A Preface to Paradise Lost*, London, 1960, pp. 62–3
5 *Eighteenth Century Essays on Shakespeare*, ed. D. Nichol Smith, 2nd edn, Oxford, 1963, p. 49.
6 J.B. Leishman, *Translating Horace*, Oxford, 1956, p. 28.
7 In *Seneca's Moral Essays*, ed. with an English translation by J.W. Basore, London, 1958, vol. ii, p. 348.
8 ibid., vol. ii, pp. 456, 458.
9 Berkeley, California, 1951.
10 See e.g. Ruth Benedict, *The Chrysanthemum and the Sword: Patterns in Japanese Culture*, Boston, 1946.
11 *Somnium Scipionis*, iii. 2, in *Ambrosii Theodosii Macrobii Commentarii in Somnium Scipionis*, ed. J. Willis, Leipzig, 1970, p. 157.
12 See *The Open Society and its Enemies*, 5th edn, London, 1966, vol. 1, p. 123, and *Conjectures and Refutations*, 4th edn, London, 1972, p. 351. Cf. Plato, *Republic*, 565C-D.
13 'Brutus and the death of Portia', *Shakespeare Quarterly*, 10 (1959), pp. 211–17.
14 '*Julius Caesar* in revision', *Shakespeare Quarterly*, 13 (1962), pp. 187–205.
15 Reprinted in *Horizon*, 15 (1947), pp. 77–90.
16 Pico della Mirandola, *De hominis dignitate, Heptaplus, De ente et uno*, ed. Eugenio Garin, Florence, 1942, pp. 104–6.
17 See e.g. Hermes Trismegistus, *Corpus Hermeticum*, ed. A.D. Nock, trans. A.-J. Festugière, Paris, 1960, vol. 2, pp. 301–2.
18 *The Elizabethan World Picture*, Harmondsworth, 1963.
19 'Letter to a Lord' (possibly the Earl of Dorset, probably 1624), in Edmund Gosse, *Life and Letters of John Donne*, London, 1899, vol. 2, p. 208.
20 *The Poems of John Donne*, ed. H.J.C. Grierson, Oxford, 1912, vol. 1, p. 44.
21 Oxford, 1960.
22 See esp. Roger Ascham, *The Scholemaster*, Bk 1, in his *The English Works*, ed. W.A. Wright, Cambridge, 1904, p. 234.
23 See e.g. J.D. Rea's note in *Philological Quarterly* (1929), pp. 311–13.
24 Shakespeare, *The Merchant of Venice*, London, 1964, p. 7.
25 See p. 235 of his essay 'Brothers and others', in his *The Dyer's Hand*, London, 1963, pp. 218–37.
26 See *The Listener*, 89 (18 Jan. 1973), pp. 79–82.
27 *Shakespeare: The Merchant of Venice*, London, 1964, p. 32.
28 *Seven Types of Ambiguity*, 2nd edn, New York, 1961, p. 44.
29 *Selected Essays*, London, 1951, pp. 126–40.
30 *The Common Pursuit*, Harmondsworth, 1962, pp. 136–59.
31 *Proceedings of the British Academy*, 41 (1955), pp. 189–205. All three essays, Eliot's, Leavis's and Gardner's, are printed in *Shakespeare: Othello: A Casebook*, ed. John Wain, London, 1971.
32 *Thomas Heywood et le drame domestique élizabéthain*, Paris, 1957, pp. 24–5.

33 See *The Rape of Lucrece*, in *The Dramatic Works of Thomas Heywood*, London, 1874, vol. 5, p. 175, and Heywood's *The Captives*, 1312–15, in the Malone Society Reprint, London, 1953, p. 53. See also Grivelet, *Thomas Heywood*, pp. 120–1.

34 In *An Apology for Actors*, B41, cited in Grivelet, *Thomas Heywood*, p. 341.

35 In *The Dramatic Works of Sir William Davenant*, ed. J. Maidment and W.H. Logan, London, 1872–4, vol. 4, p. 85.

36 Cited in Grivelet, *Thomas Heywood*, p. 212.

37 The Scolar Press facsimile, London, 1970, p. 89 of the edn of 1693.

38 *Shakespearean Tragedy*, London, 1957, p. 142.

39 *All's Well that Ends Well*, II. iii. 284–5.

40 See the New Arden edition of *Othello* by M.R. Ridley, London, 1962, p. 241.

41 See the note *ad loc.* in the New Swan Shakespeare *Othello*, ed. Gamini Salgado, London, 1976, p. 30, and H.M. Hulme, *Explorations in Shakespeare's Language*, London, 1962, pp. 153–4.

42 See above, p. 134.

43 Op. cit., p. 239.

44 *The Dyer's Hand*, p. 183.

45 Schücking speaks of 'primitiveness' and 'childishness' on p. 30 of his *Character Problems in Shakespeare's Plays*, Gloucester, Mass., 1959. He discusses Prince Hal's soliloquy, ibid., p. 218f.

46 *The Dyer's Hand*, pp. 205–6.

47 Colossians 3:1–10; Ephesians 4:17–24; Romans 6:1f.

48 Romans 6:6.

49 See Johnson's note on *2 Henry IV*, V. v. 69, in his *Notes to Shakespeare*, vol. 2, Pt 1, *Augustan Reprint Society*, Los Angeles, 1957, p. 56.

50 *The Dyer's Hand*, p. 198.

51 See Keith Thomas, *Religion and the Decline of Magic*, Harmondsworth, 1973, p. 732.

52 'What I believe', in *Two Cheers for Democracy*, London, 1951, p. 78.

53 *The Dyer's Hand*, p. 219.

54 *Advauncement of Learning*, Bk 1, in *Philosophical Works*, ed. Ellis and Spedding, revised by J.M. Robertson, London, 1905, p. 58.

Chapter 4   The new mimesis

1 See e.g. his *The Essence of Christianity*, Leipzig, 1841, in the translation by George Eliot (first published 1854), New York, 1957, pp. 12–14, 33.

2 New York, 1960. This work first appeared as *Die Entdeckung des Geistes*, Hamburg, 1948.

3 Berkeley, California, 1963.

4 ibid., pp. 1–27.

5 London, 1962.

6 Oxford, 1963.

7 Berkeley, California, 1971.

8 In 'Two unassimilable men', in *Shakespearean Comedy*, ed. Malcolm Bradbury and David Palmer, Stratford-upon-Avon Studies, 14 (1972), p. 232.

9 *The Dyer's Hand*, London, 1963, pp. 184, 203.

10 See A.W. Schlegel, *A Course of Lectures on Dramatic Art and Literature*, trans. by John Black, 1815, vol. 2, p. 192, and A.C. Bradley, *Shakespearean Tragedy*, 2nd edn, London, 1929, p. 82.

11 In *Eighteenth Century Essays on Shakespeare*, ed. D. Nichol Smith, Oxford, 1963, pp. 230–1.

12 See J.E. Sandys, *A History of Classical Scholarship*, New York, 1958, vol. 1, pp. 29–30.

13 The entry for 14 May 1845 in *The Journals of Kierkegaard*, ed. and trans. Alexander Dru, London, 1958, p. 93.

14 *The Works of Alexander Pope*, ed. W. Elwin and W.J. Courthope, 10 vols, London, 1871–89.

15 London, 1950.

16 *Life of Milton*, in *Lives of the Poets*, London, 1783, vol. 1, pp. 218–20.

17 *English Literature in the Sixteenth Century, excluding Drama*, Oxford, 1954, p. 331.

18 'The progress of Spring', in *The Poems of Tennyson*, ed. Christopher Ricks, London, 1969, p. 476.

19 From Tennyson's lyric, 'Now sleeps the crimson petal', in *The Princess*, 161–74, in Ricks (ed.), op. cit., p. 835.

20 *The Poems of Samuel Johnson*, ed. David Nichol Smith and Edward L. McAdam, 2nd edn, Oxford, 1974, pp. 226–7.

21 *Complete Poems 1913–62*, New York, 1968, p. 515.

22 *The Prelude*, i. 477, in the 1805–6 text, in the 2nd edn by E. de Selincourt, revised by Helen Darbishire, Oxford, 1959, p. 28.

23 See Diodorus Siculus, IV. vi. 7, in the Loeb edn with an English translation by C.H. Oldfather and others, London, 1960–7, vol. ii, p. 360.

Index